GW00792953

A History of The Worshipful Company of Cooks

ALAN BORG

Published by Jeremy Mills Publishing Limited
for The Worshipful Company of Cooks

Jeremy Mills Publishing Limited
113 Lidget Street, Lindley, Huddersfield HD3 3JR UK
www.jeremymillspublishing.co.uk

First published 2011

ISBN: 978-1-906600-53-2

Contents

List of Illustrations

Foreword

The Worshipful Company of Cooks is an unusual Livery in several ways. It is the only City Company to appoint annually two Masters, who, together with the new Wardens, are then crowned with ceremonial crowns. It is also the smallest of the Liveries, with its number now limited to seventy-five. It no longer has a Hall of its own, but this is not the result of the Great Fire of London in 1666 nor of German incendiary bombs in the Second World War (the most common reasons for the loss of a Hall) but of an eighteenth century fire which led to a conscious decision not to rebuild. The question of whether or not to acquire a new Hall has been discussed at regular intervals ever since, but the Cooks are now based primarily in the Hall of the Innholders' Company, a Livery to which they are related both in spirit and in history. The Guild, and later Company, of Cooks played a key role in the regulation of cooking and the supervision of cooks from the fifteenth to the nineteenth centuries, establishing their separate identity in the face of challenges from other Companies, such as the Bakers, the Brewers, the Butchers, the Fishmongers, the Grocers, the Innholders, the Poulters, the Taverners and the Vintners. In common with most other London Livery Companies, the role of the Cooks as the central regulatory body for the trade gradually diminished and by the twentieth century had all but vanished, to be replaced by the sponsorship of education in cookery and the provision of training that are at the heart of the Company's activities to this day.

I was approached by the Court of the Company in 2007 to write a new *History* of the Company, shortly after I had completed a History of the Painters' Company (2005).

This had taught me that the story of the London Livery Companies makes a valuable contribution to the history of the City, as well as giving fascinating insights into the development of the trades and professions. All the Companies were scrupulous in keeping detailed records of their meetings and activities but although these records usually survive they are often incomplete, having suffered from the ravages of time. The archives of the Cooks' Company present, as is so often the case, a frustratingly inconsistent pattern of survival; many documents were destroyed when the Hall was burnt down in 1771 and others were lost when the Clerk's office was destroyed by bombing in the Second World War. However, a considerable amount survives and, although some of it is in a very damaged condition, a few of the gaps can be filled by compilations and copies of documents that were made for various purposes by Clerks and historians of the Company over the centuries.

The great bulk of the Company archives were deposited in the Guildhall Library at the end of the nineteenth century (with subsequent additions). These have been conserved by the Library's expert staff and may be freely consulted there. Other documentary sources are to be found in the Corporation of London Record Office, the London Metropolitan Archives, the British Library, the College of Arms, and the National Archives at Kew and other libraries. I am grateful to the staff of all these repositories for their help and assistance. I have received much valuable help from current members of the Company, especially Past Masters Michael Messent and Paul Herbage, and the current Clerk, Michael Thatcher. The Cooks, in common with other Liveries, have a long tradition of family membership, often going back for many generations, and this provides an invaluable source of collective memories.

I am grateful to Hazel Forsyth of the Museum of London who provided ready access to the items belonging to the Company which are on loan to the Museum of London and to Michelle Day, Curator of the Guildhall, Hull, and Susan Capes of the Hands on History Museum in Hull, who provided information about the portrait of Master Cook John Smythson at the Old Grammar School in Hull. Numerous other people, too many to mention here, have helped me in a wide variety of ways. However, I must add the usual *caveat* that mistakes and errors are solely my responsibility.

My thanks also go to Davina Janman and Maria Samouel, respectively the proprietors of Oldlands Farm and Ladyland Farm, former Company properties, for giving me access to these beautiful houses.

This is by no means the first history of the Company and I am indebted to the work of my predecessors. The first serious attempt to chronicle the origin and development of the Company was made in the *Memorials of the Worshipful Company of Cooks, London*, a manuscript compiled by C M Phillips, Master 1901, which was deposited in the Guildhall Library in 1899. Though never printed, it remains a valuable source. Two historical essays by C M Phillips were published, *A Short Account of the Silver Plate and Miscellaneous Articles belonging to the Worshipful Company of Cooks* (1909) and *Some Account of the Hall of the Worshipful Company of Cooks* (1913) and in 1932 F T Phillips, son of C M (who became Master in 1934) published *A History of the Worshipful Company of Cooks*. This was reprinted, with minimal changes, in 1966, with the title of *A Second History*. In the Quincentenary year, 1982, a new *History of the Worshipful Company of Cooks, London* was published by P F Herbage (Master 1974) and a supplementary volume, *The Worshipful Company of Cooks: A History, 1982–2002* by P D Herbage (nephew of P F, Master 1999) and M J Messent (Master 2001) was published in 2002. All these contain much valuable information and the present book should be seen as standing alongside the previous studies, not as replacing them completely.

The dates assigned to Masters in the above paragraph need to be clarified. Here and throughout the book the date of the Master's year is given as the date on which he was elected to and took up office. This is a little misleading, since the traditional month in which the new Masters are crowned is November, following their election at the Court meeting in September, so the majority of each Master's year is in the following calendar year. Strictly speaking, the date should be give as, *eg* Master 1999–2000, but this seems unnecessarily cumbersome and so the single date of the start of the year is used to represent the whole twelve month period.

The transcription of historical sources presents another problem since the spelling of our ancestors was erratic and idiosyncratic. With very few exceptions, I decided to modernise the spelling throughout, using Cook for Coke, Dinner for Dynner and so on. Occasionally, as in Chaucer's well-known description of the Cook Hodge of Ware, I have retained the accepted fourteenth century orthography but set this alongside the modern translation by Nevill Coghill. In addition, lengthy documents, such as the Charters and Bye-Laws are printed in full in the Appendices, but only quoted selectively in the main body of the text.

History never stands still and any history of an ongoing institution will be out of date from the day it is published; nonetheless, I hope that this book gives a fair portrait of an ancient fellowship that has survived for more than half a millennium. In this time the Worshipful Company has set the standards for the profession and provided the regulatory mechanisms to enforce them. When these powers became redundant or were taken over by others in the nineteenth century, the Company developed its expertise in training and education, sponsoring competitions and prizes for young Cooks. It continues to do so today and its charitable support for research and education in cookery remains of real importance for the profession.

Alan Borg
2011

CHAPTER ONE

Cookery and Civilisation

We may live without poetry, music and art;
We may live without conscience, and live without heart;
We may live without friends; we may live without books;
But a civilised man cannot live without cooks.

(Edward Robert Bulwer, Earl of Lytton,
from *Lucile*, 1860)

Cooking is one of the oldest and most prized of human skills. Since it normally requires food to be heated the development of the art was dependent on the discovery of fire by our earliest ancestors. It was an understanding of this connection that led the Victorian essayist Charles Lamb to write his pseudo-historical fable, a *Dissertation upon Roast Pig*, which relates how roast meat was discovered when a Chinese swineherd accidentally burnt down his house with a litter of pigs inside; the alluring smell led him to pick up a burnt piglet and, licking his fingers, he discovered the joys of crackling.[1] This, of course, is make-believe thinly disguised as history, but a noted British anthropologist, Richard Wrangham, has argued that the unparalleled success of the human race is due to our conquest of fire and the subsequent development of cookery. *I believe that the transformative moment that gave rise to the genus Homo, one of the great transitions in the history of life, stemmed from the*

1 *Essays of Elia* (1823).

control of fire and the advent of cooked meals.... Cooking increased the (calorific) value of our food. It changed our bodies, our brains, our use of time and our social lives.[2] He argues that the human race owes its spectacular success to its ability to cook – a skill that developed in even the most primitive societies. If this thesis is accepted, Lamb's fable is closer to the truth than one might think and it is certainly true that many culinary skills did evolve in an accidental or experimental manner. The art of the cook through the ages has been to use the variety of available ingredients in order to present food that is imaginative, alluring and good to eat.

The Greek historian Herodotus was one of the first writers to record diet, saying of the Egyptians that *they eat loaves made from spelt* [a coarse grained wheat] *and drink a wine made from barley, as they have no vines in the country. Some kinds of fish they eat raw, either dried in the sun or salted; quails too they eat raw, and ducks and various small birds, after pickling them in brine; other sorts of birds and fish, apart from those they consider sacred, they either roast or boil.*[3]

Professional cooks are encountered in western civilisation from the time of the Ancient Greeks. The first surviving European texts dedicated to cookery were written in Sicily in the fourth century BC, notably *The Life of Luxury* by Archestratus of Gela.[4] Composed in verse, this is a sort of culinary tour of the Mediterranean, much of it concerned with the preparation of fish. All the recipes are relatively simple and this appears to have been a conscious reaction against the more heavily seasoned cooking found in Italy:

When working on fish do not let any Syracusan or Italian come near you, for they do not understand how to prepare good fish. They ruin them in a horrible way by cheesing everything and sprinkling with a flow of vinegar and silphium brine... They can bring clever ideas in a smart way to a banquet: little dishes which are cheap and sticky and based on nonsensical seasonings.

Figure 1. Edible Mediterranean Fish. Mosaic from a Roman Dining Room.

2 *Catching Fire: How Cooking made us Human*, 2009; see also *The Times*, 17 September 2009.

3 Herodotus, *The Histories*, Book 2, p. 77, Penguin Classics.

4 The best recent survey of ancient cookery is the be found in the Introduction to *Apicius, a Critical Edition*, edited by Christopher Grocock and Sally Grainger, Prospect Books, Totnes, 2006.

Archestratus seems to have been a knowledgeable amateur who probably collected his recipes from professional cooks. Such Greek cooks were mostly freemen, who worked with the support of slaves. A Master Cook was a person with a recognised if not very elevated position in society, well-educated and with time to set down his recipes in cookery books. By contrast, Roman cooks were usually slaves or freed men.

Figure 2. Baker and bread oven, mosaic originally from Saint-Romain-en-Gal, France. Roman 3rd century AD.

The Greeks also give us our first sight of cooks in literature, with poets and playwrights using cooks as stock characters. They are portrayed as people of middle social rank, but in a profession that was highly competitive. Cooks worked in rival pairs at grand dinners, each striving for the best effect. Greek comedies regularly feature such cooks and although this evidence has to be treated with caution, modern scholars have argued that the comic cook bears a close relation to his counterpart in everyday life.[5] Many of the details given are clearly based on experience and contain more than a grain of truth. From one source we learn that *Anyone can prepare dishes, carve, boil up sauces and blow on the fire, even a mere commis. But the cook is something else. To understand the place, the season, the man giving the meal, the guest, when and what fish to buy, that is not a job for just anyone. You will get the same kind of thing just about all the time, but you will not get the same perfection in the dishes or the same flavour. Archestratus has written his book and is held in esteem by some, as if he has said something useful. But he is ignorant of most things and tells us nothing.* Another extract suggests that some cooks were keen to experiment: *Sophon of Arcarnania and Demoxenus of Rhodes were fellow pupils of each other in the cook's art, and Labdacus of Sicily was their teacher. These two wiped away the clichéd old seasonings from the cookbooks and did away with the mortar: no cumin, vinegar, silphium, cheese, coriander – seasonings which old Kronos used to have. They did away with all these and said the man who used them was only a tradesman. All they asked for were oil and a new pot and a fire that was hot and not blown too often. With such an arrangement every meal is straightforward. They*

5 John Wilkins and Shaun Hill (1993) 'The Flavous of Ancient Greece', in *Spicing up the Palate: Studies of Flavourings – Ancient and Modern. Proceedings of the Oxford Symposium on Food and Cookery 1992* (Totnes).

Figure 3. Preparation for a banquet, mosaic from Carthage now in the Louvre, Paris. Roman c180–90 AD.

were the first to do away with sneezing and a running nose at table: they cleared out the tubes of the eaters.[6]

A famous book of quotations called the *Deipnosophists*, was compiled by Athenaeus, who lived in Egypt at the beginning of the third century AD. This contains many passages on the subject of food and drink from earlier writers whose work is now lost. In one description of a marriage feast we learn that each of the guests was given a loaf on a brass plate, and there were poultry, ducks, pigeons and geese, and quantities more heaped up in abundance. The guests passed all this to their slaves who served it to them. A second plate,

6 Dionysius *The Law Maker*, fragment 2.15–26KA. See John Wilkins and Shaun Hill (1994) on latis.ex.ac.uk/classics/undergraduate/food3/archestratus.htm, and Anaxippus *Behind the Veil*, fragment 1.1–26KA.

made of silver, was then placed before each guest, on which there was a second large loaf, and served with that were hares and kids, with doves, partridges and every other kind of bird imaginable.

Athenaeus also includes comments on the way other peoples dined; for example he says that the Celts made seats of grass and placed food in front of them for their guests. This was served on low wooden tables and consisted of a few loaves and a great deal of meat floating in water or roasted on spits. Those who lived near rivers ate fish, as did those who lived near the sea; this they roasted with salt and vinegar and cumin seeds.

There are many grand feasts recorded in Greek history and myth, ranging from impromptu barbeques to formal dinners. In Book II of Homer's *Odyssey* we hear how King Alcinous killed a dozen sheep, eight full grown pigs, and two oxen, which his companions skinned and dressed so as to provide a magnificent banquet. Later Odysseus himself recalls that there is nothing more delightful than to listen to a minstrel in a hall, when the tables are laden with bread and meat, and a steward is carrying round wine. *This, to my mind, is something very like perfection*, he says (Book IX). Greek banquets were normally followed by a *symposium* – literally a drinking party, although people seldom over-indulged in the wine, but rather used the occasion as a stimulant to conversation and discussion. This was the setting used by Plato for one of his philosophical dialogues, known simply as *The Symposium* – hence the word is still used today to describe academic conferences. Another Platonic dialogue, *Gorgias*, written around 330 BC, uses cookery as a metaphor for rhetoric:

Polus: *What sort of an art is cookery?*
Socrates: *Not an art at all, Polus.*
Polus: *What then?*
Socrates: *I should say an experience.*
Polus: *In what? I wish that you would explain to me.*
Socrates: *An experience in producing a sort of delight and gratification, Polus.*
Polus: *Then are cookery and rhetoric the same?*
Socrates: *No, they are only different parts of the same profession.*

Later in the same dialogue we read that *Cookery simulates the disguise of medicine, and pretends to know what food is the best for the body; and if the physician and the cook had to enter into a competition in which children were the judges, or men who had no more sense than children, as to which of them best understands the goodness or badness of food, the physician would be starved to death. Cookery, then, I maintain to be a flattery which takes the form of medicine.*[7]

The Romans continued the Greek traditions of cooking, with all sorts of exotic dishes served to diners reclining on couches and indulging in conversation (and much else

7 *Gorgias*, translated by Benjamin Jowett.

besides) late into the night.[8] Several Roman cookery books are known, the most celebrated of which is *De re coquinaria* (On the Subject of Cooking) that is attributed to Apicius and dates from the fourth or fifth century AD.[9] Once again, this seems to be a compilation of recipes first written down by professional cooks and collected together by a knowledgeable *bon viveur*. The dishes are complex, with extensive use of sauces and spices and the recent editors of the Apicius texts, Christopher Grocock and Sally Grainger, believe that we should celebrate the anonymous Master Cooks who originally designed these recipes, rather than the shadowy and possibly mythical figure called Apicius. There is some evidence that Roman cooks banded together in colleges or guilds, and an inscription near Rome reads: *A guild which welcome us for spending its life in the production of sumptuous dishes for pleasant living and festal days, who with their delicious skills and with the help of Vulcan enhance banquets and games again and again; the cooks have given this to their highest commanders* [the gods], *so they may willingly give them the good aid they desire.* These cooks seem to have had a form of apprenticeship, with young boys being trained in kitchen skills by senior slaves. Several Roman kitchens are preserved in remarkable detail in the cities of both Pompeii and Herculaneum, destroyed by the eruption of Vesuvius in 79AD.

We can imagine many of the recipes described in Apicius being used in Britain during the Roman occupation and so passing into Anglo-Saxon times, where they probably survived in monastic and royal kitchens. The first mention of cookery as a profession in England seems to come from a *Colloquy* (or instructional text) which was written in Anglo-Saxon during the second half of the tenth century by Aelfric, Archbishop of Canterbury. This takes the form of a dialogue between a Master and a pupil, in which the value of various activities is questioned:

Master: *What shall we say of the cook? Do we need his craft in any way?*

The Cook says: *If you expel me from your society, you'll eat your vegetables raw and your meat uncooked; and you can't even have a good broth without my art.*

Master: *We don't care about your art; it isn't necessary to us, because we can boil things that need boiling and roast the things that need roasting for ourselves.*

The Cook says: *However, if you drive me out so as to do that, then you'll all be servants and none of you will be lord. And without my craft you still won't be able to eat.*[10]

Here the cook is depicted as a professional craftsman, whose work can be set alongside that of the several other professions mentioned in the *Colloquy*, including bakers, blacksmiths, cobblers, carpenters, goldsmiths and silversmiths, whose distinctive skills are all recognised. The cook's arts are seen to be no less than those of other professionals; it

8 Katherine M. D. Dunbabin, *The Roman Banquet: Images of Conviviality*, 2003.

9 See *Apicius, a Critical Edition*, cited in note 4 above.

10 *Anglo-Saxon Prose*, ed & trans Michael Swanton, London 1975, 112–3.

Figure 4. The preparation of pies. Woodcut, English 15th century.

used to be thought that early cookery was a primitive business and early hygiene was virtually non-existent but in recent years medieval cookery has been the subject of much academic research and experiment. This has revealed that good cooking was always highly regarded and the standards of hygiene were generally very strict. These points are well made by Peter Brears in his valuable study of *Cooking and Dining in Medieval England* (2008); concerning the standards of hygiene; he writes *Another reason for this book is to dispel any remaining doubts of the exemplary standards of medieval food and table manners. Popular historical films from the 1930s to the present day show the Middle Ages at table in terms of dirt, squalor, belching and throwing food around. This myth has even infected 'educational' publications. In fact most medieval households were kept exceptionally clean. A medieval peasant would have been shocked by the manners on display today in fast food restaurants.* The point is also made by the German traveller Paul Hentzner, who visited England at the end of the reign of Queen Elizabeth I and noted that the people he saw *are more polite in eating than the French, devouring less bread, but more meat, which they roast in perfection.*[11]

A large number of medieval and renaissance recipes are preserved but they differ from their modern equivalents in various ways; essentially they take the form of lists of ingredients and very brief cooking instructions – there are seldom details of quantities, oven temperatures or timings. The Instructions for making Pies in the *Proper Newe Booke of Cokerye* (1557) are typical:

The mutton or beef must be minced finely for pies and seasoned with salt and pepper, and a little saffron to colour it. Also add a good quantity of suet or marrow, a little vinegar, prunes, large raisins and dates. Take the best broth, and if you would like a paste royal [pieces of pastry used as a garnish] *take butter and egg yolks and mix this broth with some flour to make the pastry.*[12]

Clearly anyone using this book was expected to understand about quantities, cooking times, and so on and a professional cook would have learned these things as an apprentice; for example, temperatures could only be gauged by eye and touch, but practice allowed remarkable accuracy to be achieved. A modern cook undertaking the preparation of early recipes may have to undergo many hours of trial and error,

Figure 5. A Cook in his kitchen. Woodcut, German 1525–35.

11 *Itinerarium Germaniae, Galliae, Angliae, Italiae, cum Indice Locorum, Rerum atque Verborum*, 1612.

12 A facsimile edition of this book, which was used by Margaret, the wife of Matthew Parker, Master of Corpus Christi College, Cambridge, was published by the College in 2002, with the aid of a grant from the Cooks' Company.

whereas his medieval predecessor would have known instinctively what was needed. Moreover, experiment has shown that when medieval dishes are properly prepared the results are both attractive to the eye and delicious to eat, and the variety is as great as or greater than today's cuisine.

It is not surprising that Thomas Cogan, in his 1584 pamphlet *Haven of Health*, wrote that a good cook is *a good jewel...to be made much of.*[13] The Devil reputedly has the best tunes but, according to Milton, he may also have the best cooks:

A table richly spread in regal mode,
With dishes piled and meats of noblest sort
And savour-beasts of chase, or fowl of game,
In pastry built, or from the spit, or boiled,
Grisamber-steamed; all fish, from sea or shore,
Freshet or purling brook, of shell or fin,
And exquisitest name, for which was drained
Pontus, and Lucrine bay, and Afric coast
Alas! how simple, to these cates compared,
Was that crude Apple that diverted Eve!

There could be hidden dangers here too. John Russell, who was Marshal or Usher in the household of Humphrey, Duke of Gloucester in the second half of the fifteenth century, wrote his *Book of Nurture* as a manual of domestic economy. In this he displays a healthy suspicion of advanced cookery: *Cooks with their new conceits, are chopping, stamping, and grinding, contriving many new dishes every day. They find that these can sometimes put people in mortal danger.* In the same book Russell emphasises that the cook takes his orders from the Marshal, whether he likes it or not – hardly surprising, since Russell himself occupied the office of Marshal.[14]

The sophistication of medieval and renaissance kitchens can be studied in a large number of examples that survive in castles, palaces and great houses up and down the land. When these kitchens are well-preserved, the complexity of the operations they contained is readily apparent. At Hampton Court, where the kitchens date from 1514, there are over fifty rooms devoted to food storage and preparation. These could accommodate some 200 staff and could easily cater for two main meals a day for members of the Royal Court, who numbered around 800 people and sometimes more. The offices included a Counting House, where all the accounts were kept and stores such as the Chandlery, where candles were stored, and a Coal House. Meats were kept in the Flesh Larder, fish in the Wet Larder,

---

13 *London Eats Out*, Museum of London 1999, '16th Century' by Hazel Forsyth.

14 *The Book of Nurture* by John Russell, *Edited from the Harleian MS. 4011 in the British Museum* by Frederick Furnivall, 1868.

pulses and nuts in the Dry Larder, with spices in the Spicery. The main area for cooking was the Great Kitchen, furnished with six great fireplaces, each with spit-racks and other cooking tools. At each end of the Great Kitchen were hatches where liveried servants would collect the completed dishes and take them to the Great Hall. There was also a Boiling House, where meat could be boiled in great copper vats, and a Confectionary, where sweetmeats were prepared.

There is a vivid description of these royal kitchens written by a Spanish nobleman who accompanied Prince Philip to England in 1554: *There are usually eighteen kitchens at full blast and they seem veritable hells, such is the stir and bustle in them.... The usual daily consumption is eighty to one hundred sheep – and the sheep are very big and fat – a dozen fat beeves, a dozen and a half calves, without mentioning poultry, game, deer, boars, and a great number of rabbits. There is plenty of beer here and they drink more than would fill the Valladolid river. In summer the ladies and some gentlemen put sugar in their wine, with the result that there are great goings on in the palace.*[15] In recent years these kitchens have been brought back to life and visitors to the Palace can both see and taste the excellent dishes that Tudor cooks could produce.

Figure 6. A Feast depicted in an Anglo-Saxon calendar, c1030. British Library Ms Cott Tib B V f.5v.

15 Simon Thurley, 'The Sixteenth Century kitchens at Hampton Court', *Journal of the British Archaeological Association*, CXLIII, 1990, pp. 1–29 and *Hampton Court Palace: A Social and Architectural History*, Yale, 2004

The staff needed to operate these great royal kitchens was commensurately large. In 1536 Henry VIII issued Ordinances detailing the members of the Royal Household. The catering department comprised well over fifty people, in the following offices:

Kitchen
Chief Clerk to the Kitchen
Two under-clerks of the same
Master Cooks
Cooks
Boilers

Bake House
Serjeant of the Bake House
Clerk of the Bake House
Purveyors
Bakers
Miller (external to the Bake House)

Pantry
Serjeant of the Pantry
Yeoman Breever
Groome Breever
Officers of the same

Cellar
Serjeant of the Cellar
Gentleman of the Cellar
Yeoman of the Cellar
Groome-receiver
Groome-Grobber
Officers of the same
Purveyors of Wines
Purveyors of Ale

Sea Fishery
Purveyor of Sea Fish

Poultry
Serjeant of the Poultry
Clerk of the Poultry
Purveyors of the same

Butlery
Butlers of Ale
Purveyors of Ale

Spicery
Clerks to the Spicery

Chandlery (candle store)
Serjeant of the Chaundry
Officers of the same

Ewery (pot store)
Serjeant of the Ewery
Officers of the same

Confectionary and Wafery
Officers of the Confectionary
and Wafery

Larder
Serjeant of the Larder
Clerk to the Larder
Officers of the same

Acatry (meat and fish store)
Serjeant of the Acatry
Clerks-Comptrollers
Two purveyors of the same office

Squillery (scullery)
Serjeant of the Squillery
Officers of the same

Pastry and Salsery
Serjeant of the Pastry
Clerk of the Pastry
Yeoman of the Pastry
Officers of the same

A glimpse of the organisation of the royal kitchen is found in a set of regulations for the King's household, dating from 1455:

Also, the clerk of the kitchen and the master cooks should be careful not to waste anything while carrying out their duties, or allow waste by those beneath them, and every man should go to the hall at meal times save those told to do otherwise. And the controller or one of his clerks, along with the clerk of the kitchen, should see that none of the said officers take fees other than those accustomed, and that none take meat from the kitchen for themselves or others, unless delivered to them by those in charge. Also, the clerk of the kitchen should decide the number of meals for the chamber and the hall, and log the deliveries that arrive each day in the pantry roll. The usher of the kitchen should allow no servant or other man into the kitchen except those who work there.[16]

The large kitchen team was kept busy and the Ordinances of Henry VIII give details of the King's Diet on both *Flesh Days* and *Fish Days*. Each meal consisted of two Messes or

Figure 7. A Helmet (Kettle Hat) re-used as cooking pot. Found near London Bridge, English 14th century.

16 Henry VI, February 1445, *Parliament Rolls of Medieval England.*

courses and on Flesh Days included the following (given here in the original used spelling, since several of the terms remain obscure):

Dinner		*s*	*d*	**Supper**		*s*	*d*
Cheat Bread and Manchett[17]	16		8	Cheat Bread and Manchett	16		8
Beare and Ale	6 gal'		9	Beere and Ale Wyne	6 gal'		9
Wyne	1 sext	2	0	Wyne	1 sext	2	
Flesh for Pottage			8	Flesh for Pottage	1		0
Chines of Beef	2	2	8	Chickens in crituary, Larkes			
Rammuners in stew or cap'	1 mess		6	Sparrows or Lambe stewed, with Chynes of Mutton	1		13
Venison in brewz' or mult'	1		4	Giggots of Mutton or Venison, stopped with Cloves	1		6
Pestells of Reed Deere	1		2	Capons of gr	2		4
Mutton	2		6	Conyes of gr'	1 mess		12
Carpes or Young Veale in Arm' farced	1		10	Pheasant, Herne, Shovelard	1	3	4
Swanne, gr' Goose, Storke or	1		4	Cocks, Plovers or Gulles	1	2	
Capons of gr'	2		4	Swete dowcetts or Orange	1		10
Conyes of gr'	1		12	Quinces or Pippins	1		2
Fryanders, baked Carpe	1		20				
Custard garnished	1		12				
or Fritters	1		8				
			Second Course				
		s	*d*			*s*	*d*
Jelly, Ipocras, Creame of Almonds	1 mess		8	Blank-mange or other dish	1 mess		4
Pheasant, Herne, Bitterne, Shovelard	1	3	4	Kydd, Lambe or Pejons	1		12
Partridges, Quailes or Mewz',	1	3		Partridge or Quailes	1	2	
Cocks, Plovers or Gulles	1	2		Godwitts Brewez' or Teales, Pullets, Chic' pip	1		18
Kydd, Lambe or Pigeons	1		14	Rabbetts or Larks	1		12
Larkes or Rabbetts	1		12	Tarte	1		12
Snyters, Pulletts or Chickens	1		12	Fruite	1		8
Venison in fine past	1		12	Butter and Eggs		3	4
Tarts	1		12	Venison, or other Baked Meates	1		12

The annual cost of this diet was assessed at the enormous sum of £1520 – 13*s* – 4*d*.

17 Ordinary or first quality bread.

Medieval and Renaissance Cooks were undoubtedly fully aware that perishable food has to be preserved. In 1553 Lord Grey wrote to Queen Mary from Calais that *another boar has come to his hand, which he sends also ready baked after the manner here, because he doubts whether it would endure the carriage unbaked.*[18] The arts of salting and smoking were developed with the highest degree of skill and the Flemish diplomat Noel de Caron wrote to Sir Robert Cecil in 1596 that the bearer of the letter *brings him a smoked salmon and is charged to tell Cecil's cook the mode they use with such. Perhaps he might also like to taste it.*[19] It was also known that many foods would last longer if kept cold and the collection of ice and snow in winter for use in ice houses in summer was common. This was an ancient practice and the first recorded ice house was built for a king in northern Iraq c.1700BC, although most surviving ice houses in Britain date from after the Reformation. Several dating from the seventeenth century have been excavated in London and by this time there was a royal official whose title was the Yeoman Keeper of Ice and Snow.

Whatever form of cookery we consider, from city cookshops that catered to the mass market to royal kitchens that produced exotic dishes for royal feasts, there can no longer be any doubt about the skills and high standards of cooks in past ages. There was a clear understanding of the dangers that could result from poor hygiene, ranging from disgruntled customers to fatal food poisoning. This was one of the important reasons for the development of the Cooks' Guild, since it was understood that cooks who tried to pass off putrid or rancid produce did the profession as a whole a serious disservice. Therefore much of the effort of the Guild and the later Company was devoted to maintaining standards and rooting out malpractices.

Little is known for certain about the way in which various trade Guilds and Associations came into existence, but a fair amount can be deduced. There were Guilds in Anglo-Saxon England – sometimes known as Frith or Peace Guilds – but these had no connection with trade or industry. Instead, they were voluntary associations formed for a variety of religious, social, and political purposes, including the protection of property and prevention of theft, not unlike contemporary Residents' Associations.[20]

The first evidence of the existence of Trade Guilds in Britain occurs in the twelfth century and their growth seems to reflect the growth of cities and towns. With increasing numbers of people coming to live in an urban environment it was natural for those who were members of the same or similar professions to gather together in the same neighbourhood. This led in many places to streets being named after the trade of those that lived and worked there – names such as Goldsmiths' Street, Butchers' Row, or Painters' Lane are commonplace and so we also find Cooks' Street in Dublin, Cooks' Row in Bristol,

18 *Calendar of State Papers Foreign, Mary: 1553–1558* (1861), pp. 15–22.

19 *Calendar of the Cecil Papers in Hatfield House*, Vol 6: 1596 (1895), pp. 255–272.

20 Two Chapters on the Medieval Guilds of England by Edwin Seligman, *Publications of the American Economic Association*, Vol 2, No 5 (Nov 1887) pp. 9–113.

Figure 8. The Great Kitchen, Hampton Court.

Cooks' Lane in Birmingham and such names are repeated in many other towns. Guilds and Companies of Cooks sprang up in most large towns and cities, including York, Exeter, Norwich, and Bristol. These were independent of the London Guild, although they developed along similar lines. The fact that the first cook recorded in Bristol in 1388 was called Thomas London does suggest there may have been some contact with the capital. There was also an early Cooks' Guild in Dublin, which received its first charter as a Company in 1444, some thirty-eight years before the first charter to the London Company.[21]

Early references to a Guild or Association are often in a religious context, for groups of professional workers living in the same area would normally worship in their parish church, supporting it by giving alms and often 'adopting' an altar or a holy image as their own special cause. Thus the Painters' Guild was also known as the Guild of St Luke, the patron saint of artists, whose altar the Guild maintained in their church of St Giles, Cripplegate. The patron saints of the Cooks are St Thomas the Apostle and St Lawrence, but there is no record of the Cooks' Guild owing special allegiance to either of these in a

21 It is of some interest to note that the Cooks of Dublin presented a snuff box to the Duke of Wellington in 1806 and this is preserved in Apsley House.

particular church. This may be because there were several areas where cooks congregated, since the need for their services was spread throughout the City and we hear of the Cooks of Eastcheap, of Bread Street, of Ironmonger Lane and so on. This meant that there was not a single parish or a single church that was adopted by the cooks and so no single altar or image was adopted by them. The fact that several communities of Cooks existed may, as we shall see, also help to explain some of the characteristics of the early Guild and the later Company, as these emerged as professional bodies.

The first dated reference to a Trade Guild is found in the Exchequer Pipe Roll of 1130, which records the payment of sixteen marks by Robert, son of Luweston, as rent from the Guild of Weavers. A little later, in 1156, there is a similar record of a payment of a mark of gold from the Guild of Bakers. From this time on there are increasing references to trade guilds, and it is clear that to begin with several of them were established without first obtaining royal or civic licenses. These unlicensed organisations became known as Adulterine Guilds and in 1180 sixteen of them were fined sums ranging from 45 marks to half a mark (a sum later traditionally rendered as *6s 8d*) by King Henry II. All the Adulterine Guilds were recognised over time as legitimate trade associations, but they serve to remind us that such legitimate Guilds and the later Companies were essentially elements in a partnership between the Royal and Civic authorities on the one hand and the urban trades on the other, intended to contribute to stability and good government. The Guilds were to achieve considerable autonomy, with royal charters and civic privileges, but they were allowed these in return for the regulation of their professions, maintenance of order and the supervision of standards.

In 1319, the citizens of London succeeded in obtaining the King's approval for a series of ordinances relating to the better government of the City. Among the articles sanctioned was one to the effect that no alien or foreigner should be admitted to the Freedom of the City, unless he happened to belong to some mistery or craft, in which case he must find six members of his mistery or craft to indemnify the City on his behalf, in the same manner as a native seeking admission and belonging to a mistery or craft was bound to do. This is firm evidence that admission to a Guild was necessary in order to obtain the Freedom of the City, both for Londoners and for 'foreigners' coming from outside the City. The role of the Trade Guilds was much enhanced by the promulgation of these ordinances. A French chronicler wrote in the early fourteenth century that *at this time many of the people of the trades of London were arrayed in livery, and a good time was about to begin.*[22] In fact it is unlikely that the wearing of a livery can be dated so precisely as this, but it is certain that by this time a close association of the Court, the City, and the Guilds was already in existence.

---

22 'The French Chronicle of London: Edward II', *Chronicles of the Mayors and Sheriffs of London: 1188–1274* (1863), pp. 248–267.

So the trade guilds that had started as social and religious associations came in time to play an increasing role in the City's government. They were frequently referred to as Misteries – the term Mistery, meaning a trade or handicraft, derived from the Latin *ministerium*, but it was soon confused with the word Mystery, which suggested that the particular occupation required secret and special knowledge – a confusion which the Guilds themselves were happy to encourage. These Guilds and Misteries gradually evolved into more formal organisations known as Livery Companies, so called because the members wore a distinctive dress or livery. They were granted Charters and operated according to rules that were set out in Ordinances and the members usually met in communal Halls. The story of how the Cooks' Guild played their part in these developments and eventually became the Worshipful Company of Cooks is the subject of the following pages.

CHAPTER TWO

From Guild to Livery

By the twelfth century the City of London was the largest and wealthiest town in England, with a population in 1100 of around 20,000 (double that of its nearest rival, York) rising to nearly 100,000 by the year 1300. The rapid growth of the City provided particular reasons for Cooks to band together. One of the defining characteristics of a town is that the population cannot feed itself. In the countryside or in villages people could and mostly did grow and cook their own food. In a large town, where houses crowded one upon another and only the rich could afford gardens, it was not possible for most people to grow their own food or keep farm animals. Moreover, the poor, who predominated in the new towns, did not normally possess ovens or cooking facilities in their dwellings, since these were expensive and posed an ever-present danger of fire. So it was that the medieval City came to depend upon what we would now call fast food, sold from premises managed by professional cooks, who could buy in ingredients in bulk and offer hot meals at economic prices.[1]

The clientele comprised not only the poor, who could only afford an occasional hot meal, but extended to include wealthy individuals who would often patronise cookshops to enjoy more expensive but well prepared delicacies. Between these two extremes there were numerous people – travellers, merchants, busy professionals and so on – who needed good food and fast service and so cooks and cookshops proliferated.

---

1 See 'Fast Food and Urban Living Standards in Medieval England', by Martha Carlin, in *Food and eating in Medieval Europe*, ed. Martha Carlin & Joel Rosenthal, London 1998, pp. 27–52.

There was another good reason for cooks to come together in their own Guild or Mistery; London was the home to an increasing number of large organisations, from the peripatetic Royal Court to the Lord Mayor's Household and City Institutions. These often required cooks to prepare large feasts – and, as we shall see, some of the feasts were on a truly gargantuan scale. So the need to regulate and organise cooks for the provision of banquets was another significant element in the establishment of their Guild. There is, however, no evidence that there were separate Guilds established for different types of cooks and it seems most probable that there was one Guild of Cooks from the outset.

This much is fairly straightforward, but problems arose when any attempt was made to define who, within the overall business of urban catering, could be termed a Cook. For some trades definition was easy enough: Saddlers made saddles and Goldsmiths produced objects in precious metal, but for Cooks the boundaries were much more blurred. It was relatively simple to separate a Cook from his suppliers, so Guilds of Butchers and Fishmongers could be distinguished (so long as they did not cook their produce). However, for several other related culinary activities it was more difficult. There were people who specialised in one particular area of cooking, notably the Bakers, the Piebakers and the Pastelers. Then there were those who operated hostelries, inns and taverns, which regularly supplied their customers with both cooked food and drink. In consequence, much of the early history of the Guild of Cooks of London was taken up with attempts to establish their monopoly in the face of competition from others practising within the broad spectrum of the catering trade.

In fact, it seems that, from the thirteenth century onwards, the terms Pasteler and Piebaker were regarded as interchangeable with the word Cook. Originally, a Pasteler was a pastry-maker, but numerous documents refer to Cooks and Pastelers jointly, while in 1421 Walter Mangeard was sworn as a Master of Pastelers, although in his will he describes himself as *Citizen and Cook of London* and he left 13*s* 4*d to the fraternity of my craft of Cooks.*[3] In 1538 John Armestronge was listed among the Pastelers, but in his will, dated 1554, he left a bequest to the Company of Cooks and we may assume that they were one and the same. Similarly, Piebakers specialised in making and selling pies from a cookshop, but they were frequently coupled with Cooks in various orders relating to food promulgated by the Lord Mayor and Aldermen – for example, in 1378 Ordinances had been granted to the *Cooks and Pastelers, or Piebakers* and in 1379 regulations regarding the sale of butter were issued to Cooks and Piebakers. The Piebakers were, however, quite distinct from the Bakers, who baked bread and were classified as either White or Brown Bakers. The Bakers formed one of the earliest recorded Guilds and resisted any amalgamation with the Cooks, which caused a series of disputes between the two trades that rumbled on for centuries.

3 Walter Mangeard is still remembered by the Company as their first benefactor.

The rapid growth of London meant that there were a great many Cooks within the City, ranging from the operators of public cookshops to Master Cooks who produced, with the help of teams of Assistant Cooks and Scullions, extravagant fare for the King's table. It is clear that successful cooks could earn a substantial income, become property owners and occupy a respected place in society. Jordan de Turri, Cook, who died in 1279, left to his sons Henry and Gilbert *all his houses, pensions, and rents*, which sounds like a substantial legacy. Similarly, John de Wolwich, Cook, who died in 1313 bequeathed to Matilda his wife and Margery his daughter a house in the parish of S. Magnus for life and *a house and shops* in Southwalk.[4] In addition, there are several instances of a cook being left property in the will of a grateful master or mistress; in 1279 Johanna Travers, a rich widow, left her cook, Roger, her best shop in the parish of All Hallows, although Henry, cook to John Preston, did rather less well, receiving from his master his second-best robe and ten shillings sterling (in addition to his wages), together with two small girdles, one having a black buckle and the other a white (1353).[5]

Figure 9. Hodge the Cook, from *The Canterbury Tales* by Geoffrey Chaucer. English School, 15th century.

Yet, despite this evidence that cooks were both skilled professionals and faithful servants who could on occasion acquire significant wealth and status, it was also widely believed that a good number of cooks were rogue practitioners, who had little regard for hygiene, would sell bad meat if they could disguise it with spices, and pass off rotting vegetables as fresh. The danger which putrid food posed to the teeming population of the City was well understood and one of the key roles of the Cooks Guild was to root out dishonest and dangerous practices which could give the whole profession a bad name. Nonetheless, the portrait of the Cook which Chaucer gives in his *Canterbury Tales*, written between 1387–1400, reflects a popular view of the profession.[6] Hodge (Roger) of Ware

4 *Calendar of wills proved and enrolled in the Court of Husting, London: Part 1: 1258–1358* (1889), pp. 43–50 and 240–248.

5 *Calendar of wills* Part 1, pp. 667–675.

6 See Constance Hieatt, 'A Cook of 14th Century London,' in *Cooks and Other People – Proceedings of the Oxford Symposium on Food and Cookery, 1995*, Totnes, 1996, pp. 138–143.

appears to have been based on a real character and the picture of him that Chaucer gives in the *Prologue* is not entirely favourable:[7]

A cook they hadde with hem for the nones	*They had a Cook with them who stood alone,*
To boille the chiknes with the marybones,	*For boiling chicken with a marrow-bone,*
And poudre-marchant tart and galyngale.	*Sharp flavouring-powder and a spice for savour.*
Wel koude he knowe a draughte of londoun ale.	*He could distinguish London ale by flavour,*
He koude rooste, and sethe, and broille, and frye,	*And he could roast and seethe and broil and fry,*
Maken mortreux, and wel bake a pye.	*Make good thick soup, and bake a tasty pie.*
But greet harm was it, as it thoughte me,	*But what a pity – so it seemed to me,*
That on his shyne a mormal hadde he.	*That he should have an ulcer on his knee;*
For blankmanger, that made he with the best	*As for blancmange, he made it with the best.*

This is clearly a double edged tribute, since in the midst of extolling Hodge's culinary skills Chaucer slips in the observation that he could easily identify London ale – *ie*. he was a drinker – and that he had an ulcerated sore on his leg. It is generally agreed that Hodge was a Cook that Chaucer knew and that his readers would recognise, perhaps from the mention of his sore leg and his heavy drinking. But this far from complimentary description is reinforced in the Cook's tale itself:

Now tell on, Roger, for the word's with you,
You've stolen gravy out of many a stew,
Manys the Jack of Dover you have sold,
That has been twice warmed up and twice left cold. [8]
Many a pilgrim's cursed you more than sparsely,
When suffering the effects of your stale parsley.
Which they had eaten with your stubble-fed goose:
Your shop is one where many a fly is loose.

This reveals that Roger was the proprietor of a cookshop, but he is accused of some of the most common offences committed by unscrupulous caterers, including reheating old food and allowing flies to foul meat, which had been specifically banned in an order made earlier in the century:

7 The English translations are by Nevill Coghill from the Penguin Books edition.
8 Probably not a fish, but a type of pie.

Also, the Assize of a Cook, who sells both flesh and fish, is that he sell only flesh and fish that is good and wholesome and seasonable, both in boiling, roasting and baking: and that he does not boil, or roast, or bake any meat twice. If this offence is proved, his fine is 40d. on each occasion and if he does not heed two warnings, the third time he shall be sentenced to the pillory.[9]

It seems that Hodge may have deserved his rather unsavoury reputation, since in 1372/3 we find that a Roger de Ware, Cook of London, was charged by a jury of twelve of his neighbours with being a common nightwalker. He confessed his offence and put himself on the mercy of the Court.[10] A nightwalker was one who was guilty of wandering the streets after curfew, contrary to numerous City ordinances, and who was presumed to about some nefarious business.[11] So Chaucer presents us with a picture of a Cook who was prepared to serve up re-heated dishes, whose shop was plagued by flies, whose personal hygiene left much to be desired, and whose night time escapades were well-known. We can probably assume that Hodge was not entirely typical of his profession, but equally it seems certain that Chaucer's audience would recognise much of what he wrote.

Figure 10. The Canterbury Pilgrims at dinner, from *The Canterbury Tales* by Geoffrey Chaucer, printed by Wynkyn de Worde, c.1485. English School.

9 Strype's edition of Stow, *History of London* 1720, Bk 5, p. 344, the spelling modernised.

10 'Roll A 18: 1372–73', *Calendar of the plea and memoranda rolls of the city of London: volume 2: 1364–1381* (1929), pp. 150–162. See also Earl D. Lyon, 'Roger De Ware, Cook' *Modern Language Notes*, Vol. 52, No. 7 (Nov., 1937), pp. 491–494.

11 For example, in 1371 John Cheddele was indicted as being a common player of dice by night and a constant nightwalker to the nuisance of the neighbours, while in 1376 the Aldermen were instructed that, in view of the affrays and robberies committed by aliens and other unknown nightwalkers, sufficient watch should be kept in the City at night to preserve the King's peace. See *Calendar of the plea and memoranda rolls of the City of London: volume 2: 1364–1381* (1929), pp. 132–149 & pp. 206–230.

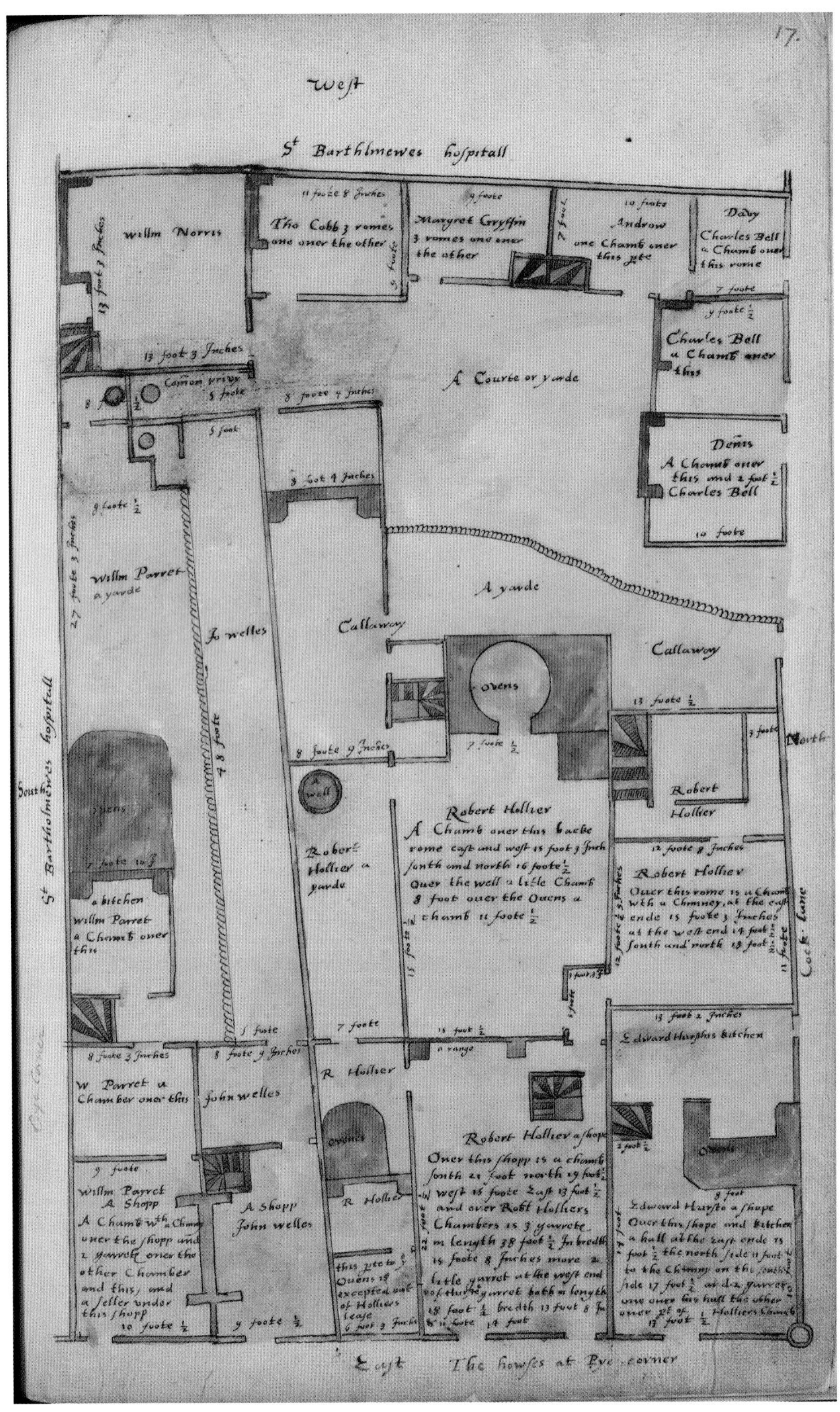

Figure 11. Cookshops at Giltspur St, near Smithfield, known as Pie Corner, drawn by the surveyor Ralph Treswell 1612. Guildhall Library Ms 12805.

Fortunately, Chaucer gives a rather more attractive description of what a generous host and a good cook could produce in his General Prologue, describing the Franklin's household:[12]

His bread, his ale were finest of the fine;
And no one had a better stock of wine.
His house was never short of bake-meat pies,
Of fish and flesh, and these in such supplies
It positively snowed therein with meat and drink
And all the dainties that a man could think.
According to the season of the year
Changes of dish were ordered to appear.
He kept fat partridges in coops, beyond,
Many a bream and pike were in his pond.
Woe to his cook, unless the sauce was hot
And sharp, or if he wasn't on the spot.
And in his hall a table stood arrayed,
And ready all day long, with places laid.

It is hardly surprising that amongst the many cooks of medieval London there were the good and the bad, honest and dishonest, skilled and unskilled. It was for this reason that the Guild or Mistery of Cooks was established, to regulate the profession, to maintain high standards and to root out malpractices of all sorts.

The first description of the London cookshops occurs as a foreword to William FitzStephen's biography of Thomas Becket, which was probably written a few years after the Archbishop's murder in Canterbury Cathedral in 1170. FitzStephen had served as Becket's legal secretary and as his chaplain. Although he was one of only three clerics who did not desert his patron, he seems to have subsequently won the favour of King Henry II (whom he avoided blaming), and was appointed sheriff of Gloucestershire in 1171; later (from 1176) he served as an itinerant royal justice. He was, like Becket, a Londoner by birth and this is probably why he included his description of the City in his biography. As a result, London is to some extent seen through rose-tinted spectacles, but it is nonetheless a vivid portrait of the growing town in the later twelfth century. His description of the cookshops is especially interesting:

Nor should I forget to mention that there is in London, on the river bank amidst the ships, the wine for sale and the storerooms for wine, a public cookshop. On a daily basis there, depending on the season, can be found fried or boiled foods and dishes, fish large and small, meat – lower quality for

12 A Franklin was a freeholder just below the ranks of the gentry.

the poor, finer cuts for the wealthy – game and fowl (large and small). If friends arrive unexpectedly at the home of some citizen and they, tired and hungry after their journey, prefer not to wait until food may be got in and cooked, or till servants bring water for hands and bread, they can in the meantime pay a quick visit to the riverside, where anything they might desire is immediately available. No matter how great the number of soldiers or travellers coming in or going out of the city, at whatever hour of day or night, so that those arriving do not have to go without a meal for too long or those departing leave on empty stomachs, they can choose to detour there and take whatever refreshment each needs. Those with a fancy for delicacies can obtain for themselves the meat of goose, guinea-hen or woodcock – finding what they're after is no great chore, since all the delicacies are set out in front of them. This is an exemplar of a public cookshop that provides a service to a city and is an asset to city life. Hence, as we read in Plato's Gorgias, cookery is a flattery and imitation of medicine, the fourth of the arts of civic life.[13]

FitzStephen is here describing the wards of Vintry and Queenhithe on the north bank of the Thames, an area of wharves and docks where merchant ships unloaded their cargoes of local fish, salt, corn and other comestibles, along with wines and exotic foodstuffs from France. The street names in this area of London, either side of the modern Southwark Bridge, reflected their association with food – Fish Street, Bread Street, Garlick Hill and of course Pudding Lane. The constant stream of merchants and traders provided customers for the cookshops. FitzStephen writes of one cookshop (*publica coquina*) but this is certainly a mistake and later references make it clear that there were numerous separate shops. The Assize of Building issued in 1212, after a serious fire in the City, ordered that all cookshops on the Thames must be whitewashed and plastered inside and out and all internal partitions taken down, so that there was only the hall and a bedroom.[14] There are other mentions of cookshops by the Thames in deeds of 1219 and 1221[15] and Stow (in his *Survey of London*) was probably correct in translating FitzStephen's words as Cooks' Row. He also mentions, in his description of Queenhithe, a *Cooks house called the Sign of King David*, which suggests that such cookshops, like taverns, were given distinctive names. The streets of this neighbourhood must have been extremely busy, with many cookshops competing for trade, their owners calling out their wares to attract custom:

Cokes and hire knaves cryden Hote pies, hote!	*Cooks and hired hands cry Hot Pies, hot!*
Goode gees and grys! Go we dyne, go we!	*Good geese and piglets! Come and dine!* [16]

---

13 Henry Thomas Riley, ed. *Liber Custumarum*. Rolls Series, no.12, vol.2 (1860), pp. 2–15.

14 Omnes coquinae super Thamisiam dealbentur et plastrientur, intus et extra; et omnia intusclaustra et diversoria deponantur omnino; ita quod non remaneat nisi simliciter domus et thalamus. *A Source Book of London history from the Earliest Times to 1800* edited by P. Meadows, London: G. Bell and Sons, Ltd, 1914; pp. 19–21.

15 *Super ripam ad coquinas* and *coquinae Vinetrie*. See Martha Carlin, *loc.cit.*

16 Langland, *Piers Plowman*, Prologue. The word grys means piglets.

There were other cookshops throughout the City, including Bread Street and Eastcheap. The latter was singled out by Stow: *This Eastcheap is now a flesh market of Butchers there dwelling, on both sides of the street, it had sometime also Cooks mixed amongst the Butchers, and such other as sold victuals ready dressed of all sorts. For of old time when friends did meet, and were disposed to be merry, they went not to dine and sup in Taverns, but to the Cooks, where they called for meat what them liked, which they always found ready dressed at a reasonable rate, as I have before showed.*[17] This is of particular interest, indicating as it does that the Cookshops were preferred to the Taverns as places to dine. There were other cookshops in the City and in nearby Westminster. When, in the early seventeenth century, the surveyor Ralph Treswell made detailed plans of large parts of London and surveyed the shops near St Bartholomew's Hospital, at Pye Corner and on Cock (Cook) Lane, he showed cookshops crowded together, each supplied with substantial ovens.

By the time the cookshops on the Thames and elsewhere were established, the London Cooks had already come together to form a Guild. However, early in the fourteenth century there seems to have been a general move on the part of several Guilds and Misteries to expand their membership. This is reflected in a remarkable surge in enrolments of Freedom of the City, then, as now, a necessary requirement for Guild membership. Between 1309 and 1312 thirty-six Cooks presented themselves for admission as citizens, along with similar numbers of Bakers, Fishmongers, Bowyers, Coopers and Skinners. Twenty-four of these Cooks applied for the Freedom of the City in 1312. The names of Cooks admitted as citizens between these years, which provides the first record of the membership of the Cooks Guild, are printed in Appendix I. This list seems to demonstrate a planned movement towards greater Guild organisation, with the aim of gaining greater participation in the City government.[18]

The Lord Mayor and Aldermen continued to claim the right to supervise all commercial activity in the City, ordering the Sheriffs to punish any Bakers, Taverners, Millers, Cooks, Poulterers, Fishmongers, Butchers, Brewers or Cornmongers who were found to be lax in their work and Misteries, and laying down that Cooks must charge no more than one penny for putting a capon or rabbit in a pasty, on pain of imprisonment.[19] However, the authorities gradually came to realise that the best way to exercise such control was through the Guilds themselves. In consequence, the Guilds and Misteries came to play the leading role in the regulation of the trade and the punishment of malpractice.

---

17 'Candlewicke streete warde', *A Survey of London*, by John Stow: Reprinted from the text of 1603 (1908), pp. 216–223.

18 See 'Introduction: Redemption, women and the unenfranchised', *Calendar of the plea and memoranda rolls of the city of London: volume 2: 1364–1381* (1929), pp. XLVII-LIV.

19 In 1327 and 1350 respectively. See Henry Riley, *Memorials of London & London Life, 1276–1419*, London 1868, p. 257.

This change can be traced in the course of the fourteenth century. At the beginning of the century the Lord Mayor was still able to operate without the help of the Guilds. In 1300 he summoned a large group of Cooks and charged them with 'forestalling', that is buying up foodstuffs, including capons, hens, geese and other victuals, before they reached the City, so depriving ordinary citizens of the chance to buy them.[20] The Cooks were also charged with purchasing goods within the City before the hour of Prime (dawn), again before the ordinary residents could buy their necessaries. A jury was summoned and, although the Cooks denied the charges, some of them were adjudged to be guilty. It is especially interesting that one of those charged was a woman, Agnes Godman, since this is by far the earliest reference to a female who may well have been a member of the Guild. For the most part women in the Middle Ages were expected to play an entirely domestic role, although in 1465 it was noted as an ancient custom that every woman married to a Freeman of the City was, after the death of her husband, a Freewoman so long as she continued a widow and resided within the City.[21] However, some Guilds had a large number of female members and the Brewers had an exceptionally strong representation, with no less than 39 recorded as wearing the Livery in 1417. There is no further evidence of female Cooks until the Ordinances of the Pastelers of 1495, which refers to *bretheren and sistern of the Fellowship*, but it seems we can presume that there were women within the Guild from at least the fourteenth century.

Forestalling remained a problem for the Cooks and in 1379 further regulations were issued by the Mayor covering Poulterers, Cooks and Piebakers, who were forbidden to go out and meet the sellers of victuals coming into the city or to resell such food in the markets before ten o'clock, on pain of forfeiting the produce and being sent to prison at the will of the Mayor. The order also states that Piebakers must bake beef pasties for one-halfpenny which would be just as good as those costing a penny on pain of paying a fine of half a mark. This presumably implies that they were selling pasties filled with cheap and possibly rotten meat at half the price of wholesome ones.[22]

---

20 The group included John de Kent, John de Paris, Agnes Godman, Laurence Schail, Richard le Barber, William Gorre, Peter le Blunt, William Crel, Hugelyn of St Magnus, John de Reigat, Edmund Sket, John Bussard, Nicholas Sket, Robert the cook of Foxle, William de Waledon, John de Mardenheth and many other cooks The defendants denied the charge and put themselves on their country. A jury, summoned from Cornhill and from each Ward within the Gates and from the suburbs, consisting of William le Lou, Nicholas le Long, John Plot, Nicholas Brun, William Poyntel, Edmund Trentemars, Walter de Bredstrate, Richard Horn and others, brought in a verdict that certain of the cooks were guilty of forestalling poultry, and that the rest bought victuals and poultry outside their doors and elsewhere in the City from persons known and unknown, against the Proclamation. See *Calendar of early mayor's court rolls: 1298–1307* (1924), pp. 46–91.

21 'Introduction: Redemption, women and the unenfranchised', *Calendar of the plea and memoranda rolls of the city of London: volume 2: 1364–1381* (1929), pp. XLVII-LIV.

22 *Memorials of London*, London 1868, p. 432.

It was malpractices of this sort that led, in the same year (1379) to the first Ordinances being granted to members of the catering trade – named in this case as the Pastelers or Piebakers. These Ordinances give authority to the four Master Pastelers to ensure that pasties containing rabbits, geese, and garbage (*ie* offal), but which are *not befitting and sometimes stinking, in deceit of the people* are banned. In addition, some Pastelers *have baked beef in pasties and sold the same for venison in deceit of the people.* In consequence of this the Master Pastelers ordered that *no one of the said trade shall bake rabbits in pasties for sale on pain of paying the first time if found guilty thereof* 6*s* 8*d and of going bodily to prison at the will of the mayor.* A further regulation was that *no one of the said trade shall buy of any cook of Breadstreet or at the hostels of the great lords, of the cooks of such lords, any garbage from capons, hens or geese, to bake in a pasty or sell under the same penalty. Also no one shall bake beef in a pasty for sale and sell it as venison. Also that no one of the said trade shall bake either whole geese in a pasty, halves of geese or quarters of geese for sale on the pain aforesaid.* Passing off beef as venison was clearly fraud, but the reason for the prohibition of goose in pasties is unclear.

The City records do also include a number of significant cases in which cooks were prosecuted with the assistance of the Guild in the fourteenth century. In 1351 Henry Pecche bought two capons baked in pastry for himself and two companions, from a cook called Henry de Passelewe who had set up his stall by the Stocks. Because they were hungry, the purchasers did not immediately notice that the first capon was *putrid and stinking* until they had eaten almost all of it; whereupon they opened the second capon, and found it was also *putrid and stinking, and an abomination to mankind; to the scandal, contempt, and disgrace, of all the City, and the manifest peril of the life of the same Henry and his companions.* The remains of the offending capon were duly produced in court, but Henry de Passelewe claimed that when he had sold the capons to Henry Pecche they were *good, well-flavoured, fitting, and proper*. He therefore requested that the evidence should be examined by men of his own trade. The court summoned Philip le Keu, JohnWynge, William Bisshop, Walter Colman, Peter le Keu, and William Miles, cooks, of Breadstreet, John Chapman, cook, of Milkstreet, and Richard le Keu, of Ismongerelane [Ironmongerlane]. This expert panel, *after seeing and inspecting the capon aforesaid, here present in Court, said upon their oath, that the same capon, at the time of the sale thereof, was stinking and rotten, and baneful to the health of man*. Henry de Passelewe was consequently sentenced to the pillory, there to remain *for the length of one league's journey in the day*; the capon which had been found to be putrid and stinking was be carried before the guilty cook on his way to the pillory, where the reason for the sentence was proclaimed to all the people.[23]

It is interesting to note that three members of one family, Philip, Peter, and Richard le Keu, were on the expert panel, while Stephen le Keu, cook, was admitted to the Freedom

23 *Memorials of London* (1868), pp. 266–269.

of the City in 1312, revealing that even from this early date there were family dynasties of Cooks. In another case in 1374, when some butchers were accused of selling bad meat, the jury included three members of the Colman family, Thomas, Geoffrey and John, along with Robert Multone, John Heurl and Thomas Ballard, all Cooks of Breadstreet, and Henry atte Boure, John Bernes, Adam Hermyte, John Birlyngham, James Scot, and John Aubrey, all City Cooks. They found the butchers guilty and in the same session condemned John West, Cook, to the pillory for being found with a basket of bullock's flesh that was unfit for human consumption.[24]

Four years later, in 1355, Henry de Walmesford, Cook, was charged by Robert de Pokebrok, a chaplain, that he had sold him some veal for his supper the preceding day, which, when it was served, was found to be re-heated [*recalefactas*], stinking, and abominable to the human race, and a manifest danger to the plaintiff and his friends. Once again the offending meat was produced in court and submitted to the inspection of Thomas Maluele, John Wenge and Geoffrey Colman, Cooks of Breadstreet, and of John de Ware and John de Stoke, Cooks of Ironmonger Lane, each of whom certified on oath that the meat was good. In order to be absolutely sure and perhaps not trusting the judgement of the Cooks, the Mayor and Aldermen ordered the meat to be submitted to public inspection, when, after careful examination inside and out, it was again declared to be good and wholesome. Henry de Walmesford was duly acquitted.

In 1365 John Russelle of Abingdon, Poulterer, was prosecuted for offering for sale thirty seven, putrid, rotten, and stinking pigeons. The carcases were examined by John Vygerous, Thomas de Wynchestre, Pyebakers, and John Wenge, Geoffrey Coleman, John Lowe, Thos Coleman and Richard de Daventre, Cooks, who all agreed that pigeons were not good or wholesome. Russelle was sentenced to the pillory and his pigeons were burnt beneath it.

Other trades were equally guilty of trying to pass off false ingredients as something else: in 1394 Edmund Fraunceys and Mark Ernelee, Masters of the Mistery of Grocers, brought before the Mayor and Aldermen *three bags of dust, made of rape, radish roots and old, rotten cetuall* (the root of the zedoary, a plant having qualities resembling those of ginger) *unhealthy for human use, found in the house of Walter King, Grocer, and exposed for sale by the said Walter's apprentice as being good powdered ginger, in deceit of the people and to the scandal of the whole Mistery of Grocers. The said Walter admitted this and other offences committed by his servants and put himself on the mercy of the Mayor and Aldermen. Thereupon it was considered that he pay a fine of £200 to the Chamber.*[25] The fact that the Cooks were not involved on this occasion can be put down to the fact that the Grocers were by this date sufficiently well organised to be able to exercise control of the trade themselves, without recourse to outside help.

---

24 *Calendar of letter-books of the city of London: G: 1352–1374* (1905), pp. 327–334.
25 *Calendar of the plea and memoranda rolls of the city of London: volume 3: 1381–1412* (1932), pp. 205–227.

A particularly interesting case that did come before the Cooks involved a man named as Reynald atte Chaumbre. The scale of his dishonest operation is remarkable, for in 1382 he was charged with bringing into the City a boatload of 7,000 herrings and 800 mackerel, all of which he knew to be putrid and corrupt. A jury of five Cooks, John Lowe, Geoffrey Coleman, John Westerham, Reynald Coleman, and Robert Multone, with John Filiol, Fishmonger, and six other honest citizens, decided that the fish was *corrupt and unwholesome for man*. The accused pleaded guilty and threw himself on the mercy of the Court, which sentenced him to stand in the pillory for one hour each day for six days and to have his rotten fish burned beneath him. At this point Reynald played his trump card, claiming that he held office under the King and implying that His Majesty would be displeased if one of his servants was placed in the pillory. The sentence was therefore postponed until a conference could be held with one of the King's Council. In the meantime Reynald was remanded to Newgate prison. Unfortunately we do not know the final outcome of his case, but it seems probable that he escaped severe punishment.[26]

Similar cases, though not on the same scale, can readily be found and they were to give rise to the characteristic right of Guilds and Livery Companies to carry out Searches, in order to discover those who were trading illegally or selling defective goods. What appears to be the first record of these dates from 1373, when Geoffrey Colman and Thomas Ballard, Cooks of Bread Street, and Edmund Cadent and William Longe, Cooks of Eastcheap, were sworn to make *scrutinies* and exercise supervision over the men of their trade and the Pyebakers, to prevent the sale of unhealthy food and the charging of unreasonable prices, and to report offences from time to time to the Mayor and Aldermen.[27]

In several of the above cases Cooks are described in terms of the location of their business – namely *of Breadstreet* or *of Eastcheap*, or *of Ironmongerlane*. What exactly these geographic distinctions implied is not clear, but on at least one occasion, in 1393, there is a record of separate Masters of the Mistery of Cooks being sworn in: on 21st June William Baldeswelle and Edward Brydde were sworn as Masters of the Cooks of Eastcheap and John Wyldbournham and William Goldynge were sworn as Masters of the Cooks of Breadstreet. It is, however, clear that these were not Masters in the sense that the term is used of later Masters of Livery Companies. There are several early lists of Masters sworn in a range of Misteries and the number elected varies between two, three and four at a time. Thus, in the same year that the Masters of the Cooks of Eastcheap and of Bread Street are sworn, we find Robert Austyn, Richard Dyne, Martin Godard, and Richard Twyford, sworn as Masters of the Cutlers, while in 1377 and again in 1379 four Masters of the Pastelers were sworn. In 1416 four Masters of the Cooks were sworn, while two years later the Cooks and the Pastelers jointly swore four Masters. Confusingly, the Pastelers go

26 *Memorials of London* (1868), pp. 455–476.
27 *Calendar of the plea and memoranda rolls of the city of London*, vol 2: 1364–1381 (1929), pp. 163–181.

back to having four Masters in 1421, as do the Cooks in 1425. It may well be that the term Master, as it is used in these fourteenth and early fifteenth century lists, denotes men who carried out similar functions to the Wardens of the later Livery Companies, which commonly elect two, three or four Wardens.

The earliest Ordinances of Cooks that survive date from 1378, but Ordinances existed in some form before this. In 1376 Thomas Blome, a foreigner (*ie* not a Londoner) attempted to sell six cheeses at Leadenhall market, but this was judged to be *against the liberty of the City and the ordinances of the Cooks* and the offending items were confiscated.[28] Strengthening the membership and organisation of the Guild certainly allowed the Cooks to play a growing role in the affairs of the City. This was seen over the question of paying for the water supply, which was essential for cleanliness and hygiene. Initially, water supplied by the Great Conduit in Cheapside was available to all without charge, but by the early 14th century commercial demands were threatening the domestic supply and a charge was levied on those who used the water in the pursuit of their trade. In 1312 the Wardens were appointed to collect the sums assessed on brewers, cooks, and fishmongers for the use of the water, and to spend the money on the maintenance of the Conduit.[29] It is not known whether this also involved paying, in the same year, for the huge celebrations held in London to mark the birth of a son (the future Edward III) to Queen Isabella, consort of King Edward II. However, it is recorded that *the Conduit in Cheap ran with nothing but wine, for all those who chose to drink there* and that the Mayor and Aldermen all dined at the Guildhall, which was *excellently well tapestried and dressed out* for the occasion.[30]

A further indication that the Cooks, the Pastelers and the Piebakers had come together as a single Guild, whatever the status of their various 'Masters', is provided by the joint Ordinance of the Cooks and Pastelers, and Piebakers, ordered by the Mayor and Aldermen in 1378, with regard to the prices of different sorts of flesh, meat and poultry, both roasted and baked in pasties. These prices also give a good indication of the variety of meat and poultry that was available:

The best roast pig for 8d. Best roast goose 7d. Best roast capon for 6d. Best roast hen 4d. Best roast pullet 2 ½d. Best roast rabbit 4d. Best roast river mallard 4 ½d. Best roast dunghill mallard 3 ½d. Best roast teal 2 ½d. Best roast snipe 1 ½d. Five roast larks 1 ½d. Best roast woodcock 2 ½d. Best roast partridge 3 ½d. Best roast plover 2 ½d. Best roast pheasant 13d. Best roast curlew 6 ½d. Three roast thrushes 2d. Ten roast finches 1d. Best roast heron 18d. Best roast bittern 20d. Three roast pigeons 2 ½d. Ten eggs a penny. For the paste fire and trouble upon a capon 1 ½d. For the paste fire and trouble upon a goose 2d. The best capon baked in pastry 8d. The best hen baked in a pasty 5d. The best lamb roasted 7d.[31]

---

28 *Calendar of the plea and memoranda rolls*, vol 2:, pp. 206–230.
29 St. Mary Colechurch: the great conduit, *Historical gazetteer of London before the Great Fire* (1987), pp. 612–616.
30 *Memorials of London* (1868), pp. 93–107.
31 *Memorials of London* (1868), pp. 415–428.

Figure 12. Norman cooks preparing meat, depicted on the Bayeux Tapestry c.1070–80.

There are obviously some exotic delicacies listed here, including expensive roast heron and bittern, so it is not surprising that the King from whose reign it dates, Richard II, had a widespread reputation as a *gourmet.* His Court employed many Cooks and some of them produced the first real Cookery Book in English. Entitled *The Forme of Cury* (The Proper Method of Cookery), its preface states that it was *compiled by the chief Master Cooks of King Richard the Second, King of England after the Conquest; the which was accounted the best and most royal vyaundier* (*ie* generous host) *of all Christian Kings.*[32] Stow relates that the Court regularly fed 10,000 people a day and although this seems a vast number it may not be too far from the truth. The Cooks were clearly kept busy!

There was a parallel development in France, where the first *celebrity chef* is recorded in the fourteenth century. This was Taillevent, born Guillaume Tirel in Normandy around 1310, who started his career as a kitchen boy for Jeanne d'Evreux, Queen of France in the 1320s and subsequently served as cook to the Kings of France, becoming Chief Cook (*premier queux*) to Charles V and Supervisory Cook (*Ecuyer de Cuisine*) to Charles VI. He retired in 1392 aged over eighty. At some point, probably the 1370s, he wrote a cookbook called *Le Viandier* which gave details of the royal feasts he prepared and was to influence French cooking for generations. When he died in 1395 he was buried with all the panoply of a knight and the effigy on his tomb showed him in armour, with his personal arms on his shield, including three cooking pots.[33]

---

32 Constance Hieatt & Sharon Butler, *Curye on Inglysch: English Culinary Manuscripts of the 14th century*, Early English Text Society (OUP), 1985.

33 He was buried in the priory of Notre Dame in Hennebont, Brittany. The tomb is destroyed but is known from nineteenth century engravings.

Providing feasts and banquets was to become one of the main occupations of the London Cooks. On the Bayeux Tapestry Cooks are depicted preparing and serving a banquet for King William I on campaign, when the feast was cooked in the open air, the meat roasted on spits and with a cauldron heated over an open fire. It also shows bread being baked in a field oven. The cooked food was passed to the servants, who served their masters sitting at table. Most feasts were, of course, cooked indoors and served in banqueting halls. One of the first such London occasions of which there is a record occurred in 1257 when the Scottish King Alexander and his Queen Margaret came to Westminster and enjoyed a *marvellous great dinner* with John Mansel, chaplain to King Henry III, when over seven hundred dishes were served to a multitude of guests. The chronicler Froissart records a great feast when Edward III married Philippa of Hainault in 1329, and there is no doubt that such royal events – births, marriages, coronations, and military victories – all provided good excuses for elaborate banquets. One of the most famous was that given in 1356 by the fabulously wealthy Sir Henry Picard, Vintner and

Figure 13. A Norman feast, depicted on the Bayeux Tapestry c.1070–80.

Lord Mayor, who entertained on one day King Edward III, John, King of France, the King of Cyprus, David, King of Scotland, Edward the Black Prince, and a large assemblage of the nobility. *And after*, writes Stow, *the said Henry Picard kept his hall against all comers whosoever that were willing to play at dice and hazard*.[34]

Unfortunately, there is little detail of the way in which these medieval feasts were organised. A rare exception is the extraordinary enthronement feast for George Neville as Archbishop of York in 1466; a great deal is known about this, although it was clearly an exceptional event. The Nevilles were the most powerful and influential family in Britain and this feast was designed to advertise their supreme status. There were over 2,000 guests and more than 1,000 officers and servants, who also needed to be fed, requiring vast quantities of food – the meat alone comprised 6 wild bulls, 104 oxen, 304 calves, 204 kids, 1,000 sheep, 304 pigs and 2,000 suckling pigs.[35] There were 57 Cooks and 115 scullions and other assistants, who served what were essentially four separate three-course dinners; which of these meals guests received depended upon where they were seated in the Archbishop's Palace.

For London, there are records of dinners held by the Brewers Guild in their Hall in the 1420s [36] – Brewers Hall was itself an early example of a Livery Hall and it was used by other Guilds, including on three days by the Cooks, for their own dinners. The Guild paid 7*s* 4*d* on each occasion to the Brewers for the use of their Hall, which indicates that they were a growing organisation, albeit one that did not yet possess a Hall of its own.

Several of the Brewers' own menus are recorded, including that for the Election Dinner in 1419, which consisted of brawn in mustard, cabbage soup, roast swan, venison broth and roast partridge, pears in syrup, fritters, and custard. A dinner on 29 August, 1424, consisted of a first course of loin of deer soup, pheasant stewed in syrup, swan in a spicy sauce, and for the second course cream of almond soup, rabbit, pigeon, and sweetmeats. The total cost was £3 11*s* 11 ½*d*. By contrast, the Election Dinner in 1425 was more elaborate and cost the enormous sum of £38. Another dinner that year featured seafood (eels, whelks, mussels, sturgeon, salmon, pickerel, plaice, halibut, pike and stockfish) rather than meat. A well documented dinner, also in 1425, included stewed sirloin of beef, roast goose and capons, glazed chicken, roasted pigeons, and sweetmeats, with each Guild member contributing 6*d* towards the cost. Three and a half barrels of ale and 35 gallons of wine were provided, while two dozen earthenware pots, four dozen cups, and eight dozen

---

34 *Old and New London*: Volume 1 (1878), pp. 550–565.

35 Peter Brears, *Cooking and Dining in Medieval England*, Totnes, 2008, pp. 465–484. This book gives the most detailed modern account of the subject and is especially informative about the design of kitchens and the provision of food to households. The evidence for catering operations in London is not considered in great detail.

36 R.W. Chambers and Marjorie Daunt, eds., *A Book of London English 1384–1425*, Oxford: Clarendon Press, 1931, pp. 178–80.

Figure 14. The Dukes of York, Gloucester and Ireland dine with Richard II, by Jean de Batard Wavrin (on vellum). British Library Ms Roy 14 E IV f.265v.

pewter vessels were rented, and service fees were paid to a cook, turnspits, water-carrier, butler, and pantry-keeper. Arrangements were made to clean the vessels and wash the dinner linen, and to empty out the privy after the feast. It may be safely assumed that the cook was a member of the Cooks' Guild and that it was already established practice for all City Dinners to be placed in the hands of a member of the Guild.[37]

By the beginning of the seventeenth century, such feasts are recorded in more detail. King James I dined with the Merchant Taylors Company on 16 July 1607. Immediately after the King had announced that he would come and dine with the Company elaborate preparations began. One of the first things to do was to appoint two Caters (*ie* catering managers): *Lansdale the Lord Mayor's Cater, and Sotherne one of the Sheriffs' Caters are appointed to be in attendance upon the Stewards to inform them of all things necessary for such an*

37 *Medieval English Political Writings*, Kalamazoo, Michigan: Medieval Institute Publications, 1996.

entertainment, and to consider what number of messes are requisite and how many and what dishes, and how and where the same shall be disposed, and to draw out Bills of the Diet to be considered of by the Committees, and to do all such services as doth appertain to Caters to perform.[38] Messes were groups of diners seated at one table (the word survives in this sense in terms such as Officers' Mess), on which the various dishes were set out and the guests would help themselves. A member of the Livery was appointed Chief Butler, to supervise all the actual Butlers that would be needed. The Company also undertook to provide *a competent and sufficient number of the Officers attending the Lord Mayor and Sheriffs to wait at the Dinner.* Ben Jonson was employed to write an Ode for the occasion and, since the King would dine in the King's Chamber above the Hall, a hole was to be cut in the wall so that His Majesty could observe the proceedings below. Every Lord that was in London was invited, along with Ambassadors and many members of the Royal Court.

The feast was a great success and Henry, Prince of Wales, who accompanied his father, was made free of the Company, along with many other of the distinguished guests. But then came the reckoning and information about this is contained in the detailed bills and accounts that survive. The entire feast cost more that £1,000, an enormous sum, but hardly surprising in view of the range and extent of the food provided. The poultry and game birds alone included 17 swans, 28 pheasants, 16 geese, 63 capons, 158 pullets, 36 turkey chickens, 57 large chickens, 162 smaller chickens, 114 baking chickens, 172 quails, 45 herons, 10 bitterns, 13 shovelers, 17 godwits, 81 partridges, 14 ruffs, 14 brewes, 52 peewits, 66 ducklings, 57 pigeons, 10 owls, 2 cuckoos, 2 ring doves, 2 peacocks, 1 great turkey, 24 teals, and 1,300 eggs. An equally extensive range and quantity of meats, puddings and fruit was provided, together with seemingly endless gallons of wine and beer. All this was prepared by the Company Cook, Henry Beaumont, assisted by thirty-two other Master Cooks, each employed for between one and four days. The Cooks were assisted by forty-three kitchen labourers. Beaumont himself prepared some of the speciality dishes, including a swan pie and an owl pie, and he was also responsible for providing dinner for the other thirty-two Cooks on the day of the feast; unfortunately, there was *no cold meat left for them*, presumably because the guests had eaten it all.

Such extraordinary feasts occupied the grandest of the Cooks, but most members of the profession still catered on a daily basis for the popular market. The cookshops continued to flourish, as was demonstrated in the satirical poem, *London Lickpenny*, attributed to John Lydgate and written at the end of the fifteenth century, which portrays a young innocent from the county abroad in London and Westminster:

38 The Banquet given to James I, 1607, *Memorials of the Guild of Merchant Taylors: Of the Fraternity of St. John the Baptist in the City of London* (1875), pp. 147–181.

Then to Westminster gate I went
When the sun was at high prime.
Cooks to me, they took good intent,
Called me near, for to dine,
And proffered me good bread, ale, and wine.
A fair cloth they began to spread,
Ribbs of beef, both fat and fine;
But for lack of money I might not speed.

So he travels into the City, in search of cheaper fare:

Then I hied me into Eastcheap.
One cried, "Ribs of beef, and many a pie!"
Pewter pots they clattered on a heap.
There was harp, pipe and sawtry (psaltery).

Eastcheap had long been a centre for cookshops and this combination of food and drink led the area acquiring a reputation for licentious and riotous behaviour. On Midsummer's Eve, 1410, the Princes Thomas and John, sons of King Henry IV, came to Eastcheap between two and three o'clock in the morning, in order to dine. A fight broke out among their supporters, and it took more than an hour for the Mayor and Sheriffs to get the situation under control. This resulted in a series of City Ordinances that tried to control the opening hours of the cookshops and taverns in the City. Before Midsummer's Day in the following year a proclamation was made forbidding Vintners, Taverners, Brewers, Cooks, and others to keep their doors open after 10pm on the Eves of the feast of St. John the Baptist (24 June) and that of St Peter and St Paul (29 June) and ordering that a light or lantern be kept burning in front of every house on the street on the same evenings.[39] Further restrictions were imposed over the years such as the

Figure 15. A stout cook in his kitchen surrounded by cooking utensils. Woodcut, German, 1530.

39 *Calendar of letter-books of the city of London: I: 1400–1422* (1909), pp. 101–111.

order by Mayor Thomas Calworth in 1444 that no Cook was to bake or roast meat on a Sunday and a ban on Cooks and Innholders selling uncooked meat on the Sabbath.

At the same time the Guild was tightening its control over the membership, settling disputes between individuals and making sure they presented a united front. Typical of this, in 1422 Gilbert Page, Cook, and William Audley, Cook, issued mutual bonds of £20 each to John Bederenden, chamberlain, swearing good behaviour towards each other and towards the Masters and Goodmen of the Mistery of Cooks and Pastelers and promising obedience to all the Ordinances and Rules laid down by the said Masters and confirmed by the Court.

The growing status of the Guild was recognised on 31st May, 1461, when the Cooks received a Grant of Arms from John Wrexworth, Guyenne King of Arms.[40] This stated that the Wardens of the Craft of Cooks of the City of London had presented themselves to Wrexworth, *requiring me to devise a sign and a cognisance in form of arms for them and their successors to bear and use for perpetual memory*. Consequently, he had *devised, given and granted unto the said craft…a sign and conysaunce* (knowledge) *of arms…which blazon I witness not thus borne by none other person what so ever he be within the Realm of England.*[41] The arms were to be *Argent three Columbine flowers Azure*. It is not clear why the grant was made by Guyenne, since the Guild was in the province of Clarenceux King of Arms, William Hawkslowe. To rectify this anomaly Hawkslowe confirmed the grant on 13 October, 1467, as *Argent a Chevron engrailed Sable between three Columbine flowers Azure*. For some reason the Sable (black) of the Chevron was changed to Gules (red) in the eighteenth century, but the correct tincture (colour) has now been re-adopted. The choice of Columbine flowers is also puzzling, as they do not have any obvious connection with cooking. It has been suggested that they may represent the form of Ginger known as Colambyne, and in Russell's *Book of Nurture* (c1460) we read *For good ginger Columbine is best to drink*. The Columbine flower was also held to have medicinal properties, particularly beneficial for the liver, so this sense too may have been intended.

A Crest and Supporters were added to the Arms by William Camden, Clarenceux, on 1 August, 1612 and these were approved and entered in a Visitation in 1634,[42] where they were described as *On a Wreath of the Colours A Mount Vert thereon a Cock Pheasant proper* (Crest) and *Dexter a Buck*, *sinister a Doe both proper* (Supporters) with the Motto *VULNERATI NON VICTI* (Wounded not Conquered). Why this motto was chosen is not at all clear, but it may have been intended as a pun, since the word VICTI could be derived

40 Earlier histories of the Cook's Company incorrectly name him as Gwyan Wraxworth, King of Arms. John Wrexworth, Guyenne King of Arms was created in 1446 and died some time before 1472, when a new Guyenne King of Arms was created.

41 'Devises of Arms during the Fifteenth Century, Pt III' Colin Cole in *The Coat of Arms*, c1960.

42 In Tudor and Stuart times it was obligatory for those who had arms to furnish the Heralds with proof and have those arms recorded. The Heralds made a Visitation for this purpose about every thirty years.

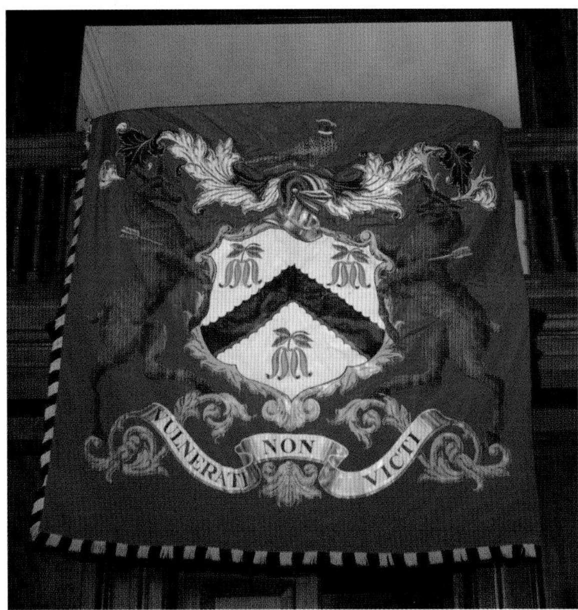

Figure 16. The Banner bearing the Company's Arms, acquired through a bequest of Liveryman Arthur Fordham, who died in 1976.

from VICTUS, meaning food or victuals, in which case the words could also be construed as *Do not harm food* and such a double meaning would be entirely in tune with the sort of wordplay that was popular in late medieval England.

The supporters were drawn with an arrow piercing them at the shoulder, but these arrows were crossed out on the drawing and a note reading *The Arrows left out of the Supporters* was added. A subsequent Visitation in 1687 confirmed the removal of the arrows and added the word SED (but) to the Motto: *VULNERATI SED NON VICTI.* The choice of a buck and a doe as Supporters is readily understood, given the importance of venison to the Cooks and the Motto made more sense when these animals were portrayed pierced with arrows –the reason for the removal of the arrows is not clear.

The Grant of Arms was followed in 1475 by a petition from *the good men of the Mistery of Pastelers* that certain Ordinances might be approved. This is a rather obscure set of rules and the meaning and purpose of several of the clauses are also unclear, serving only to remind us that many details of the trade are not fully understood. They included a demand that only Cooks should be permitted to draw and pluck poultry, that they should not sell fish and flesh together on Wednesdays, no twice-baked fish or flesh should be sold, that no one *sell any victuals to any huckster, that is to say Elys Tartes or Flans or any such bake meats, save only to free persons of the said City or no mould ware be made by hand or by mould to sell in their Shoppes or to any huckster to retail or to any other but if it be bespoken fore to the Feasts*, that no Cook should employ any *foreign person* as long as there is a freeman of the Guild who can do the work, and that cooked food must be paid for before it is delivered.[43]

The Ordinances do at least demonstrate that all aspects of the profession of cookery were coming under scrutiny and so they can be seen as anticipating the full Incorporation of the Company. This occurred on 11th July, 1482, when King Edward IV granted a Charter that set out the rights and privileges of the Guild and Mistery of Cooks. It is the document that marks the true foundation of the Company. The full translation of the text of this

43 *Calendar of letter-books of the city of London: L: Edward IV-Henry VII* (1912), pp. 110–130. See Appendix 4.

Charter (originally in Latin) is set out in Appendix 5, but the key points may be summarised here.

The Charter notes that the Cooks have served the King well, since they *have for a long time outside the aforesaid City, personally taken and borne and to this day do not cease to take and bear great and manifold pains and labour, as well at our great feast of St George as at others according to our command.*[44] This indicates that the Guild was already well established as the Royal caterer. However, since the members were also charged with carrying out public duties such as serving on assizes and juries, which presumably interfered with their role as royal servants, in future they would be excused from such service. They would now be constituted as *one Body and one Commonality perpetual* and two of their principal members would choose annually two Masters or Governors, who are most expert in the same Mistery, *to superintend, rule and govern the Mistery and Commonality aforesaid.*

This clause explains the unique right of the Company, which survives to this day, to elect two Masters each year. It is not, however, clear why this unusual arrangement was made; a tradition within the Company relates that the King and the Lord Mayor both required the attendance of the Master on the same day, leading the King to insist on the appointment of a second Master. Alternatively, it has been suggested that when serving at Court feasts one Master attended the Sovereign, while the Second Master was below stairs. There is no firm evidence for either of these explanations and it has already been noted that the earlier records of Guild elections of two Master Cooks along with two Master Pastelers can be discounted, since these were paralleled by the election of two, three or four Masters in several other trades. The later Minute Books of the Company regularly refer to the election of one Master and three Wardens, although the meetings of the Court are shown at the same time as taking place in the presence of two Masters and two Wardens. The evidence is confusing but the most likely explanation is that the two Masters of the Cooks should be seen as the equivalent of the Master and Upper Warden commonly found in other Livery Companies. In the eighteenth century there are many references to the *Second Master or Upper Warden*, indicating that the two terms were interchangeable. Nonetheless, although the precise reason for designating two Masters remains unknown, the custom certainly does date from the first Charter and it is therefore appropriate that it is still in operation. However, it is only from the first half of the twentieth century that the term Second Master has been exclusively used and no reference has been made to an Upper Warden.

The Charter also made the Guild a legal entity, with the right to purchase and hold property and to take actions in court. The Masters and Court could hold meetings and

44 The St George's Day Feast, at which the monarch entertains the Knights of the Garter at Windsor, still takes place each year on 23 April.

enact Ordinances for the regulation of the profession, provided these were not in contravention of the laws of the realm. The Guild should have *supervision, scrutiny, correction and government of all and singular men of the said Commonality of Cooks....and the punishment of them for their defaults in not perfectly executing, doing and using the Mistery aforesaid, so as the punishment of this sort be executed by reasonable and fit means*. Finally, the Guild should have the right to admit members who are *sufficiently instructed and informed in the said Mistery of Cooks*. The regulations set out in the Charter were to remain in place for ever.

The provisions of the Charter are expressed in the elaborate legalistic language that is usual in such documents, but the content is relatively slight. However, its clauses form the basis of all the future rights and privileges of the Company, although they were soon to need expanding, to cover more aspects of the profession. The most important of the early additions to the clauses in the Charter were the Ordinances of the Pastelers of 1495, which provide a much more detailed series of regulations for the new Company.

The Cooks or Pastelers obviously felt the need to defend their newly-won independence from encroachment by related trades and in 1495 the Wardens of the Art or Mistery of Pastelers came before the Mayor and Aldermen and complained that whereas in the past they had been *of power to have a company of them self in one clothing* and been able to afford the charges imposed on them by the City, they had now fallen into such poverty that they could no longer appear in one clothing, nor could they bear the City's charges. The reason for this was that they were being deprived of their living by Vintners, Brewers, Innholders, and Tipplers. They therefore requested new Ordinances and these are printed in Appendix 4 but the main points included:

Disputes between members must be submitted to the Wardens.

The Wardens should have authority to search and oversee all dressed victuals in open shops, to see if they were wholesome and *whether the pennyworths thereof be reasonable for the common weal of the Kings liege people or not.*

All persons *that seethe, roast, or bake victuals for sale in the City* must pay the same quarterage to the Wardens as Freemen had been accustomed to pay in support of the Craft. This seems to be the first direct reference to the payment of quarterage, and this clause was intended to extend the monopoly of cooking that the Company claimed.

No one should in future sell any ready-dressed victuals in the streets or lanes. Confiscated victuals would be sent to the poor prisoners in Ludgate and Newgate jails. The purpose of this is presumably to ensure that cooked food was only sold through authorised cookshops.

No members of the *Craft of Pastelers* shall prepare any of the great Feasts, such as the Sergeants' Feast, the Mayor's Feast, the Sheriffs' Feast or the Merchant Taylors' Feast, without informing the Wardens and all such feasts must be *well and worshipfully dressed for the honour of this City and also for the honour and profit of the persons that shall bear the charges thereof.* Any member that is employed as a household cook to the Mayor or the Sheriffs may not dress any *Feasts, Breakfasts, Dinners or Suppers, for any Weddings, Obits, Crafts or otherwise out of the Mayor or Sheriffs houses without such Feast, Breakfast, Dinner or Supper be made at the cost and charge of the said Mayor and Sheriffs.* This is so that *every man of the same Fellowship may have a competent living.*

Figure 17. Medieval cooking pot found in excavations at St Bartholomew's Hospital.

Henceforth there shall be only one cookshop open on Sunday in Breadstreet and one in Bridgestreet, so that *the good Folks of the same Craft may serve God the better on the Sunday as true Christian men should do.* The Wardens would prescribe which two shops should open on Sunday, based on a strict rotation by all the owners.

If a member of the Company contracts with an individual or institution to prepare any feast, dinner or supper he shall not be prevented from carrying out this work by any other member of the Company.

If any foreigner or stranger is found making or dressing a feast, dinner or supper within the City it will be lawful for the Wardens, together with a Sergeant of the Mayor assigned to them, to arrest the offender and consign him to prison, to await the punishment imposed by the Mayor and Aldermen.

Every brother *of ability and power* is to pay 4*s* quarterage yearly, for the benefit of the priest and the clerks and for his dinner.

No freeman of the Craft shall slander or revile another. Any brother making an unreasonable complaint to the Wardens shall forfeit 20 pence.

No one of the Craft shall *make or do to be made upon one day more than two dinners and one Supper.*[45]

45 *Calendar of letter-books of the city of London: L: Edward IV-Henry VII* (1912), pp. 303–313.

The Charter and these Ordinances formally established the Cooks as a corporate body within the City, responsible for all aspects of the trade and for all the actions of their members. In fact, as we have seen, this seems to have been the case in practice for most of the fifteenth century and the Charter was little more than the official and legal confirmation of the position of the Guild, or, as it could now be called, the Company. Following the pattern of other Companies, it may be presumed that there were two classes of members – freemen and liverymen. The first use of a livery by the Cooks is not recorded, but there are references to various trades wearing a livery from at least 1319.[46] In 1382, one Adam Carlelle, appeared before the Mayor on a charge of abusing fishmongers who were legally selling their fish by the Stocks and, having been found guilty, was debarred from holding public office and from wearing a livery. In 1415 we hear of Richard Merlawe, Alderman, who had originally been admitted into the freedom of the City as an Ironmonger, but was now a Fishmonger, and who received annually the livery and clothing of both crafts, which was contrary to the ordinance made of King Henry V.[47] In the same year it was laid down by the Mayor that the custom for Officers of the City to receive each year either a hood or clothing from each of the Guilds should be abandoned and each officer was only entitled to wear the livery of his own craft. By 1475 it had been agreed by Common Council that, for the election of a new Mayor and Sheriffs, the Masters and Wardens of the Misteries, together with all the membership assembled in their halls, should go together to the Guildhall, clothed in their livery.

So, by the end of the fifteenth century the Guild of Cooks had become the Company of Cooks, furnished with a Royal Charter, reinforced by Ordinances, bearing Arms, wearing a Livery and thirty-fifth in order of seniority in the City Livery Companies. It seemed that all the Cooks were lacking was a Hall and this was something that was shortly to be remedied.

---

46 See Chapter 1, p 16.
47 *Calendar of letter-books of the city of London: I: 1400–1422* (1909), pp. 146–157.

CHAPTER THREE

The Company under the Tudors

During the eighteenth century a manuscript book was compiled, containing extracts from documents relating to the history of the Worshipful Company of Cooks of London. It was most probably penned by Richard Wood, who was Master of the Company in 1767 and fortunately it survived the fire which destroyed the Hall in 1771 and subsequent disasters, including the loss of many original documents during the Second World War.[1] This small book is now one of the few sources for much of what we know about the early history of the Company. It is particularly important for the history of the Hall since it includes the deeds to the property dating back to 1350.

In that year one John De Gheyntion (presumably a Dutchman) sold William Beaver, Citizen and Merchant Taylor of London, a tenement in the parish of St Botolph without Aldersgate, together with the houses, buildings, and other appurtenances belonging to it. This was between the City Ditch, known as Houndsditch, on the east and the King's Highway of Aldersgate on the west. The property passed through several hands over the next hundred years, but it does not seem to have had any connection with the Cooks until it was acquired by Richard Cornish of London, Gentleman, and Elizabeth his wife in 1473. By a Deed Poll of 15th May 1500 Cornish granted the freehold of the property to John Woodall and Thomas Nelson, *Masters or Governors of the Art of Cooks in the City of London.* We do not know whether Richard Cornish himself was a member of the Cooks' Company

1 Now Guildhall Library Ms 9989. On 13 September, 1766, the Minutes record that Mr Wood was ordered to deliver the Company's deeds and writings to Mr Henshaw, the clerk, and to compare the same with the abstract.

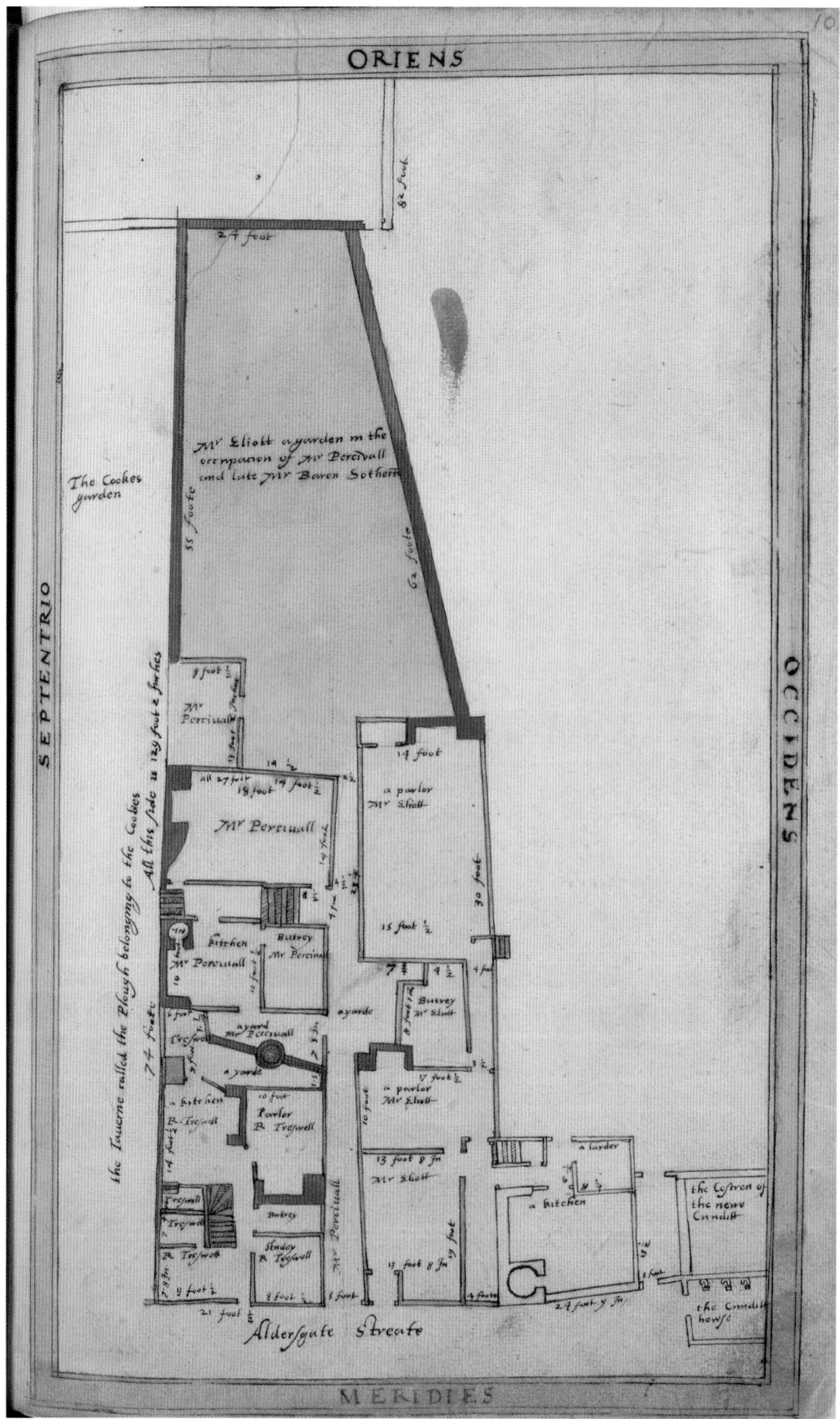

Figure 18. Numbers 7–10 Aldersgate Street facing the Cooks' garden, drawn by the surveyor Ralph Treswell, 1612. Guildhall Library Ms 12805.

but he may perhaps be identified with a Londoner of the same name who died in 1504, leaving lands in Hertfordshire and at Shacklewell in Hackney. These he had inherited from his father, Thomas Cornish, a Saddler, who is recorded as a tenant in Shacklewell in1490.[2]

The terms of the Deed are that the entire tenement, with the shop, cellars, sollars (upstairs rooms) and the rest of its appurtenances is for the use of John Woodall and Thomas Nelson and their successors as Governors or Masters of the Cooks forever. The property, situated in *Aldersgate Street in the Suburbs of London*, lay between a tenement belonging to the church of St Botolph on the south and a tenement late of John Rowthe on the north, with the ditch of the City of London towards the east and Aldersgate Street to the west.

It is not known exactly when the Cooks built their Hall on this plot – there are references to other tenements abutting Cooks' Hall by the middle of the century and in 1561 John Wilcokes, Citizen and Cook of London made a bequest *to the Master and Wardens of his Company of the Mistery of Cooks within the City for a dinner in their Common Hall.*[3] There is also an indenture relating to the Hall, dated 28th September, 1561. This is a contract between the Master and three Wardens of the Cooks Company on the one hand and John Leoff, Citizen and Carpenter of London on the other, for Leoff to pull down the roof of the Hall, together with all the glass and part of the wainscot, and build a new roof of well seasoned oak, covered with lath and tile, and re-glaze it, repairing the wainscot and ceiling as well. The Company agreed to pay him £13 – *6s* – *8d* for this work. It may well have been at this time that the Long Gallery was constructed. Such a radical refurbishment suggests the Hall had been built some time earlier and it is likely that it was put up shortly after the tenement passed to the Cooks in 1500.

By the reign of Queen Elizabeth I, Cooks' Hall had acquired a reputation for fine dining which was reflected in popular entertainment. In 1575 the Queen was received by Robert Dudley, Earl of Leicester at Kenilworth Castle with feasting, masques, and plays. In one of these entertainments a comical ancient minstrel is asked how he comes to bear the arms of *the worshipful village of Islington, well known to be one of the oldest and best towns in England near London.* He explains that he was granted the arms for his *faithful friendship demonstrated over many years, at the Cooks' feast in Aldersgate Street, held every year on Holy Rood day* [14th September] *and at solemn bridal feasts in the city of London throughout the year, where he properly served guests with Furmenty* [hulled wheat boiled in milk] *for porridge, not overboiled until it is too weak; milk for their flans, not watered down and covered in chalk; cream for their custards, not frothed or thickened with flour; and butter for their pasties and pie paste, not*

2 'Hackney: Shacklewell', *A History of the County of Middlesex: Volume 10: Hackney* (1995), pp. 35–38.

3 From: 'Wills: 1–10 Elizabeth I (1558–68)', Calendar of wills proved and enrolled in the Court of Husting, London: Part 2: 1358–1688 (1890), pp. 668–682.

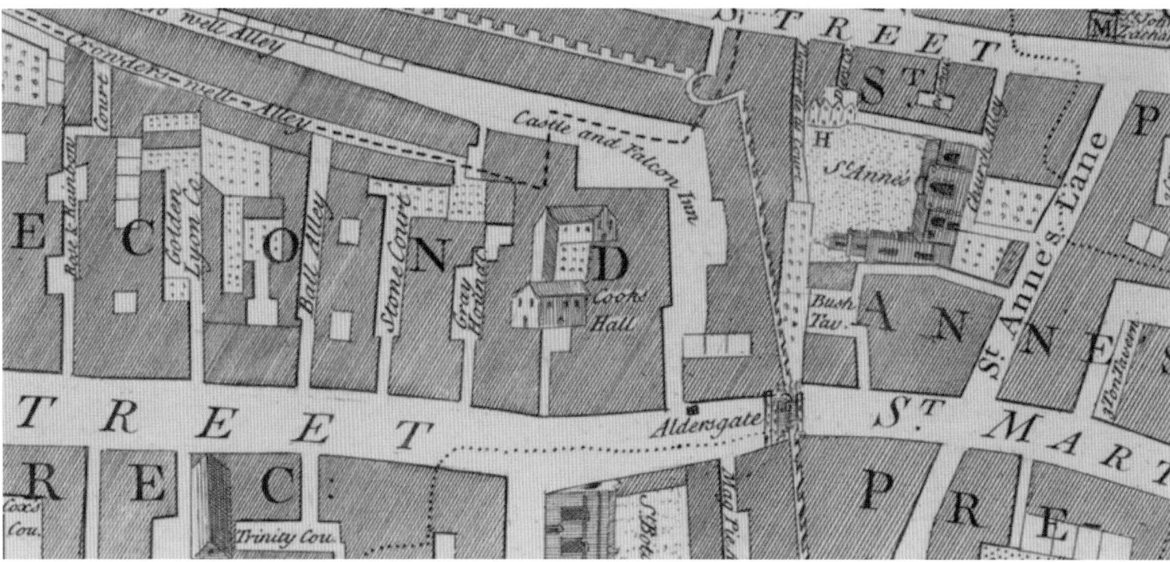

Figure 19. A Plan of the Ward of Aldersgate, 1740.
Detail showing the Cooks' Hall. British Library, Crace Collection Maps.

made of well curds or gathered from whey in summer, or mixed with salt butter in winter, watered or washed.[4] The implication seems to be that the Minstrel had been a cook at some point in his career, perhaps in the tradition of Chaucer's Hodge of Ware, but his words confirm that Cooks' Hall would have been recognized by the audience as a place noted for the quality of its dinners.

Unfortunately, no detailed pictures of the Hall have come to light. Early in the seventeenth century the surveyor Ralph Treswell made a series of plans of buildings in London, including the tenements at 7 – 10 Aldersgate; on the left hand side of this plan is an open area marked as *The Cooks' Garden*, with a frontage of 124 feet. A further annotation within the garden space refers to *the tavern called the Plough belonging to the Cooks.*[5] The Company was obviously proud of its garden, since in 1687 the Renter Warden's accounts include *Paid the gardener for pruning the trees and planting new ones and fitting up the garden, 5/-* and in 1690 *paid for gravel and fitting up garden, by order of the Court, 9/-.*[6] One of the earliest maps of London, printed in 1633 and attributed to Ralph Agas (but derived from the largely lost 'Copperplate Map' made in the 1550s) clearly shows Aldersgate and St Botolph's church and what may be Cooks' Hall and garden, but the identification is uncertain.[7] There is a small scale depiction of the Hall on a Map of Aldersgate Ward, published in 1740, showing how the building was set back from Aldersgate Street and

4 Robert Laneham's [or Langham] Letter, *New Shakespeare Society*, London, 1890, 39.

5 *The London Surveys of Ralph Treswell*, edited John Schofield (London Topographical Society No 135) 1987, Fig 4.

6 Guildhall Library Ms 9989.

7 *London: A Life in Maps*, Peter Whitfield, British Library, 2006.

consisted of two large Halls joined by a Long Gallery, these elements together enclosing a garden on three sides of a rectangle.[8]

The Hall was clearly kept in good repair, and in July, 1666, only two months before it was badly damaged in the Great Fire of London, John Blunkett, glazier, presented his bill for glazing and repainting the windows in the Hall, the Gallery and the Parlour. Blunkett was paid and engaged to keep the glass windows in good repair for seven years. It was probably the damage caused by the Great Fire that necessitated the provision of an additional new Hall in 1674, as part of a major building campaign and restoration of the entire site (see Chapter 4 pp. 88–9). The result of this was that the Cooks now had a very large property on Aldersgate Street and maintaining it was consequently an expensive operation.

The earliest printed histories of London are generally uninformative about the Hall; Stow (1598) simply states that *Without Aldersgate, on the east side of Aldersgate street, is the Cooks hall. From thence along unto Hounsditch or Barbican street, be many fair houses. On the west side also be the like fair buildings till ye come to Long lane, and so to Goswel street.*[9] In 1756 Maitlaind wrote that the Hall was *mean and ordinary*, while according to Entick (1776) it was *to be more admired for its conveniency than elegance of building*, although Richard Skinner thought it was *an old convenient building.*[10] William Harvey, a journalist and antiquary who wrote under the name of *Aleph*, called it *a spacious building which escaped the Great Fire, but was consumed by a comparatively insignificant conflagration in 1771.*[11]

Further evidence is provided by an Inventory drawn up in 1746 (printed in Appendix 7), which allows the general lay-out to be understood. It stood on three sides of a roughly rectangular plot on Aldersgate Street, with a frontage of some 124ft (38 m).[12] The original or Old Hall was built some way back from the Street and was 41 x 35 ft (12.5 x 10.5m) in size, behind two houses that fronted onto the street, one of which was presumably the tavern that belonged to the Cooks and the other was probably the house in which John Fish, the saviour of the Hall, was living at the time of the Great Fire.[13] The Old Hall was partially damaged in the Fire and this led the Company to construct the New Hall, 55 x 26 ft (16.8 x 7.9m) in 1674, at the end of the Long Gallery, which itself was constructed at right-angles from the side of the Old Hall. The Gallery was raised up above a ground-level undercroft. The new Hall was therefore parallel with the old one and presumably at the same elevation. The garden or courtyard was open on the south side.

---

8 British Library, Crace Collection of Maps, drawn by Jacob Ilive, engraved by R W Seale.

9 *A Survey of London*, by John Stow: Reprinted from the text of 1603 (1908), pp. 303–310.

10 *A History of London*, William Maitland, 1756; *History & Survey of London*, John Entick, 1764, Richard Skinner, *A New & Complete History of the Cities of London & Westminster*, 1795.

11 Quoted by Walter Thornbury, *Old and New London*, 1878, vol.2.

12 This is the frontage given by Ralph Treswell in his Survey, see note 5, above.

13 See Chapter 4 p. 88.

An early glimpse of the Hall in use is provided by a letter written on 13th September, 1580, by Peter Osborne to the Lord Mayor and Aldermen. He asks them to admit his servant, Robert Nicholls, to the Freedom of the City by patrimony, because his father, Thomas Nicholls, was presented in the Cooks' Hall by John Johnson the elder, as his apprentice, and so was enrolled in the Chamber of London. He served as Chief Cook to the late Lord Cromwell, Earl of Essex and he subsequently married Widow Green, a Grocer, who lived *next the Cow's Face, in West Cheap, towards the great Conduit*. Thomas was always reported to be Free and a search had been made for his certificate of Freedom in the Cooks' Hall and the Chamber of London. However, it appeared that because of negligent record keeping this could not be found and the date could not be proved.[14]

The building of the Hall was not the only sign that the Company was now firmly established as one of the important City institutions. The Charter of Incorporation was confirmed twice in the sixteenth century, by Henry VIII and Elizabeth I (see Appendix 5). The first occasion was in 1519, when the original grant of 1482 was set out in full and ratified and confirmed by the King; the second, in 1559, follows exactly the same formula and appoints *a Master and three Wardens*, a phrase that also occurs in the 1561 indenture with John Leoff (quoted above), indicating that there was still an amount of confusion as to whether there were to be two Masters (as specified in 1482) or one Master and three Wardens.

The growing status of the Company is demonstrated by the leading role which the Cooks played in a great feast and military pageant that took place in 1559 on the open fields at Mile End, a favourite gathering place for Londoners. The event was vividly recorded by Henry Machyn in his Diary:[15]

The 21st of March the Queen's Master Cooks and other officers dined at Mile-end, [with] all manner of meat and drink; and there was all manner of artillery, such as drums, flutes, trumpets, guns, Morris pikes, halberds, to the number of 105; the gunners in shirts of mail and . . . pikemen in bright harness, and many swords and 5 great guns and shot . . the which did much hurt to glass windows; and came a great giant dancing, and after [that a] Morris Dance dancing, and guns and Morris pikes; and after came a cart with a great whip[?] and 2 [bears?] within the cart, and beside went a great [cart?] of great mastiffs; and then came the Master Cooks riding in embroidered coats, and chains of gold, and many of the Queen's servants in their livery, to the Court, and there they shot their pieces, and ...the Queen's grace standing in the gallery; and so every man went into the park, showing them in battle array, shooting and playing about the park; and before the Queen one of the bears was baited, and afterwards the Morris dancers went into the Court, dancing in many offices.

14 *Analytical index to the series of records known as the Remembrancia: 1579–1664* (1878), pp. 145–164.

15 *The Diary of Henry Machyn: Citizen and Merchant-Taylor of London (1550–1563)* (1848), pp. 184–201; see also 'The first public playhouses, especially the Red Lion', by Herbert Berry, *The Shakespeare Quarterly*, 1989, Vol 40, no 2, pp. 133–48.

Figure 20. John Smythson, Master Cook to Queen Elizabeth I, painted in 1568.

The reference to the Cooks' embroidered jackets and gold chains shows that they were people of standing in society. Such a jacket adorned with two gold chains can be seen in a portrait of John Smythson, Master Cook to Queen Elizabeth I, painted in 1568. He is shown as a Gentleman, richly dressed, with rings on his fingers and a general air of status and well-being.[16] John Smythson is in fact the first Royal Master Cook whose appearance is known from a portrait and about whom we have a number of details. He was the illegitimate son of John Taylor, an officer in the Wardrobe of Henry VII and Elizabeth Smythe, a royal Laundress; as was common at the time, he took his mother's name, in the form of Smythson, and he himself married another Elizabeth, who was also a royal Laundress.

John Smythson is recorded as the Master Cook to the Queen, giving a New Year gift to his Sovereign on several occasions.[17] He lived in Eltham in Kent, where he held properties, but his main landholding was granted directly to him by the Queen in 1562 and included the *Vyne Garden* and a close called the *Mylbancke* within the sanctuary of St Peter's Abbey, Westminster. The *Vyne Garden* was on the site of what is now Romney Street, between Horseferry Road and Smith Square on the Embankment and consisted of a flourishing vineyard. He left this property to his son-in-law, Hugh Miller, in his will of 1590, which was witnessed by various friends from the Court, including Ambrosio Lupo of Milan (1505–91), one of the Queen's Musicians, who was a significant figure in the development of Tudor court music. When his wife died, three years later (1593) she left a considerable amount of property, including a ring with a diamond and a ring with a Turkish stone, taffeta and cloth gowns, and all her ruffs to her cousins, while her daughter was to receive all her mother's *best apparel, my best rings, my great ring with the stone and my chains* – presumably the gold chains that her husband wore for his portrait as Master Cook. Both husband and wife were buried together in the chancel

16 This picture is currently in the Hands on History Museum in Hull, and was there incorrectly identified as John Smith, who was Mayor of Hull in 1563. The arms shown are certainly those of John Smythson, Master Cook.

17 John Nichols's *The Progresses and Public Processions of Queen Elizabeth*, Society of Antiquaries, 1788.

of Eltham parish church, but their tomb was destroyed when the church was rebuilt at the beginning of the twentieth century.

The year after the Mile End pageant, 1560, the Queen made a ceremonial passage through the City of London on 10th April, when 920 members of the Guilds and Companies guarded her way; ten of these were Cooks, with an equal number of Poulters, Fruiterers and Woodmongers – by comparison, the Horners, Paviors, Founders, Loriners, and Weavers provided only four each.[18]

We also have the first indication that the Company had lands outside London. Marsh Manor in Buckinghamshire seems to have formed part of the original endowment of the Company from the time of its incorporation in 1482. It was retained by the Cooks until 1529, in which year they sold it to Robert Dormer. The property passed to a John Howel, who died in 1575, whereupon the Masters of the Company trumped up an *odious suit*, to the effect that the original sale to Robert Dormer had been void because the corporation was misnamed in the indenture. They accordingly put in a tenant of their own, Edmund Croft, against whom John Howel's son, Henry, brought an action and won his case. Despite this setback, the Cooks continued to acquire properties and these were to contribute significantly to the development of the Company in the following century.[19]

Figure 21. A Cook holding a Bird Pie, representing the month of February. Engraving by Theodore Matham, Dutch, 1645 .

18 *The Worshipful Company of Poulters*, P E Jones 1981, p. 155.

19 *A History of the County of Buckingham: Volume 4* (1927), pp. 205–209.

The same period sees some of the first gifts and legacies coming to the Company. In 1552 John Armestronge, Citizen and Cook of London (who was listed among the Pastelers in 1537) died and in his will he left to the Company of Cooks *forty shillings to make them a recreation or banquet.* Several of his other bequests are of interest: to John Styrley, Vintner, *his best gown faced with damask, and also a Jerkin of Branched Velvet* [*ie.*patterned] *to shoot in;* to Robert Watles, Citizen and Grocer, *a pot parcel gilt with a cover with his name, with an arm and a hand open on it;* to John Sturtle, Citizen and Cook, *his bow with small pins and half a dozen shafts; also his gown of brown blue faced with lezardes* [lynx fur] *also a pot with ears without cover, parcel gilt, and a dogeon*[?] *mould;* to John Starkye, Citizen and Fletcher, *his gown without velvet faced with foynes*; and to his cousin William Armestronge, a Man at Arms, *a Target with a mace.* To a former servant of his he left *two moulds, the one of pear tree bearing dise square* [with a square device] *the other having a pelican with a cluster of grapes.* He left his wife Alice a life interest in all his lands and tenements in the City of London and the county of Middlesex. Most interestingly, he left George Frisingefelde a property in Bridge Street in the parish of St. Leonard Eastcheap, *on condition that the said George and his successors continue to keep it as a cook shop for ever.* [20]

All this points to John Armstronge being a man of considerable wealth, who liked fine clothes and possessed substantial properties. He is also recorded elsewhere, for in 1537 a list of Livery Companies and their members was drawn up and, while there is no list of the Cooks, there is a list of the Pastelers. It has already been established that the two terms were interchangeable by this date and this is confirmed by the fact that both Armstronge and John Wilcokes are on the list of Pastelers but both left bequests to the Company of Cooks.[21]

The 1537 list of Pastelers (printed in full in Appendix 1) is of considerable interest as it is the first list of members of the Company to survive. There are forty seven names, divided into three groups. The first group is presumably the Court, the second the Liverymen and the third the Freemen. Some of those listed can be identified elsewhere and whenever it is possible to trace a Cook whose name occurs in the 1537 list of Pastelers he turns out to have been a person of substance, wealth and position. For example, one member of the Court is John Mirfyn, who was almost certainly a relation of Thomas Mirfyn, Lord Mayor in 1519; this John Mirfyn, Cook, is found again in January 1551, living in the parish of St. Giles without Cripplegate and engaged in a dispute with William Harper, Merchant Taylor, concerning a garden plot.[22] Thomas Lorkyn may well be

20 From: 'Wills: Mary I (1553–58)', Calendar of wills proved and enrolled in the Court of Husting, London: Part 2: 1358–1688 (1890), pp. 655–668.

21 It is unusual find the word Pasteler in legal documents but William Jurdayn's will, dated 1510 but proved in 1526, describes him as a Pasteler (Sharpe's Calendar of Wills in the Hustings).

22 *London viewers and their certificates, 1508–1558: Certificates of the sworn viewers of the City of London* (1989), pp. 104–118.

identified with a man of the same name recorded as Mayor of Winchester in 1532, while John Armstronge, Rafe Iswell, John Cooke and Richard Townshend were among the Master Cooks attendant on Anne Boleyn at her Coronation Feast in 1533.[23] Thomas Bateman and George Briges are listed in the London Subsidy Roll of 1541 with the latter assessed for the enormous sum of £400 (the average was £20), indicating that he was seriously rich.[24]

A glimpse of the meals prepared in the kitchens of early Tudor London is given by an Italian visitor, Andrea Francisci, who visited the City in 1497. *They delight in banquets and variety of meat and food, and they excel everyone in preparing them with an excessive abundance. They eat very frequently, at times more than is suitable, and are particularly fond of young swans, rabbits, deer and sea birds. They often eat mutton and beef, which is generally considered to be better here than anywhere else in the world. This is due to the excellence of their pastures. They have all kinds of fish in plenty and great quantities of oysters which come from the sea-shore.*[25] In 1578 Lord Burghley recorded a list of presents of food given to him at Richmond by his household over the Christmas season and this demonstrates the range available:

from Sir Harry Lee, 2 *dowes* [doves]
from Mr. Comptroller, half a doe, half a cheese.
from Mr. Lewes Dyve, 4 *vesants* [pheasants], 4 little cheeses.
at two several times from my Lord Admiral's, 2 pheasants.
from Mr. Edmondes, 2 pheasants.
from my Lord of Arundel, one pheasant.
from Thomas Keyes, a cook of the kitchen, a pullet in grease, one woodcock, 6 plovers, 4 *snytes* [snipe],12 larks.
from Mr. J. Croftes, a capon, 2 pullets, 2 conies.
from Serjeant Bore, 3 *snytes*, 3 dozen of larks.
from my Lady Knightsley, 2 cheeses.
from Sir Christopher Heydon, a card of sprats.
from my Lord Riche, 12 plovers, 8 curlews, 10 *marles* [?small birds], 2 woodcocks.
from Mistress Walter, 10 puddings.
from Mistress Lyfeld, 8 puddings.
from Mr. Bridges, 7 puddings.
from Mr. Fitton, a pie of woodcocks.
from the Earl of Hertford, a pasty of wild boar.

---

23 *'Henry VIII: May 1533, 26–31', Letters and Papers, Foreign and Domestic, Henry VIII: 1533*, Volume 6 (1882), pp. 234–262.
24 *Two Tudor Subsidy Rolls for the City of London*, R G Lang (editor), 1993.
25 *Two Italian Accounts of Tudor England*, translated by C V Malfatti, Barcelona, 1953, p. 37.

Figure 22. A Confectioner's Kitchen with workers making pastry. Etching by Abraham Bosse, French 1632–5.

from my Lord Admiral, 12 larks, 2 plovers.
from the Serjeant of the Pastry, an orange pie.
from my Lady Dacres, one fat doe.
from Mr. Dacres, 3 pheasants, 8 puddings.
from Mr. Plum, the master cook of the Lord Syee [? Say], a pot of jelly and 2 dishes.
from Mr. Stokes, 2 *pastives* [?pasties] of red deer, one pasty of wild boar, one of *Hever* [?heifer]
from my Lord Admiral, 1 partridge.
from Mr. Jo. Croftes, 12 *snytes*, 2 pullets, 2 conies.[26]

Many Cooks were still in the business of owning and operating cookshops, although there seems to have been a period of inflation in the 1520s, since it was said that *Beef and*

26 *Calendar of the Cecil Papers in Hatfield House*, Vol 2: 1572–1582. (1888), pp. 225–230.

mutton is so dear, that a pennyworth of meat will scant suffice a boy at a meal.[27] Despite this, the number of such shops continued to increase and Sir Thomas More told Dean Colet that on a late night walk in Westminster *Whithersoever we cast our eyes, what do we see but victualling-houses, fishmongers, butchers, cooks, pudding-makers, fishers and fowlers, who minister matter to our bellies.*[28] For this reason the Steward, Dean, and Burgesses of Westminster, issued Ordinances in1585 regulating trade *for the better municipal government.* These Ordinances stipulated *That no person or persons that keeps or that hereafter shall keep any cooks shop, shall also keep a common ale-house (except every such person shall be lawfully licensed thereunto) upon pain to have and receive such punishment and pay such fine as by the statute in that case is made and provided.* A further article prohibited the reverse of this, laying down that tavern-keepers and inn-keepers could not operate cookshops.[29]

Numerous Cooks would set up temporary stalls at fairs and markets and the eighteenth century regulations for Bartholomew's Fair perpetuate rules that had been in operation from the middle ages:

That no manner of cook, pie baker, nor buckster, sell or put to sale any manner of victual, except it be good and wholesome for man's body, upon pain that will fall thereof.

And that no person or persons whatsoever within the limits and bounds of this fair presume to break the Lord's Day in selling, showing or offering to sale, or in buying or offering to sale, or in buying or offering to buy, any commodities whatsoever; or in sitting, tippling or drinking in any tavern, inn, alehouse, tippling house, or cook's house, or in doing any other thing that may tend to the breach thereof, upon the pains and penalties contained in several Acts of Parliament, which will be severely inflicted upon the breakers thereof.[30]

It clearly remained necessary to maintain standards and punish dishonesty within the profession. The most unusual instance of this was in 1531 when *a cook* [was] *boiled in a cawdren* [cauldron] *of brass in Smithfield for the poisoning of the bishop of Rochester's servants.*[31] It seems that some sixteen members of the Bishop's household had died from eating poisoned broth, but the Bishop himself, the intended target, had survived. A century later there is a record of two Portuguese cooks being tried at Windsor for poisoning a Mr. Beninge; the jury found them guilty, but no sentence was passed as it transpired that Mr. Beninge was not dead after all.[32] These grisly incidents remind us that the members of the

---

27 Robert Whittington in *The Vulgaria* (1524) quoted in *Old Cookery Books and Ancient Cuisine*, William Hazlitt, London, 1886, pp. 245–9.

28 *Old Cookery Books* , p. 256.

29 *Old Cookery Books*, p. 259.

30 *The records of St. Bartholomew's priory [and] St. Bartholomew the Great, West Smithfield: volume 1* (1921) pp. 298–317.

31 *Two London Chronicles from the Collections of John Stow* (1910), pp. 1–17 and Entick's *London*, I, p. 474.

32 *Calendar of State Papers Domestic: Charles II, 1682* (1932), pp. 224–279.

profession who worked for the Royal Court or for great Lords were in an extremely privileged position and it was essential they could be trusted.

In 1599 John Danyell wrote to the Secretary of State Robert Cecil, that *The wicked minds of some are not yet ceased, as appears by their writing upon walls, and it is to be feared they will attempt further mischief; I beseech the Omnipotent to preserve Her Majesty, and to confound all such as mean harm towards her or you. To prevent their wicked attempts for poisoning, it is meet that command be given to the Master Cook, the Yeoman for the Mouth and for the Bottles, the Grooms of the Privy Bakehouse, and the other officers of the pantry, pastry, &c., that they be circumspect in their several charges, so that no one may touch anything but themselves, and I wish you would use the like course with your own officers. To prevent others their wicked practices, I will endeavor to find out their villainy, without respect to persons, and discover it to you. You had need be careful of yourself, for you are the chiefest and only man they envy.*[33] This same concern about poisoners is reflected in Shakespeare's *Romeo and Juliet* (Act 4 scene 2):
Capulet: *Sirrah, go hire me twenty cunning cooks.*
Servingman: *You shall have none ill, sir, for I'll try if they can lick their fingers.*
Capulet: *How canst thou try them so?*
Servingman: *Marry, sir, 'tis an ill cook that cannot lick his own fingers, therefore he that cannot lick his fingers goes not with me.*

Few Cooks were going to risk dabbling with poison and, to make sure, most great Lords employed tasters to test their food. Simple dishonesty or theft was always a more common offence, so it is not especially surprising to find cases such as that of William Baynard of London, Cook, who stole 10*s* 10*d* from Richard Skelton of Dunstable in Bedfordshire in 1559; he was found guilty and sentenced to be hanged.[34]An interesting case occurred in 1595 when one Owen Saintpire, a Cook of the City, was imprisoned for refusing to pay his taxes and for disobedience to the Lord Mayor and Government of the City. Saintpire had retaliated by starting an action for wrongful imprisonment in the King's Bench against the Chamberlain and other officers of the City and seeking to call the matter to the Court of Chancery. He was clearly a man of substance, for when he died in 1613 he left to his son, also named Owen Saintpire, his leaseholds in the parish of St Mary Bow, his apparel, and a gold seal ring engraved with his arms, along with several other bequests of land and property. This second Owen was also a member of the Company and was listed as an Assistant of the Court in 1639.[35]

33 *Calendar of State Papers Domestic: Elizabeth, 1598–1601*, Volume 273 (1869), pp. 355–367.
34 *Middlesex Sessions Rolls: 1559–60, Middlesex county records*, Volume 1: 1550–1603 (1886), pp. 34–37.
35 *Memorials of the Worshipful Company of Cooks, London, compiled by CM Phillips, 1899* [Guildhall Library Ms 11764].

Others broke rules that were laid down by Church and State and the Company had to intervene. In 1545 the Lord Mayor ordered the Wardens of the Butchers, Cooks, and Poulters to search diligently for those who killed, dressed or uttered flesh in Lent, since eating meat was prohibited during this period.[36] To make sure that all professions followed lawful practices an Act of Parliament in 1562 laid down that the members of specified Livery Companies, including the Cooks, Clothiers, Weavers, Tuckers, Fullers, Clothworkers, Sheremen, Dyers, Hosiers, Tailors, Shoemakers, Tanners, Pewterers, Bakers, Brewers, Glovers, Smiths, and Saddlers must have completed a seven year apprenticeship. This requirement was already enshrined in the Charters and Ordinances of many of the Companies and the legislation was designed to regularize the position for those where the terms of Apprenticeship had not been formally set out.

One particular problem that the Company faced was set out in a letter of 1585 from the Lord Mayor, Thomas Pullyson to Lord Walsingham, Principal Secretary to the Queen, which stated that Queen Elizabeth was concerned about the amount of her venison that was being stolen by poachers and which found its way into London to be sold by the Cooks. Her Majesty therefore required every Cook to subscribe to a bond of £40 *per annum* in order to insure that they would not sell such stolen meat. If anyone was found to be selling royal venison illegally his £40 bond would be forfeit. In addition, each Cook must keep a note of the names of every dealer from whom they received venison, so that checks could be made. The Mayor called the Wardens of the Cooks to appear before him, explained the position and attempted to raise the bonds the Queen required. However, the Cooks replied that this would be a great inconvenience to the members of the Company, especially as the Tabling Houses and Taverns received much more stolen venison than they did; they therefore requested that, in fairness, either the members of these other trades should be subject to the same regulations or the Cooks should be given *carte blanche* to search the premises of the Taverners and Innholders for stolen meat. The letter asks Lord Walsingham what the Lord Mayor should do and, as no more is heard of it, presumably the advice was to let the matter drop, since to have pursued either of the courses the Cooks suggested would have caused huge problems for the City.[37]

The Company had other dealings with the Crown. Queen Elizabeth, like most monarchs of the time, was always short of money and in 1567 she determined to raise a substantial sum by way of a Lottery, in order to promote shipbuilding and restore the ports. The Lord Mayor issued orders to the Livery Companies that required them to take part. The attraction of the scheme was that there were to be no blank tickets and the top prize was a staggering £5,000. Each Company was to use a motto for the occasion, with the Cooks adopting:

---

36 2 & 3 Edw VI, c19 [*Butchers of London, London*, Philip Jones, 1976, p. 124].

37 *Calendar of State Papers Domestic: Elizabeth, 1581–90* (1865), pp. 244–249.

We Cooks of London, which work early and late
If anything be left, God send us part.

There were 400,000 tickets costing 10*s* each and the result of the draw was that Richard Tomson, who was presumably the Clerk, won for the Company the paltry sum of 1*s* 2*d*.[38]

A little later, in 1573, the Common Council ordered a new large loan to be raised *by indifferent taxation* towards the purchase of wheat for the City; the Cooks were assessed at £37 10*s* but this is put into perspective by comparison with the rich Mercers, whose contribution was £500.

It is unfortunate that the Company's own records do not survive from the sixteenth century, but other sources give us some further insights into the way the Cooks operated. In the list of expenses for the reception of Queen Elizabeth by Lord Keeper Bacon at Gorhambury in 1577 the wages paid to the Cooks of London are given as £12. This suggests that the Queen expected her Master Cooks from London to accompany her on her progresses round the realm.[39] Similarly, at the funeral feast for Mary, Queen of Scots, in Peterborough (where she was first buried in 1587) Thomas Kayes, Chief Cook, asked for an allowance to cover the cost of twenty-four labourers hired to turn the spits and carry water for the kitchens, at 6*d* each, giving a total of 12*s*. Thomas also claimed his own expenses and those of his man, for 16 days at 4*s* per day, totalling 64*s*.[40]

There is also information about the costs of catering generally. A record of the dining expenses for the Lords of the Council at Westminster in 1539 on Tuesday 16th April included *for boiling beef, loins and necks of mutton, rumps of beef, loins and breasts of veal, kids, geese, rabbits, marybones* [marrow bones], *capons, pigeons, bacon, butter, cream, chickens to bake, spices, onions and herbs, sauce and salt, cups and trenchers, pippins, oranges, cooks' wages, and boat hire* ; the sum total was 45*s* 11*d*. On 29 April they had fish, including *ling, haberden* [salt cod], *and other kinds of fish, quinces, spices, and other kinds of fruit.* This, together with the hire of cups and trenchers, the cook's wages and boat hire came to the larger total of 49*s* 7*d*, but the explanation may be found in a letter that John Hussee wrote to Lady Lisle in 1536: *as for salt fish, you will not believe how dear it is, both ling and haberden.*[41] The payments made for boat hire suggest that the Lords may have dined on barges in the Thames.

---

38 *The Loseley manuscripts*, ed. Alfred John Kempe, London 1836, pp. 185–214.

39 *Old Cookery Books and Ancient Cuisine*, William Hazlitt, London, 1886, pp. 245–9.

40 *Calendar of State Papers, Scotland: volume 9: 1586–88* (1915), pp. 457–481.

41 *Letters and Papers, Foreign and Domestic, Henry VIII: 1539*, Volume 14 Part 1 (1894), pp. 470–488. The inclusion of boat hire in both of these bills suggests that the Lords may have been dining on the River Thames.

In this context it is of interest to compare the extent of the daily rations that were laid down for the King's troops in 1546: bread *at 7 men to a peck* [a small two gallon barrel] *a day*; beer *at 3 quarts for a man a day*; beef at *a piece for a man a day* (a 2*1b.* piece when *watered and sodden* weighed only 1*1b* 1½ *oz*, and there were *five flesh days* each week); haberden, *at one fish for two messes of four men each* (once a week); stockfish (twice a week); butter (for every mess 1½*lb*); cheese (for every mess 1*lb*) and forty flitches of bacon, to be consumed over an unspecified period.[42] It may be assumed that soldiers were not fed as lavishly as Lords or their officials and these quantities indicate the vast amounts of food that was needed to cater for the Court or the Lord Mayor's household.[43] Some idea of the Lord Mayor's table is provided by Thomas Platter, a Swiss medical student, who came to England in 1599. Rather surprisingly, he managed to get himself invited to lunch with the Lord Mayor and described the experience: *Straightway all manner of lavish dishes were served most decorously. And there were two servers or carvers who removed one plate after another from the table to another covered table nearby, and they did nothing else but carve and serve. They laid the food in small pewter bowls, placing these before each person upon plates, one course after another, all most perfectly and richly prepared and served with delightful sauces, while diverse other dishes to stimulate the appetite surrounded one. After two helpings of roasts, stews and other things, dessert was served, consisting only of sweetmeats, tarts, and pastries, not to be compared for delicacy with the entrees.*[44]

Figure 23. The Coconut Cup, the oldest of the Company's cups, bearing the hall-mark of 1588 and with the maker's mark R.F.

42 *Letters and Papers, Foreign and Domestic, Henry VIII: September 1546–January 1547*, Volume 21 Part 2 (1910), pp. 2–12.

43 *Letters and Papers, Foreign and Domestic, Henry VIII: September 1546–January 1547*, Volume 21, Part 2 (1910), pp. 2–12.

44 *The Journals of two travellers in Elizabethan and early Stuart England, Thomas Platter and Horatio Busino*, London, 1995.

It was becoming increasingly common for the Company to cater for important civic events, although this was not always a success. In 1521 the Lord Mayor, Sir John Brugge, attended the annual feast given by the Serjeants-at-Law. Although he had no cause to complain of any want of deference paid to him officially, the banquet itself left much to be desired. *To show what the fare was is but loss of time. I suppose that the worshipful citizens were never worse served.* To avoid such problems all Cooks were required to inform the Company when they attended civic functions, so that the feasts should be *well and worshipfully dressed*, for the honour of the City and the honour and profit of those who had to pay for the entertainment.[45] This was to lead to the appointment of full-time Cooks, who were members of the Cooks' Company, to most of the other Livery Companies. For example, the Founders' Company first recorded a salaried cook in 1579; he was Richard Kempe who received 13*s* 4*d* for his year's service. His successor was John Tyffine, appointed 1605 but presumably dead by 1617, when a series of payments to his widow begin. In 1606 William Greene was appointed Cook to the Turners' Company *to be paid from time to time according to his desserts and labour*; while in 1615, William Green was *entertained* to be Chief Master Cook to the Company.[46]

Master Cooks were also employed in the households of successive Kings and Queens of England. It is clear that these were members of the Company, for the preface to the Charter of King Edward IV (11 July, 1482) states that *We bearing in mind how our well beloved honest and freemen of the Mistery of Cooks of our City of London have for a long time outside the aforesaid City, personally taken and borne, and to this day do not cease to take and bear, great and manifold pains and labour as well at our great feast of St George as at others according to our command.* Similarly, the Charter of James I, (19 May, 1616) opens with the words *The many services heretofore done and performed and as yet continued to our noble progenitors, Kings and Queens of England, as also to ourselves since our first coming unto the Imperial Crown of this Realm by our well beloved subjects, the honest freemen of the said Mistery of Cooks of our said City of London, in their own persons as well as at the Royal Feast of our Coronation, at the entertaining of our dear brother the King of Denmark, the marriage of my well beloved daughter the Lady Elizabeth, our annual Feasts of St George, as at the entertaining of foreign Princes and upon all other occasions when they are thereunto required.*

We have the names of several of these royal Cooks and among the earliest recorded were William Scudet in 1086, Humphrey, who was Cook to King John in 1213 and Henry Wade, Cook to Henry III, who was granted land in Oxfordshire in 1260.[47] Another was the somewhat inappropriately named John Hunger, who was commemorated by a brass effigy in 1435 in the church of All Saints, Hertford. Sadly, only the feet of the figure now

45 'Introduction', *Calendar of letter-books of the city of London: L: Edward IV-Henry VII* (1912), pp. I-XLIV.
46 *The Worshipful Company of Turners*, Roland Champness, 2nd ed 2004, pp. 84.
47 *A History of the County of Oxford: Volume 6* (1959), pp. 56–71.

survive but there is an inscription in Norman French identifying him as Master Cook to Katherine, wife of Henry V.[48] It is also recorded that in 1348 King Edward III employed three Master Cooks who were paid the not inconsiderable sum of 12*d* per day.[49]

In 1455 John Gourney was Master Cook to Henry VI and William Heckling was Master Cook to the Hall. The catering department was under the supervision of the Senior Clerk and the Kitchen had a staff, including cooks, of thirty-one; when all the other offices, such as the bakehouse, pantry, cellar, buttery and so on, are included the total number involved in the production of meals was in excess of one hundred and fifty.

Many individual Royal Cooks are known by name in the Tudor period, when they often carried the title of Master Cook or Yeoman to the King's Mouth. John Hunt was Master Cook to King Henry VIII in 1522,[50] while Robert Hogan held the post in 1532

Figure 24. The 'old' Crowns, used in the crowning ceremony of the Masters & Wardens. These were restored in the 19th century but probably date from the 17th century.

---

48 Others described as Kings Cooks in the Middle Ages included Geoffrey de Bath (1235), Master Richard (1253), Henry Lovel (1260), John de la Beche (1293), Richard of Cleobury (1310), Master John de Sutton (1317), Henry de Thornhill (1318), and John Goderich (1363).

49 *A Collection of Ordinances and Regulations for the Government of the Royal Household*, published by the Society of Antiquaries of London in 1790.

50 National Archives REQ 2/7/79.

Figure 25. All that remains of a monumental brass to John Hunger, Master Cook to Queen Katherine, wife of King Henry V, 1435. All Saints Church, Hertford.

and on his death in 1534 he was succeeded by George Lufkin. John Breket was similarly listed between 1538–41 and was in charge of a staff of thirty-three other Cooks.[51] In November 1540, the King gave John Dale, Master Cook to the King's household, and his wife Elizabeth the lease of his tenement in All Hallows, Honey Lane, for life rent- free.[52] Perot le Doulce, was *cook pro ore* to both Henry VII and Henry VIII. In 1533 it was *the King's pleasure that Pero, his yeoman cook, shall have his dwelling in one of the new houses at Charing Cross* and this same man, his name now given as *Piro Doux, yeoman cook for the King's Mouth*, was awarded £10 annually for his apparel in 1539.[53] He was a Frenchman[54] and two other Frenchmen, Estienne Havet and Astyan Hana, were Master Cooks to Queen Mary, while Hugh Pigott was Master Cook to Princess Mary in 1533. In 1609 a warrant was issued under the Signet to the Master of the Great Wardrobe for an allowance of £50 a year to Hance Popleman (presumably a German), Master Cook to the Queen in succession to William Morkeley, and *divers parcels of stuff for his livery yearly at the feast of All Saints during his Majesty's pleasure.*[55]

In the Household Ordinances of 1526 the duties of Henry VIII's Master Cooks are recorded: *It is ordered that every of the Master Cooks give their daily attendance in serving the King, the Queen and his Household, and that their meats be good and sweet, and to see the same well-dressed; and to cause the cooks under them to see all such victuals as shall come to their hands*

51 *Letters and Papers, Foreign and Domestic, Henry VIII: 1540*, Volume 15 (1896), pp. 118–132 and Volume 18 Part 2 (1902), pp. 282–378.

52 *Historical gazetteer of London before the Great Fire: Cheapside; parishes of All Hallows Honey Lane, St Martin Pomary, St Mary le Bow, St Mary Colechurch and St Pancras Soper Lane* (1987), pp. 97–101.

53 *Letters and Papers, Foreign and Domestic, Henry VIII: 1533*, Volume 6 (1882), pp. 306–313 and Volume 14 Part 2 (1895), pp. 303–358.

54 He was referred to as Piro, the French cook in 1540, when he received 66*s* 8*d* in wages, while at the same time Hugh Pigot, cook, received only 30*s* 5*d* . *Letters and Papers, Foreign and Domestic, Henry VIII: 1540–1541, Volume 16* (1898), pp. 178–210.

55 *Calendar of the Cecil Papers in Hatfield House*, Vol 21: 1609–1612 (1970), pp. 352–362.

be well and seasonably dressed, and the same to serve out at the dressers by the oversight of the said Clerk of the Kitchen, without embellishing or taking away any part of the same; according to the old custom of the King's house.[56] Under Elizabeth I we learn that her Master Cook received an annual stipend of £11 8*s* 1 ½ *d* and *hath five dishes of meat every meal, and likewise the assay of meat carved to the Queen; he, and his fellow the Master Cook for the Household, hath for their fee all the fat that comes from the beef boiled in this house and all the lamb skins yearly spent; he is Governor of the Privy Kitchen and the Queen's Side Kitchen.* The Master Cook for the Household also received £11 8*s* 1 ½ *d* along with £10 a year for his meat and half the fat, as mentioned above.

The names of some other Master Cooks to Queen Elizabeth are known from the lists of New Year Gifts presented to her. It seems it was a tradition that her Master Cook should give her a special marzipan cake, known as a marchpane, while her Pastry Cook gave a pie. Thus in 1561–2 George Webster presented *a marchpane being a chessboard* and John Betts, Servant of the Pastry, gave *one pie of quinces.*[57] John Smythson, whose portrait was painted in 1568, is recorded in 1577–8 as presenting *a feyer*[fair] *marchpan* and John Dudley, now Servant of the Pastry, gave *a great pie of quinces and wardens* [pears] *gilt.* The following New Year, 1578–9, Smythson is recorded as giving *a fair marchpan with a cattle in middle* and in 1588–9 he presented *one fair marchpan, with St. George in the middle* and John Dudley *one fair pie of quinces orangeado* [candied orange peel].[58] By 1599–1600 the kitchen seems to have expanded as gifts are recorded from William Cordall, Master Cook, of one marchpane, from Daniel Clarke, Master Cook of the Household, of one marchpane, from Thomas Frenche, Servant of the Pastry, *one pie of orangeado* with a similar pie given by Ralph Batty, another Servant of the Pastry. Daniel Clarke, who is mentioned as Master Cook to the Household is recorded in 1591 living in the manor house known as Tottenham Court. He served as a Master Cook to the Queen and afterwards to James I for a total of twenty-nine years and is listed as one of four Master Cooks who each presented a marchpane as a New Year gift in 1605–6, the others being Willam Cordall, John Murray, and William Morkley. Daniel Clarke was buried in Old St Pancras church in 1626, where his inscription reads:

A Memoriall Of Daniell Clarke Esq Who Left
This Life Most Comfortablie The Last Of Ivne 1626
A° Ætat. Svæ 79. Having Bene Master Cooke To Qveene
Elizabeth & To King Iames 29 Yeare

56 *Ordinances and Regulations*, 1790, p. 142.

57 Perhaps the son of Roger Betts who is listed amongst the Pastelers in 1538.

58 All these Master Cooks to the Queen and of the Pastry are listed as donors in the New Year Gifts to the sovereign printed in John Nichols's *The Progresses and Public Processions of Queen Elizabeth I*, 1809.

Figure 26. The 'new' Crowns, designed by Jane Arkwright in 1995; the two Masters Crowns are based on a 19th century Cook's Hat, while the two Wardens Crowns are derived from a 14th century Cook's cap.

Another Master Cook to Elizabeth was Edward Wilkinson, who died in 1567 and whose tomb is in Charlton Church at Blackheath.[59] These Elizabethan Master Cooks were almost certainly all members of the Company and perhaps it was one of them who presented the earliest surviving piece of plate, the Coconut Cup. The exotic shells of coconuts had been prized in Europe since the Middle Ages and many were mounted in silver or gold to form drinking cups. They were especially popular in Tudor and Stuart times and the Company's cup is typical in form, with a round foot and baluster stem, the

59 *The Environs of London: volume 4: Counties of Herts, Essex & Kent* (1796), pp. 324–342. He may well have been the son of Richard Wilkinson who is listed as a member of the Livery of the Pastelers in 1538.

shell itself being held in place by three silver straps surmounted by a silver-gilt rim. It bears the hallmark for 1588 (the year of the Armada) and the maker's mark R.F. within a shield. The initials may stand for Robert Frye or Roger Flint, both of whom were London Goldsmiths active at this time. It was very common for Masters and senior Liverymen to make gifts to their Livery Company. Since the number and cost of such gifts is a measure of both the health and the wealth of the Company; it is notable that the largest number of such gifts to the Cooks' Company took place in the seventeenth century. This reflects the fact that the solid basis of the organization was established under the Tudors in the sixteenth century, leading to a period of unprecedented growth over the following hundred years.

One custom of the Company, the Crowning of the new Masters and Wardens, also dates from at least the sixteenth century. We know this because of a case that came before the Court of Aldermen on 21st January, 1570: *Item; forasmuch as William Stokes, Cook, in the Cooks' Hall, did very cruelly and disrespectfully, to the evil example of evil doers, pull the garland from the head of one Robynsone, Cook, elected one of the Wardens of that Company; it was therefore ordered by this Court that the said William Stokes, for his lewd and evil behaviour therein, be discharged from the freedom and liberties of this City and Mr Chamberlain commanded to shut up his shop windows.*[60] This tantalizingly brief record of what was clearly a scandalous event at least indicates that the Officers of the Company had by this date a distinctive form of headgear and the term *garland* is found in the records of other companies describing a round cap of the sort used by the Cooks. It may therefore be presumed that the crowning ceremony was in existence by this time. Warden Robinson may well be the William Robinson who is listed as a Freeman of the Pastelers in 1538, while the William Stokes could be a relative of John Stokes, who is named as one of the Masters in James I's Charter to the company in 1615. Similar ceremonies took place in other Livery companies. One of the 17th century '*garlands*' used to crown the Master and Wardens of the Leathersellers' Company survives, and their ceremony is recorded from 1487 onwards. New crowns were acquired in 1540 and in 1638. Other Companies that Crown their Masters are the Grocers, Drapers, Skinners, Barbers, Girdlers, Carpenters, and Gunmakers. It seems likely that the custom was first adopted by the Cooks in the fifteenth century.

The Crowning Ceremony remained in use during the eighteenth century, for in 1739 the Court ordered that the Renter Warden, Leonard Pead should *procure the three crowns belonging to this Company to be new covered and the Company's arms worked thereon and do also buy one more new crown with the Company's Arms thereon for the use of the Masters and Wardens*. Again, in 1803, the Court required *the wardens' caps to be new covered and the Arms revarnished.* The custom seems to have died out in the nineteenth century, but was revived in 1930 by Master Daniel Duff and now takes place annually at the Confirmation Dinner in November.

---

60 *The Repetories of the Court of Aldermen* are now lodged in the London Metropolitan Archive. The dates given are in the 'old style' so this entry is under January 1571 in the original manuscript.

CHAPTER FOUR

The Company under King and Commonwealth

The seventeenth century was a turbulent period for the City of London and the Livery Companies. Civil and religious unrest was growing during the reigns of James I and Charles I, culminating in the Civil War and the Protectorate. The Restoration brought rejoicing in 1660, but the Great Plague in 1665 and the Great Fire in 1666 changed the face of London for ever. While there is not a great deal of surviving evidence relating to the role of the Cooks' Company in these national events, a certain amount can be discovered or deduced and it seems most likely that, in view of the important relationship with the King and the Court, the Company was normally Royalist in sentiment.

The most conspicuous project that involved the City of London and the Crown was the Ulster Plantation and this was to test the loyalty of the Livery Companies most severely.[1] The problems of Ireland had long pre-occupied the Government and James I regarded the Irish as the prime instigators of Counter-Reformation plots. His solution was an attempt to settle or, in contemporary parlance, *plant* Ulster with a loyal population from the mainland. Many of these plantations were undertaken by wealthy English landlords, who thereby acquired vast Irish estates, but there was one area, County Coleraine, which was notoriously lawless and which private citizens were unwilling to take on. It soon became apparent that, if he were to succeed, the King needed a body that was both rich and well organised, which could be invited or, if necessary, ordered to take on Coleraine. The City of London seemed the obvious answer and discussions took place between the Privy

---

1 James Stevens Curl, *The Londonderry plantation, 1609–1914 : the history, architecture and planning of the estates of the city of London and its livery companies in Ulster*, 1986.

Council and the Lord Mayor. It was agreed that a delegation of four eminent citizens would go to inspect the territory. The visit was organised by Sir Arthur Chichester (1563–1625), the founder of Belfast, who made sure that the deputation saw only the attractive parts of the country and were not exposed to the dangerous and lawless conditions which existed in reality. Consequently, the four Londoners formed a favourable impression and even asked that the area of plantation should be increased, to include parts of Antrim and Derry. The Government suggested that this enlarged area would form a new County, to be called Londonderry, and the delegation recommended that £15,000 should be raised to undertake the settlement of it.

It was decided that the Plantation itself should be organised and paid for by the Livery Companies. Unsurprisingly, the idea was not welcomed, since each Livery consisted of businessmen who could recognise an expensive white elephant when they saw one. It took considerable persuasion and not a little coercion before the City agreed to raise the funds for the Plantation. In 1609 the Wardens of the Mercers' Company said they could not produce the sums of money required of them, so they were imprisoned and only released when they had paid up. The following year it was the Cooks' turn to object and on 29th June *Owen Semper, one of the Wardens of the Company of Cooks, for that he refused to make payment of £25, being part of the sum rated upon the said Company towards the Plantation in Ireland, according to several Acts of Common Council, and former precepts to them in that behalf directed, is by this Court committed prisoner to one of the Compters of this City, there to remain until further Order of this Court be taken for his enlargement.*[2]

From the outset it was clear that the richest 'Great Twelve' Companies would have to shoulder much of the burden, but the sums of money involved meant that the other Liveries must contribute too. Eventually forty-four of the fifty-five Livery Companies were involved in contributing funds to the general pot. In most cases the Companies were grouped together in Associations, each headed by one of the Great Twelve. The Cooks, together with the Innholders, the Masons, and the Broderers, came under the Mercers. They were to be responsible for raising the money for building and fortifying towns and arranging for settlement. These responsibilities were transferred in 1613 to a separate *Society of the New Plantation in Ulster*, later known as *The Honourable The Irish Society*, which had powers to convene Courts and to determine all the business relating to the Plantation. This arrangement was similar to that found in the governing bodies of other seventeenth century joint-stock companies established for purposes of trade and colonisation, such as the East India Company or the Newfoundland Company, and the Irish Society enjoyed similar wide-ranging powers.

Twelve estates, known as Proportions, were created for the Associations, consisting of lands separated from each other by property granted to the Established Anglican Church

---

2 This is quoted in an article on the *Cooks Company* which appeared in the *City Press* of 9th November, 1861. The only source given is 'City Records'.

or to *Native Irish Gentlemen.* Irishmen who lost their own land in this process were to settle in these buffer zones, which would be surrounded by planted immigrants. The London settlers were supposed to outnumber the natives, but there were never enough of them and consequently security was always an issue. The Mercers' Proportion consisted of some 33.5 square miles of land west of the River Bann, forming a manor to be called Mercers and centred on Movanagher and Kilrea. This was formally conveyed to the Associates in 1617. The Association also had to contribute substantial sums to the building of the new city of Londonderry and the fortification of Coleraine.

The initial financial estimates had to be revised and the sum of £40,000 was raised, with each 'Great Twelve' Company responsible for one twelfth of this – £3,333 *6s 8d.* Within the Association, the Mercers contributed by far the largest amount, £2,680, with the Cooks producing £200, the Broderers £153 and the Masons £100. The Innholders appear to have got away without paying. There were inevitably further demands for funds, with the total required soon rising to over £100,000, and although the Cooks only contributed another £100 this was still a considerable sum for the Company. Indeed, in 1642, when further sums were demanded, many Companies pleaded poverty; the Plumbers said that they had mortgaged their Hall and the Cooks claimed to have melted down their plate.

Under King Charles I the Associates were accused of having broken the Articles of Agreement for the Plantations and they were forced to find more money to defend themselves in court. Nonetheless, the City was found guilty by the Star Chamber, and the Irish estates were confiscated by the Crown and a fine of £70,000 imposed. This judgement was overturned in 1641 by the House of Commons and the estates were restored to the Liveries. Nonetheless, the King's action turned much of the City against him and was a contributory factor to his downfall and execution after the Civil War. It also allowed the Irish to rise in rebellion against their English masters and Cromwell only crushed the uprising in 1653 with much bloodshed.

Figure 27. The Trinity Cup, a copy of a cup from Trinity Hospital in Greenwich and dated 1616. This was presented to the Cooks' Company by the Mercers' Company in 1909 to mark three hundred years of the Association for the Irish Plantation.

After the Restoration in 1660, a new charter confirmed the Livery Companies' ownership of the Plantations, and *six and twenty honest and discreet citizens of the City of London* were constituted for ever as The Irish Society, which exists to the present day.

The Mercers initially managed their Irish Estates, on behalf of the Associated Companies, paying out dividends from time to time. In 1658 they granted long leases on the whole Plantation, but when the last of these expired in 1831 the Company reverted to direct management through an agent. Eventually, under the terms of the Irish Land Purchase Act of 1903, the estates were sold and in 1909 the Association was formally closed. There is, however, a continuing special friendship between the former Associated Companies. In 1910 the Mercers presented each of the Associate Companies with a silver cup, copied from their own Trinity Cup of 1616, and the Associates presented the Mercers with a cup of Renaissance form made by Edward Barnard & Sons. A tradition was established in the nineteenth century whereby each of the Associates invited the Officers of the others to dine annually, and this still continues. In 1948 the Mercers' Company became involved in Chartered Estates Ltd of Southern Rhodesia, which comprised a Cattle Ranch of some 100,000 acres near Salisbury, and invited the former Associates to become joint subscribers. This they did, although the venture was sold in 1980 after the Declaration of Independence by the Rhodesian Government.

The City placed other burdens on the Companies. The Liveries had long been expected to produce funds for corn, which should be stored in their granaries of London, in case of emergencies or a failure of supply to the City. Despite threats, many companies did not comply with these orders and in September 1631 the Wardens of eleven companies – the Cooks, Cutlers, Dyers, Haberdashers, Innholders, Leathersellers, Saddlers, Salters, Scriveners, Skinners, and Tallowchandlers, were summoned to Hampton Court and castigated by the Privy Council for non-co-operation; they were to make a provision of corn and this would be overseen by two Aldermen. But eighteen months later it was noted that *the Companies are not stored and provided with grain for the service of this City*. The problem grumbled on, with Companies fined and Wardens from time to time imprisoned, until the granaries were themselves destroyed in the Great Fire and the custom was not revived. Other calls were made on the Liveries by Charles I, who called upon the City to raise forced loans to finance his wars with France and Spain. In 1634 the City was ordered to fund seven new warships for the Crown, causing further resentment and refusals. In 1690, under William and Mary, the Renter Warden's accounts included *paid Mr Moseley per order of Court the whole charge of the loss upon the account of the horses and furniture that were bought for their Majesties Service £16 15s.*

The Company also contributed to the City Militia, which policed the streets by day and night. The accounts regularly bear witness to this duty: *Paid two men for going out with the Company's arms the whole duty & for match and powder*, *7s 4d* (1674) and again *paid for 2 soldiers for going out a day & night, 6s* (1689). The arms themselves had to be maintained and the Renter Warden frequently records this: *Paid a gunsmith for a new stock and fire lock to the musket, 11s, paid for a new pair of bandoleers, 7s* and *Paid for fitting and cleaning the three old muskets and for hooks to hang them up, 9s 6d* (1678) or *Paid for mending and cleaning the muskets and for a new trigg catch sight and brass to them, 6s 6d* (1690).

Relations with the King were sometimes strained, but not always. The reign of King James I had brought the Worshipful Company of Cooks no less than three new Charters. The first, in 1604, just a year after the accession of the new monarch, again confirmed the rights and privileges set out in the original Charter of 1482 and appointed John Harte Master and Richard Scarlett and Arthur Harte, Wardens. However, the second Charter was much more controversial. There was obviously a dispute going on between the Company and the City about the relative rights and privileges of Cooks and Innholders to sell beer and wine, although few details are known about this. However, in 1614 the Company obtained a completely new Charter, which brought them into head-on conflict with the Lord Mayor and Aldermen. This Charter was described as *Non Obstante*, words used to express an act by the King in which he dispensed with existing law, effectively authorising its violation. This Charter permitted the Company to ignore all previous Statutes, Proclamations and Orders and presumably to devise an entirely new set of rules for themselves. In a panic, the Lord Mayor wrote on 21st May to the Lords of the Council that the Cooks had *secretly and surreptitiously* obtained this new Charter from the King. He therefore begged the Council to mediate and get the new Letters Patent referred to a judge, who could say whether they were agreeable to the law, and compatible with the existing Charters that had been established for the good government of the City.

The matter was referred to Lord Justice Coke, who was asked to suspend the new Charter pending further orders from the Council. On 16th October the Council ruled that the new Charter was against Common Law and the existing Charters of the City because it gave the Company *unlimited powers to search and seize unwholesome victuals and dispose thereof at their pleasure, whereby they might take it from others and make benefit of it themselves*. It was also contrary to many Statutes against forestalling and engrossing victuals and specifically against a recent Order of Council, dated 26th March 1614, by which Cooks were prohibited from having more than twenty barrels at one time in their houses, or from keeping beer or ale in other vessels than barrels, or from selling beer or ale in or out of their houses without meat. These clauses, which were clearly detrimental to Innholders and Tavern Keepers, appear to have been the nub of the issue and the real reason behind the sweeping new Charter; the very fact that the Cooks were in a position to get such a far-reaching document from the King testifies to their influence in Court circles.

Nonetheless, the Council declared that the Charter should not be enforced but ordered it to be suspended and remain in the Council Chest. At the same time Lord Chief

Justice Coke certified that the Cooks had a just grievance and although many Ale Houses had been suppressed, there were still far too many of them; so the Council directed the Lord Mayor to legislate against the excessive number of Ale Houses within the City and its suburbs, so that the Cooks Company might have no further cause of complaint.

This led James I to issue his third Charter on 19th May, 1616, which confirmed the Charters given by his predecessors and included a lavish tribute to the Company:

The many Services heretofore done and performed and as yet continued to our noble Progenitors, Kings and Queens of England, as also to ourselves since our first coming unto the Imperial Crown of this Realm by our well beloved Subjects the honest Freemen of the said Misterie of Cooks of our said City of London, in their own persons as well at the Royal Feast of our Coronation, at the entertaining of our dear brother the King of Denmark, the Marriage of my well beloved daughter the Lady Elizabeth, our annual Feasts of Saint George, as at the entertaining of Foreign Princes and upon all other occasions when they are thereunto required.

No doubt by reason of this faithful service to the Crown, the Charter gave the Company the power to sell beer and wine with food at home without a licence, so retaining some of the benefits of the 'suppressed' Charter of 1614. It also appointed two Masters, two Wardens and twenty-two Assistants and a Clerk. The Masters were Thomas Norman and John Stokes with their Wardens Nicholas Pinfold and Robert Wood; the clerk is named as Robert Glover. The Court of Assistants is mentioned here for the first time.

The new arrangements were obviously rather delicate, causing one Lythan Price, who wished to continue his trade as a cook, to admit that he had bought the lease of a house and shop in Southwark, and set up a tippling-house without licence in 1617; he had done this in ignorance of the law, so he prayed the Master of the Rolls to petition the Lord Mayor in his favour.[3] A sidelight on a related issue is a Proclamation of 1619 prohibiting Innholders, Cooks, Chandlers, Alehouse Keepers, and Victuallers, from drawing off their beer into wine-casks, or other large vessels, which made the beer heady, which also resulted in the casks themselves becoming scarce for the use by the Navy.[4]

To the disputes over the sale of beer and wine was added another old problem – the sale of stolen venison. The idea of taking a bond from the Cooks against the selling of stolen meat, which had been tried unsuccessfully under Queen Elizabeth, was revived in the seventeenth century and in 1608 the Lord Mayor received a letter from the King, requiring him to restrain the Cooks within the City from buying and selling venison, as this tended to encourage the Under Keepers of His Majesty's Forests, Chases, and Parks, to become hunters or stealers of venison. The Mayor assured him that he had called the Cooks before him, and had taken bonds from them to ensure that they would not sell the

3 *'Vintners, victuallers and taverners', Analytical index to the series of records known as the Remembrancia: 1579–1664* (1878), pp. 539–549.

flesh of red or fallow deer in the future.[5] But the problem did not go away and in 1622 there was a Commission to the Justices of the Peace for Middlesex to suppress and punish the insolence of Cooks, Victuallers, and others who keep dogs to hunt down the King's deer to sell it.[6] On another occasion, in 1633, Sir Sanders Duncombe, one of the King's Gentlemen Pensioners wrote of the burden placed upon the good people of Norfolk, Suffolk, Essex, and Middlesex by thieves stealing the King's deer and his subjects' horses and cattle. The problem was made worse because there was no Watch [Guard] at Bow Bridge, as there was in other places, allowing the criminals to get into London without being intercepted. Once there, they were sheltered by Cooks, Butchers, and other *extravagants, so that no hue and cry can take hold of them, whereby the penalty of the statute is levied on the township or hundred.*[7]

One of the dubious practices that some unscrupulous Cooks reserved for stolen meat was described in 1615: *Indeed, I could instance in some kind of coarse venison, not fit for food when first killed; and therefore cunning cooks bury it for some hours in the earth, till the rankness thereof being mortified thereby, it makes most palatable meat.*[8] This was no doubt one of the reasons for a proclamation issued in 1635 to redress *the abuse of persons of the inferior rank killing game*.

In 1635 a commission was given to Sir William Uvedale, Treasurer of the Chamber, and Sir Thomas Hatton, Surveyor General of the Revenue of the King, for the preservation of His Majesty's game, allowing them, for a term of 31 years, to take bonds of £20 from the Cooks, Vintners, and Keepers of Ordinaries to prevent them from buying or selling any of the King's deer, pheasant, partridge, or heath-pout,[9] (unless they had been brought

---

4 *Calendar of State Papers Domestic: James I, 1619–23* (1858), pp. 100–111. The role of Cooks in the armed services, especially in the Navy, is outside the scope of this study, but it is of interest to note a report to Trinity House in 1619 on the placing of galleys on ships: *Reasons for maintaining the cook's rooms amidships in the king's ships: (a) Ordnance and men will not be hindered, which is of prime importance. (b) It is freer from enemy shot than in the forecastle. (c) Foul air created by the great number of men, stinking water, beer, beef and the closeness, lies between the 2 lower orlops and in the hold. When the lower hatches are opened, it ascends and settles between the 2 orlops, endangering health and lives. The cook's fire, always burning at sea, purifies the air. (d) In their present place the cooks do not trouble others, nor are they troubled. (e) They have their provisions (beef, fish, fresh or salt water) close at hand. (f) If the cook's rooms were in the forecastle, the operation of 2 or 4 of the most serviceable pieces [of ordnance] would be hindered. The cook's provisions (trays, platters, kettles, pots, buckets, tallow, tubs, etc.) would inconvenience the men working in the forecastle where there are many ropes, namely fore-halyards [tackle to operate the lower yards], tacks, jeers, bowlines [rope to keep taut the weather edge of the sail] and other ropes belonging to the foremast and bowsprit. (g) The siting of the cook's rooms in the forecastle would spoil one of the best parts of the ship, for it would become noisome and offensive to the crew and gentlemen who come to see the ship. (h) In the forecastle, the cooks would be remote from their provisions.* See *'Transactions – vol. 1: 1619', Trinity House of Deptford Transactions, 1609–35: London Record Society* 19 (1983), pp. 36–42.

5 *Remembrancia: 1579–1664* (1878), pp. 539–549.

6 *James 1 – volume 127: February 1622', Calendar of State Papers Domestic: James I, 1619–23* (1858), pp. 341–353.

7 *Calendar of State Papers Domestic: Charles I, 1634–5* (1864), pp. 421–436.

8 *'Holborn: Inns of Court and Chancery', Old and New London: Volume 2* (1878), pp. 553–576.

9 The black grouse, also known as heath-cock. A heath-pout was a young specimen.

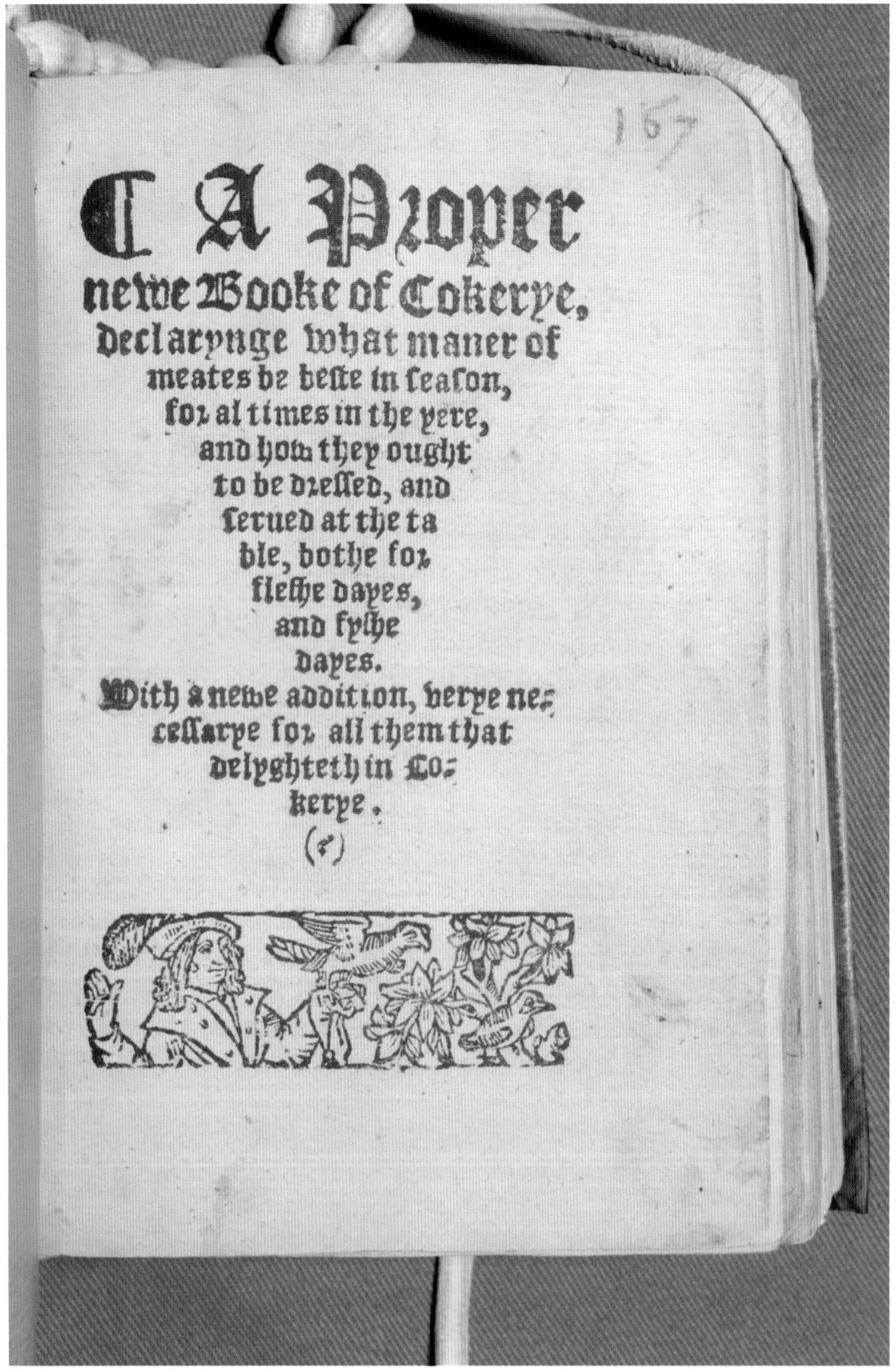

¶ A Proper
newe Booke of Cokerye,
declarynge what maner of
meates be beſte in ſeaſon,
for al times in the yere,
and how they ought
to be dreſſed, and
ſerued at the ta
ble, bothe for
fleſhe dayes,
and fyſhe
dayes.
With a newe addition, verye ne-
ceſſarye for all them that
delyghteth in Co-
kerye.
(✠)

Figure 28. Frontispiece of *A Proper Newe Booke of Cokerye*, 1557–8.

from abroad or were domestic birds). The fines were set at the same rate usually paid by those who broke the rules about trading in Lent.[10] These last regulations seem to have been equally unsuccessful, for in 1630 the Justices of the Peace for Westminster had fined forty-two people, chiefly Cooks and Innholders, for breaching the King's recent proclamation of abstinence from flesh, and against dressing any meat in taverns or inns on fish days and in Lent.

All of these issues suggest that there was a clear distinction within the Company between the Master Cooks who served the Royal Court and the great City institutions and those who operated the fast food cookshops, some of whom were clearly involved in illegal activities. The continued popularity of cookshops was noted by John Stow, who wrote in 1603 that Eastcheap was *a Cooks Row*. However, he also observed that *this Eastcheap is now a Flesh Market of Butchers there dwelling, on both sides of the street; it had sometime also Cooks mixed amongst the Butchers, and such other as sold victuals ready dressed of all sorts. For of old time when friends did meet, and were disposed to be merry, they went not to dine and sup in Taverns, but to the Cooks, where they called for meat what them liked, which they always found ready dressed at a reasonable rate.* The cooks had also moved from the banks of the Thames, where FitzStephen had described them in the twelfth century. By the early 17th where there had been *a common cookery or Cooks Row whereby it appears that in those days (and till of late time) every man lived by his professed trade, not any one interrupting another, the cooks dressed meat, and sold no wine, and the Taverner sold wine, but dressed no meat for sale* and in place of the cookhouses were *many fair and large houses with vaults and cellars for stowage of wines and lodging of the Bordeaux merchants have been built in place.*[11] Some of the areas where new cookshops appeared were regarded as insalubrious; we hear of *rough Ram Alley* [that] *stinks with cooks' shops vile* and *Pottage Island* by St-Martins's-in-the-Fields, near the Strand.[12]

The Spanish Catholic missionary Luisa de Carvajal, who came to England in 1605 and remained till her death in 1614, was not impressed with the food which was *of poorer quality than in Spain. The food looks good but has no smell and almost no taste and is not very nourishing; you can't keep it, even in winter, for four whole days without it going off. Since they sell things in pieces and not by weight, you are obliged to buy more than you need for a small household. They get round this by roasting things and keeping them as cold meats or by putting them in pastry. Chickens usually cost a shilling to a shilling and a half, but there is nothing to them and, on their own, they are insufficient to the point of being uneatable, as well as being on the small side. This is why they prefer capons, which are like good chickens in Spain, although not really in taste, and these cost half a crown or three shillings and rarely have I seen them for two shillings.*[13]

10 *Calendar of State Papers Domestic: Charles I, 1635* (1865), pp. 519–559.

11 *'Candlewicke streete warde', A Survey of London, by John Stow: Reprinted from the text of 1603* (1908), pp. 216–223.

12 *'Fleet Street: Southern tributaries', Old and New London: Volume 1* (1878), pp. 135–146.

13 Glyn Redworth, *The She-Apostle: The Extraordinary Life and Death of Luisa de Carvajal*, Oxford, 2008, p. 131.

Figure 29. Gold Bowl c.1675, engraved with the Company's Arms that were in use up to 1612. Purchased in 1938 but the records relating to its acquisition were destroyed in the Second World War.

Perhaps the most vivid description of the cheaper end of the market was provided a few years later by Ned Ward, known as the London Spy, who went to the St Bartholomew's Day fair and then visited the Cooks at Pie Corner: *Having trespass'd, like misers, too far upon nature and spent most of the day without giving our bodies that refreshment which was requisite to enliven our spirits, and preserve health, after a short consultation we agreed to gratify our importunate appetites with a quarter of a pig, on purpose to be fools in fashion. In order to accomplish our design, with a great deal of elbow-labour and much sweating, we scrambled throh the throng, who came pouring into the Fair from all adjacent streets, each stream of rabble contending to repel the force of its opposite current and striving, like tide and stream, to overcome each other.*

At last, with as much difficulty as a hunted buck gets thro' a wood with his horns on, by inch and inch we gain'd Pie Corner [the Smithfield end of Giltspur Street and famous for its cookshops], *where cooks stood dripping at their doors, like their roasted swines-flesh at their fires, each setting forth with an audible voice the choice and excellency of his pig and pork, which were running as merrily round upon the spit as if they were striving who should be first roasted. Some pigs as big as large spaniels were hanging in the shop windows, half-baked by the sunbeams, and look'd as red as the thighs of a country milk-wench in a frosty morning.*

After we had gaz'd round us, to examine what cook was most likely to accommodate our stomachs with good entertainment, at last we agreed to step into a large shop where we had great expectancy of tolerable meat and cleanly usage. But no sooner had we enter'd this suffocating kitchen, than a swinging fat fellow, the overseer of the roast to keep the pigs from blistering, who was standing by the spit in his shirt, rubbed his ears, breast, neck, and arm-pits with the same wet-cloth which he applied to his pigs, which brought such qualm over my stomach, that I had much ado to keep the stuffing of my guts from tumbling into the dripping-pan; so scouring out again thro' an army of flies, encamped at the door in order to attack the pig-sauce, we defer'd our eating till a cleanlier opportunity.[14]

14 *The London Spy by Ned Ward (1703)*, The Folio society, 1955, pp. 186–7.

This was clearly at the rough end of the catering market, although some of the owners and managers of these simple cookshops were probably members of the Company. However, there was a superior type of cookshop, serving the middle classes and providing meals on the premises and as well as 'take-away' services. A great patron of these better-class shops was Samuel Pepys and, as so often, his *Diary* gives us an unprecedented glimpse into the way of life of a well-to-do London family in the 1660s. There are many entries similar to those for the year 1660: *I went to a cook's and got a good joint of meat, and my wife and I dined at home alone* (1st July) or *dined with Mr Luellin and Salsbury at a cook's shop* (8th July). The take-away dishes were usually good, although when he sent his wife to buy something for supper she returned with *a Quarter of lamb, so we eat it but it was not half roasted* (17th July). Pepys could also be the victim of sharp practices – on 16th October, 1661 he went *with Dr Thomas Pepys and my brother Tom to a venison pasty, which proved a pasty of salted pork.*

Sometimes domestic concerns meant that Mr Pepys' kitchen was unusable: *To dinner at home of roast beef from a Cook's (which of late we have been forced to do because of our house being always under the painters and other people's hands, that we could not dress it ourselves)* (22nd October, 1660). But ordering dishes to be brought in from a Cookshop was in fact a regular practice. On Christmas day, 1662, he sent *for a mince-pie abroad, my wife not being well enough to make any herself yet.* There were some hazards to contend with that ring a clear bell in contemporary ears. On 6th October, 1663, Pepys had invited guests to dinner whom he clearly wanted to impress: *we had no meat dressed; but sent to the Cook's and my people had so little wit to send in our meat from abroad in the cook's dishes, which were marked with the name of the cook upon them; by which, if they observed anything, they might know it was not my own dinner.*

The alternative to buying ready-made dishes was to bring in a Cook to dress dinner.

Figure 30. A Newcastle engraved glass goblet of c.1670, given by H.H. Tickler, Master 1962. It shows a Cook preparing a turkey on a table, a dressed peacock on a side table, with other poultry hanging on a circular rack. The motto reads *Prosperity to the Company* and the Company's Arms are engraved on the reverse. It would originally have had a cover or lid, now lost.

Figure 31. St Bartholomew's Day Fair, by Egbert van Heemskerck (d.1744), oil on canvas.

Before the seventeenth century this would only have been possible for members of the Court or the aristocracy, but one of the effects of the Civil War was to open up society for the middle classes, and men like Samuel Pepys took full advantage of the new opportunities that were available to him. The result might be a combined effort, as on 13th January 1663 when *my poor wife rose by 5 a-clock in the morning, before day, and went to the market and bought fowls and many other things for dinner – with which I was highly pleased...Things being put in order and the Cook come, I went to the office...* On the following 28th November Pepys held a dinner party for guests and *had six noble dishes for them, dressed by a man-cook, and commended, as indeed they deserved, for exceedingly well done.* This was another occasion on which he set out to impress his visitors, since all the food was served *in silver plates, and all things might rich and handsome about me.* Such was the success of the occasion that he hired the same cook again two days later.

Good cooks were not always easy to come by and on 13th March 1668 Pepys had a lot of trouble organising another dinner party: *And thence to Whitehall to have got a cook of Mrs Turner's acquaintance, the best in England as she says. But after we had with much ado found him, he would not come; nor was Mr Gentleman in town, whom I next would have had; nor would Mrs Stone let her man Lewis come, whom this man recommended to me; so that I was at a mighty loss what in the world to do for a Cook, Philips being out of town. Therefore, after staying at*

Westminster a great while, we back to London and there to Philip's and his man directed us to Mr Levett's [Mr Levitt kept an eating house called *The Ship* in Bartholomew's Lane], *who could not come; and he sent to two more and they could not; so that at last Levett, as a great kindness, did resolve he would leave his business and come himself, which set me in great ease in my mind.* Fortunately, the evening was a great success. The eventual cook, William Levitt was a member of the Company, as was Mr Philips.

Figure 32. Portrait of Samuel Pepys by John Hayls, 1666.

Pepys liked to think of himself as a man of fashion and it is interesting to find that he comments in 1669 on the fact that dinner was brought up from the kitchen, one dish after another, but a dish at a time. This was the French manner of dividing the meal into courses which was still fairly novel in Britain at that time.

Pepys's fellow diarist, John Evelyn, was also interested in food and collected recipes which he put together in a manuscript book.[15] His diary reveals that Cooks sometimes had to give practical demonstrations of their skills before they were employed. On 27 October 1685 he wrote that he *was invited to Sir Stephen Foxe's, with my Lord Lieutenant, where was such a dinner for variety of all things as I had seldom seen and it was so, for the trial of a Master Cook, which Sir Stephen had recommended to go with his Lordship into Ireland; there was all the Dainties not only of the season, but of what art could add: Venison and plain solid Meat, Fowl, Baked and Boiled Meats, Banquet*[16] *and in exceedingly plenty and exquisitely dressed.*

The hiring of private cooks for the home should be set alongside the increasingly common practice of the Livery Companies of employing a full-time Cook. The first such appointments are recorded in the sixteenth century and they continued apace in the

15 *John Evelyn, Cook: the Manuscript receipt book of John Evelyn,*ed Christopher Driver, Prospect Books, 1997.

16 Here the word banquet is used in its archaic sense of a course of sweetmeats.

17 *The Worshipful Company of Turners*, Roland Champness, 2nd ed 2004, p. 95.

seventeenth. It was the rule that the Cook to any Company must first be a member of the Cooks' Company, and if this was not the case then he (or she) would be fined. Moreover, members of the Company were not permitted to work for Liveries that were assigned to another Cook. At the Girdlers' Company in 1626 one of the Stewards employed James Ellis, a member of the Company, to dress two of the quarterly feasts, and consequently Thomas Smith, also a member of the Company, *procured Mr Ellis to be fined twenty shillings or thereabouts at Cooks Hall*. This may have been part of a private dispute between Smith and Ellis, since when the Court heard about the fine, *it was ordered that the said Thomas Smith shall pay all such fine and charge as shall be imposed upon the said Mr Ellis for the dressing of the said dinners, or otherwise he shall no longer remain Cook to this Company*.

In 1606 William Greene was appointed to be Cook to the Turner's Company *to be paid from time to time according to his desserts and labour*; he was still there in 1615 when he was described as Chief Master Cook, suggesting that he now had one or more Assistants.[17] The appointment of a new Company Cook was a matter to be taken seriously. At the Carpenters' Hall in 1659 *the place of Cook to this Company being a long time void, by the death of Albert Gurney late Cook*, the Court held an election for a replacement. Eight names were put forward, including William Levitt, whom we have already met with Samuel Pepys. The other candidates were John Johnson, Ralfe Trunckett, William Hughes, John Jackson, Symon Mawe, Thomas Palmer, and, it is interesting to note, Katherine Gurney, widow of the late Albert. *The Choice by most voices fell upon William Levet, a cook dwelling in Bartholomew Lane, near the Royal Exchange, to be Cook to this Company in the place aforesaid, who was presently admitted thereunto accordingly.* He was to enjoy the same place and receive the same remuneration that the late Mr Gurney had lawfully enjoyed, during the Company's pleasure and no longer. In fact, like most of these appointments, Levitt remained in post for a long time and he is recorded in 1688 receiving a *laced Cap with the Company' arms, to be worn and used by him upon all public dinners of the said Company*, which cost 40*s*.

The most intriguing account of the appointment of a Cook concerned the Grocers' Company. The process was recorded in detail and reveals that the King took a very close interest in the affair in order to make sure that his preferred candidate got the job. The election took place in December 1622, when the office of Cook to the Grocers fell vacant following the death of the incumbent, Arthur Hollingsworth. Hollingsworth was a cook of considerable note, mentioned in the introduction to Robert May's *The Accomplisht Cook* (1665) as *one of the ablest workmen in London, cook to the Grocer's Hall and Star Chamber*.[18] The names of six candidates were put forward for the post. It was agreed that only two of these should be put to the vote, the other four being rejected; the two leading contenders were William Norringroet, Cook to the Lord Mayor, and *by his Lordship commended to this*

18 May's opinion was probably coloured by the fact that he had been apprenticed to Hollingsworth.

Court to be both very sufficient in his profession, and of an honest and civil behaviour in his course of life, requesting the whole Court, for his sake, to take consideration of his suite. The second was Francis Acton, Cook to Sir Humphrey Handford, one of the Sheriffs of the City. He came with a letter of recommendation from Sir George Calvert, Principal Secretary to the King. This ran as follows:

To my very loving Friends, the Master, Wardens, and Assistants of the Company of Grocers in the City of London.

After my very hearty commendations; I have received a commandment from his Majesty to recommend unto you earnestly and effectually, in his name, one Francis Acton to be the Cook of your Company; a very honest man, singularly skillful in his profession and so known unto his Majesty as having served the late Queen Anne of happy memory for divers years and by that means hath been oftentimes employed in his Majesty's own service; I can assure you that his Majesty will take it in very gracious part the favour that you prefer this man upon his recommendation and will expect from me an account of the success, which I wish with all my heart to be such as may give his Majesty contentment and that he may acknowledge it unto you with his Princely thanks, as I doubt not but he will, and so I bid you heartily farewell;

Your very loving friend,
George Calvert.

This was extraordinarily direct interference by the King in the affairs of the Company and we can assume that Acton had done some very special service for his monarch. The letter was duly read out to the Court and the two candidates were then put to the vote *by the balloting box.* This involved dropping a small ball into the box which was divided into two sections marked 'Yes' or 'No' – a traditional method of voting still employed in many London Clubs. Acton receive nineteen balls, Norringroet fourteen, while two balls were found to be the *utter box* [*ie.* blackballs] and one was lost putting it into the box, because *as it was affirmed, some of the assistants being not acquainted with the said kind of election, were mistaken in putting their balls into the box*. For this reason the Court moved to hold a second ballot and this time Norringroet got nineteen and Acton eighteen – but since there were only thirty-five people present a rat was smelt! It was then discovered (how, we do not know) that the Lord Mayor and Mr Warden Wynch had each put in two balls. This was judged by the Court *not fitting nor usual* and the vote was not valid; so a third vote was taken and this produced eighteen for Acton and seventeen for Norringroet. The Lord Mayor then claimed to have the right to a casting vote, making it eighteen each. *Whereupon the Court being all this time unresolved of the said election, deferred the same till another Court*. A few days later Sir George Calvert summoned the Master and Wardens of the Company to come and speak with him. He demanded to know why they had not acceded to the King's request and insisted a speedy resolution and the right answer. Faced with a clear threat of reprisals, a new Court was summoned and it was agreed that Acton was indeed the successful candidate.[19]

This case illustrates the close connection between the Master Cooks and the Court and the extent to which the King was prepared to intervene in the private affairs of a Livery Company in order to obtain a position for a faithful servant. It was not an isolated case, for in November, 1663, Richard Pierce, a Yeoman Cook in the Royal Kitchens, petitioned the King to send a letter to the Merchant Taylors' Company asking them to admit him as their Cook. The letter was duly sent, recommending Pierce, *who has long served as yeoman cook, but is now dismissed on reduction of his family, to serve them as Cook, he having particular ability in his profession*.[20]

There was no shortage of work for Cooks in royal service. In addition to the usual round of entertainments and feasts, both James I and Charles I adopted the medieval custom of eating in public once a week, when they could be seen by their subjects. There is a painting of Charles I and his family doing so in his Banqueting House, where they are served by relays of footmen.[21] Several of the Royal Cooks also served for long periods; we have already met Daniel Clarke, who was Master Cook to both Elizabeth I and James I, while in 1619 John Ferris, Master Cook of the late Queen, petitioned to be taken into the King's service, and to have wages and livery as heretofore.[22] Many of the Cooks' concerns related to their remuneration. In 1635 John Sparkes, Master Cook to the young Prince Charles petitioned for an allowance and the Earl of Pembroke, who was appointed to investigate, found that *upon search made in the great wardrobe, he is informed that John Lisle, Master Cook to his Majesty when Duke of York and Prince of Wales, had an allowance of livery out of the great wardrobe of 9l. 5s. 4d. payable yearly, as the King's Master Cook then had, and as his Majesty's Master Cook now has, and is the same that Sparkes craves*.[23]

Lavish feasts and extravagant entertainment were less common during the Civil War and under the Protectorate, but there was still an amount of fine dining in the service of diplomacy. So we find John Mushee, Master Cook, producing dinners for ambassadors from Venice and Genoa in 1655, while the members of Parliament were all invited to dine with Cromwell in the Banqueting House in February, 1656. In fact the Lord Protector was not averse to a good meal and the City of London sought to exploit this uncharacteristic weakness by offering him a grand feast in the Grocers' Hall in February 1653, shortly after

19 *Some Account of the Worshipful Company of Grocers*, Baron Heath, 1869.
20 *Calendar of State Papers Domestic: Charles II, 1663–4* (1862), pp. 324–342.
21 By Gerrit Houckgeest, in the Royal Collection.
22 *Calendar of State Papers Domestic: James I, 1619–23* (1858), pp. 20–32.
23 *Calendar of State Papers Domestic: Charles I, 1634–5* (1864), pp. 554–581.

he had assumed power. At Temple-Bar he was met by the Lord Mayor and Aldermen and conducted through the streets, which were lined with seats in which sat all the Companies of the City, no doubt including the Cooks, in their livery gowns. Arriving at the Hall, Cromwell *sat in the middle of a long table; his son, the Lord Henry on the left hand, and the Lord Mayor on the right; and on each side of them the Council, with General Monk, Commissary-general Whalley, and Mr. Claypole, Master of the Horse to his Highness; being entertained, besides cheer, with music, voices, drums, and trumpets. After this, his Highness was conducted up-stairs again, by my Lord Mayor, to a noble banquet. This being done, his Highness departed, being played out by hautboys and other loud music.* John Evelyn was not impressed, however, noting in his Diary that *In contradiction to all custom and decency the usurper, Cromwell, feasted at the Lord Mayors, riding in triumph thro the City.*[24]

With the Restoration came a return of royal employment and grants were made to several Cooks for their past services, some of whom had been suspended or curtailed during the Commonwealth. In 1661 John Sawyer, Master Cook to the King, petitioned for a salary of £200 – a very large sum – in lieu of fees that he had been receiving *for sayes* [saye was a textile similar to serge that was made in East Anglia and Sawyer had presumably been given the concession for trading it]. He argued that a salary of £100 had been granted to Cooks by the three last Sovereigns and increased by King Charles [I] to £150 to each of his two Master Cooks. Moreover, the profit from the sayes, if taken, would bring in much more than £300. Despite this argument, Sawyer only received remuneration of £150 a year for his position as Chief Cook in Ordinary.[25] But there were probably some additional perks, similar to those received by William Austin, the King's Master Cook, who had an allowance of £9 5*s* 4*d* for his yearly livery.[26]

It was not just the King's own servants who came back to work. William Hobbs petitioned to be placed in the Queen's household as Second Cook; he had served the late King and held the same position under the late Duke of Gloucester. John Ferris, Master Cook to the late Prince Henry, successfully begged a pension of £50, while John Sayers, Master Cook, asked to be allowed to benefit from any money as he could find that had been collected and concealed in 1641. This was the duty due on French and other imported sweet wines, which should have been paid to Sir David Cunningham, the late King's Cofferer.[27] What seems to have been a particularly hard case was set out in a letter from Captain William Hickes to Samuel Pepys (then an official in the Admiralty), in which he commends Thomas Fortescue, Cook of the *Colchester*, the King's pleasure boat, as a truly honest and loyal person. Under the former regime he was due to be hanged on account of

---

24 *'Guibon Goddard's Journal: December 1653 and commentary', Diary of Thomas Burton esq, volume 1: July 1653 – April 1657* (1828), pp. XIV-XVI.

25 *Calendar of State Papers Domestic: Charles II, 1660–1* (1860), pp. 482–500.

26 *Calendar of State Papers Domestic: Charles II, 1661–2* (1861), pp. 610–632.

27 *Calendar of State Papers Domestic: Charles II, 1663–4* (1862), pp. 36–63.

Figure 33. King Charles I, Queen Henrietta Maria, and Charles, Prince of Wales dining in public, by Gerrit Houckgeest, 1635.

his love for the King, but instead was forced to become the hangman to save his skin; he had now become an object of charity himself.[28] Lastly, there was an order for the Treasurer of the Household to pay Elizabeth, widow of John Sparkes, late Master Cook to the King, a pension of £40 per annum, in full satisfaction for the arrears due to her late husband.[29]

In line with the Royalist spirit of the age, the Company petitioned for a new Charter in 1663, which was issued on 16th February of the following year, in return for a payment of twenty nobles [1 noble was valued *6s 8d*], which was raised by a subscription amongst the members. This new Charter is a very lengthy document, which begins by reciting and confirming the previous charters. It then ratifies the Act of Common Council by which all Freemen practising as Cooks within the City, but not being Free of the Company, should be translated to it. There follow a series of rights and privileges, many of which the Cooks had long coveted but which were only now explicitly stated in their favour.

28 *Calendar of State Papers Domestic: Charles II, 1663–4* (1862), pp. 263–284.
29 *Calendar of State Papers Domestic: Charles II, 1661–2* (1861), pp. 329–357.

Among these privileges was the statement that *the Mistery of Cooks and their successors, and all men free of the said Mistery and who exercise the said trade, shall not at any time hereafter be taken, called or reputed to be Common Victuallers, Tipplers, or Alehouse Keepers, but that they shall for ever hereafter be persons able to sell, as well within their houses, shops, cellars and other places, as also out of them, meat, bread, beer, ale, salt, sauce and all other victuals, fit and wholesome for the bodies of men, freely, according to the aforesaid custom of the said Mistery of Cooks, without any other license from Us, our heirs or successors, from any of our Justices or other officers and without any let, trouble, disturbance, interruption or denial of Us our heirs or successors or of any Mayors, Sheriffs, Bailiffs, Justices of the Peace, Constables, Head-boroughs or any other of our officers or ministers whatsoever, and Law, Statute, Act, Ordinance, provision, Proclamation or other restraint, matter, cause or thing whatsoever to the contrary thereof in anywise notwithstanding*. To this was added the right *to search and survey shops, Cellars. Houses, Rooms and other places of Cooks and to seize Works and Stuff which they shall find falsely made.*

These clauses give the Company pretty much *carte blanche* to operate within the City, allowing its members to trade with virtually no external restrictions and with no interference from other Companies. It was not to work out exactly like this, however, as other Companies were also obtaining new Charters from the King at the same time, with equally sweeping and often similar powers. The potential for overlap and conflict with those who produced food (such as the Butchers and the Bakers) or with those who sold it (such as the Innholders and the Alehouse Keepers) remained, but it is not surprising that this Charter of Charles II is still the one under which the Company operates down to the present day.

The Charter also set down the administrative structure of the Company, allowing the Court annually to *chose and elect of the most ablest and expert men of the said Mistery, of the Assistants who have not borne the office or charge of one of the Masters of Governors of the said Mistery, two discrete persons, freemen of the same Mistery of Cooks, to be the two Assistant Wardens of the said Company for that year, the one whereof who is the last elected to be called the Renter Warden.*

On the feast day of the Holy Cross (14th September), the Masters or Governors, Wardens and Assistants of the Company are to nominate two persons, who have formerly been in Office as Wardens, to be the two Masters or Governors for the year. At the same time, they should elect from among the Assistants, two others to be Assistant Wardens who should serve as Masters or Governors and Assistant Wardens of the Company for the entire year. Edward Corbett and John Knowles were then appointed the two Masters and Thomas Paine and John Symonds were appointed two assistant Wardens for the coming year. A number of practical clauses follow:

If one of the Masters died in office then a new Master should be appointed; similarly in the case of an Assistant. The Court was given the power to elect annually an *honest and discrete person* as Clerk, to hold meetings in the Common Hall, to make Ordinances and to fine for transgressions of them, with the proceeds going to benefit the poor and decayed members of the said Company. There would be a common seal, and the Company had the power to *break, deface or alter and make new the same seal as to them shall seem most meet*. Very importantly, there was the also the right to raise quarterage and the power to *have, purchase and enjoy any messuage, lands, tenements and hereditaments not exceeding in yearly rent two hundred pounds*. All Masters, Wardens, Assistants and Officers were to take oaths of allegiance and supremacy, in front of the Lord Mayor and the Chamberlain of the City, before acting as Officers.

The sort of problem that could arise from such a wide-ranging Charter was demonstrated only a few months later, when the Tobacco-Pipe Makers complained to Parliament that the actions of others threatened their ruin, because Cooks, Bakers, and Alehouse Keepers were making pipes, but so unskillfully *that they are brought into dis-esteem*: they therefore requested that the Statute of Labourers be enforced, to ensure that only those who had been apprenticed to the trade for seven years were entitled to make pipes.[30] A more serious dispute arose in 1670, when it was alleged that *several members of the Company of Bakers of London have for several years past baked pies, puddings and other baked meats and things properly belonging to the Cooks Trade and to them as Bakers; and do daily blow horns, ring bells and make cries by their boys or other servants about the streets of this city of London and suburbs thereof, thereby inviting people to bake their pies and other bakemeats at their respective houses, to the great detriment, loss and damage of all or most of the Members of this Company.* The solution proposed was a boycott. Cooks must not buy any form of bread from a baker who also made and sold *pies, puddings or other bakemeats*. Anyone offending against this Order would be fined *10s* and *20s* for every subsequent offence. It is not recorded if this achieved the desired result, but it was no doubt partly because of such cases that the Company sought to gain formal recognition for its Bye Laws. These, setting out the various offences and the fines attached to them, were examined and approved by the Lord Chancellor and two Lords Chief Justice in 1686 and a summary of their provisions is given in Appendix 6.[31]

Despite such problems, the Charter of 1663 confirmed that the Cooks' Company was well-established and flourishing. Nevertheless, it was prudent to keep in with the King, even if political circumstances required behaviour worthy of the Vicar of Bray. In 1687 James II issued the Declaration of Liberty of Conscience, a first step towards allowing the freedom of religious worship, and the Cooks sent him an extraordinarily flowery address praising his wisdom and justice.[32] However, only nine years later, in 1696, after the

30 *Calendar of State Papers Domestic: Charles II, 1664–5* (1863), pp. 100–116.

31 Guildhall Library MS 3354, a copy of the Bye Laws made 14th April, 1686 by Richard Bromhill, Clerk.

32 This was published in the *London Gazette*, 14 Nov 1687.

discovery of a plot to assassinate William III and restore James II, the Company sent the new Monarch a loyal address stating that in view of the *horrid and detestable conspiracy founded and carried on by papists and other wicked and traitorous persons for assassinating his Majesty's Royal person, …we heartily, sincerely and solemnly profess, testify and declare that his present Majesty King William is Rightful and Lawful King of these Realms*….and they will defend him against *the late King James and all his adherents*. This was signed by 181 members of the Company –only four Members, whose names were listed at the bottom of the document, refused to sign.

Not long after the Company received its Charter from Charles II two terrible events occurred in the City, the Great Plague in 1665 and the Great Fire in 1666. The Plague started in the east end of London in April 1665 and, in the course of a long hot summer, carried off around 100,000 people, or nearly a quarter of the city's population. Of course, plagues were not new and there had been regular visitations over the centuries. In 1603 the Lord Mayor had banned all public feasting because of a plague and there were no doubt many Companies that followed the Merchant Taylors and adopted a special prayer in times of sickness: *Good Lord, keep this noble city of London, and defend it from grievous plagues, and contagious sickness that we may often in brotherly and true love assemble and meet together, to thy glory, and our mutual comfort in Christ Jesus*.[33] But the plague of 1665 was exceptionally severe and caused many to leave the city for the healthier air of the country. In common with others, the Cooks had to suspend meetings of the Court during the height of the epidemic and in September it was recorded that Richard Pierce, Master, *could not make his Master's dinner according to the ancient custom of this company by reason of the present visitation*. He offered instead to give either a piece of plate or money or a dinner at another time; the Court voted for a piece of plate to remain *as a remembrance thereof*. They also agreed to pay Thomas Palmer and other poor members of the Company, 20 shillings towards their relief *in the time of this said visitation*.[34] In July of the following year the Minutes record that *in the late visitation several Livery men of this Company died and there now being a necessity to call others in their place*, nine of the Freemen were summoned to *come on the Clothing of this Company*. A further consequence of the Plague was seen when Henry Peirson, Wiredrawer, asked to lease a Company property in the parish of St Giles Cripplegate; this was debated by the Court and agreed, *taking into consideration the deadness of trade and that many houses are now standing empty in London by reason of the late visitation*.

33 *Memorials of the Guild of Merchant Taylors: Of the Fraternity of St. John the Baptist in the City of London* (1875), pp. 128–131.

34 The Minute Books of the Company survives for the period 1663– 1682; the Minutes then continue, with some breaks, until 1807 (Guildhall Library, Ms 3111/1–3). These references come from the Minutes for September, 1665.

Then, hard on the heels of the Plague, came the Great Fire. Fires, like plagues, were commonplace in the City, where the majority of the buildings were still constructed of wood, but the conflagration of 1666 was on an unprecedented scale. Fires could be started in many ways, and ovens and open hearths were always a potential source of danger. They were also an important source of revenue to the Crown and a Hearth Tax had been introduced in England and Wales in 1662, to provide a regular income for the newly restored King Charles II. Over 44,000 London households paid this tax, according to the number of fireplaces and ovens they contained, with the Cooks and the Bakers being prominent contributors. The Hearth Tax return for the household and shop of the Baker, Thomas Farrriner, in Pudding Lane records five fireplaces and an oven, and it was the latter that he forgot to douse on the evening of the 1st of September 1666, with disastrous results. Nevertheless, a few years later in 1672, the Cooks had discussions with the Bakers and they jointly resolved to resist paying the Hearth Tax on their ovens in the future. They argued, incorrectly, that they had not paid in the past and so henceforth both Companies would each support members of either Company who were taken to court for non-payment.[35]

The Great Fire of 1666 lasted for four days and destroyed much of the City. Miraculously, the Cooks' Hall was spared, although subsequent entries in the Minute Books reveal that it was a close run thing. On 14th September the Court decided that the Hall should be let out to *any Tradesman, Company or Corporation, whose Halls are now destroyed by the late dreadful fire.* This was not mere altruism, since it would bring in additional income; *and taking into account the goodness of God in sparing this Hall being surrounded with those dreadful flames* it would be *more beneficial for several members of this Corporation, especially those who are Cooks to such Companies whose Halls now burnt.* The rental rate was set at £10 a year for the Great Twelve Companies, and £8 for the rest, while the Clerk personally received a fee of 40*s* a year for attending the Hall when it was used by other Companies. The fact that he was also instructed to hire workmen *to put that part of the Hall and Gallery which is now defaced by the late fire in good repair* indicates that the building had been damaged to some extent. It is, therefore rather surprising that we have to wait until September 1672 for the following entry in the Court Minutes: *Renter Warden shall at the cost and charge of the Company get a piece of plate to the value of five pounds to be given to Mrs Fish as an acknowledgement of her husband's particular care and diligence in preserving this Hall in the time of the late dreadful fire which happened in London in 1666.* We do not know what Mr Fish did during the fire, but it has been suggested that he was the tenant of one of the houses in the Cooks' Garden.[36] We may presume that he died in 1672 and the gift was made retrospectively to his widow.

35 Court Minutes ,12 July 1672.
36 Peter Herbage, *History*, 1982, p. 134.

There are other indications of the effect of the fire – in October, 1666, Ralph Russell, having been elected Second Warden, asked to be excused from serving, because *he has sustained great losses by the late fire*, and several others asked to be excused for the same reason. The offer to allow other Companies to make use of the Hall, while their own premises were repaired or rebuilt, was widely taken up. Of the fifty-five Livery halls that were standing before the fire only eight survived intact and we know that the Haberdashers, Salters, Bowyers, Brewers, Distillers, Farriers, Fruiterers, Glovers, Painter Stainers, Stationers, Upholders, Working Goldsmiths, the Charterhouse Men and the Society for the Propagation of the Gospel all made use of the Cooks' Hall. This provided a good source of income, although in 1667 the Renter Warden and the Clerk had to go to the Haberdashers and the Stationers to demand the rent owed for their meetings in the Hall. Both Companies paid up, but by 1681 the Farriers' Company had got so far behind with their rent that they were warned that from next quarter day they must find another Hall.

It was probably the result of exceptionally heavy usage, combined with the damaged caused by the Fire itself, that necessitated a major restoration in 1674 of the entire site, which included the provision of a new Hall. On 11th May the Minutes record that *Whereas at this Court the several members having taken a view of the Long Gallery, and finding the same insufficient and very dangerous and no way to be well supported or repaired and for the safety of the Company or any others to dine or meet therein, it was thought fit upon serious consideration, the premises being fully debated and altogether agreed upon by the members present, that the said Old Gallery shall be taken down and a new Hall to be erected for the accommodation of this Company, upon that part and so much more of the Garden as shall be thought convenient by the several persons named or any five of them; and for the better management and care to be had and taken with the said intended building; it is ordered and agreed at this Court and hereby declared that the Masters or Governors and Wardens of this Company (for the time being) together with Mr James Ellis, Mr Edward Corbett, Mr Richard Pierce, Mr Ralph Russell, Mr Wm Dynes, Mr John Marshall and Mr Anthony Spencer, or any five of them shall have full power and authority to treat, contract and agree with any person or persons for the erecting and building of the said new intended Hall and for the making of such additions or alterations as shall be thought most convenient at such rates and prizes as they or any five of them shall think fit for the best advantage of the Corporation and for their future accommodation at all public meetings.*

The work was clearly carried out very swiftly, but not entirely to the Company's satisfaction, as only a year later, on 19th March 1675, *it was ordered and agreed that the ceiling of the new Hall shall be taken down and made into the frame and model agreed upon between them and the workmen who have undertaken the same, for which they are to have the sum of five and twenty pounds, and are to make good all damages whatsoever, save only the braces which are to be altered at the charge of the Company*. In the following May it was *ordered and thought fit that the Joyner shall go on and make a handsome cornice round the Hall, the value of which is to be left*

Figure 34. The Company's Poor Box, 1722 (on loan to the Museum of London).

to the consideration of the Court. There is further evidence that the major renovation of 1674 may have been a rushed job, since in 1687 the considerable sum of £130 had to be paid to the bricklayer for rebuilding the kitchen and a further £94 expended for work done in the Hall by carpenters and painters.

The survival of the Minute Books from 1663 gives us, for the first time, a detailed insight into the way the Company conducted its business. It is apparent that Freemen and Liverymen were, on election, expected to make a presentation to the Company and this normally took the form of a silver spoon.[37] On 4th May 1664 Thomas Osborne paid £5 and one knobbed spoon as a Freeman, but as a workman half of the money was returned to him; in January of the following year several apprentices gave spoons and were bound as Freemen. On 27th November, 1663, the Clerk placed in the Till[38] two gilt, five knobbed, and seven plain spoons. At various times we hear of spoons being taken out of the Till in the Iron Chest – in 1672 thirteen gilt spoons and three and half dozen silver ones were removed. Two years later William Dynes, Master, received *five dozen and one* silver spoons, to be disposed of for the use of the Company. This was *Spoon Money* and regarded as part of the Company's working capital. The custom of presenting spoons seems to have died out by the middle of the eighteenth century.

There is also regular mention of *Oyster Money*, but this was a sum paid by the Master and Wardens on their election for an Oyster Supper that was held in the spring. The Renter Warden was responsible for most financial transactions, including the provision of equipment for the Hall; for example, in January, 1665, the Master (Richard Gay) ordered the Renter (Thomas Carpenter) to sell the old brass and iron that was stored in the Armoury and to buy in its place six new brass candlesticks and other things needed by the Kitchen.

37 The Innholders Company had a similar tradition of presenting spoons and a good number of these survive and are displayed at Innholders' Hall.

38 The till was a compartment or box for keeping valuables. The Minutes of 29 November 1664 state *This day the Auditor did put into the till within the Iron Chest eight silver spoons.*

The Minutes record the social and religious side of the Company as well. In 1669 the ancient custom (we do not know how old) of meeting together on Candlemas Eve (February 2nd) was revived, in order to hear a sermon and to have a dinner. This lasted until 1723, when the practice was abandoned. Each year Stewards were elected, among whose duties was arranging a dinner for the Assistants, the Livery and their wives. Dinners were not only held in the Hall; and it was also customary for the Masters and Wardens to entertain smaller numbers in their homes.

Figure 35. The head of the old Beadle's Staff, 1671 (on loan to the Museum of London).

Occasionally, the Minutes include an intriguing but obscure entry; on 16th January 1694 it is recorded that *Whereas a complaint hath been made unto this Court of an ill conveniency as by binding a girl as an Apprentice to any Member of this Company. It is ordered by this Court that no girl shall be bound as an Apprentice for the future and that the Clerk shall not presume to bind any girl, notwithstanding the Master's or Wardens' order, upon pain of forfeiting the sum of ten pounds.* The unusual word *conveniency* was a late seventeenth century term for a mistress or a whore and we must assume that some female apprentices were taken on as cover for an illicit relationship. The new rule was apparently enforced, for on 26th March, 1795, the order *that no Member shall be allowed to take a Girl apprentice, under penalty of £10* was re-enacted, because the original had been burnt in the fire that destroyed the Hall in 1771.

Most Court business recorded in the Minutes was more ordinary, but not without human interest. The annual election of Officers was normally contested; for example, in August, 1664 the following were nominated:

For Master: Richard Pierce, Richard Gay and George Thorpe;
For Upper Warden: Wiliam Johnson and Thomas Payne;
For Second Warden: Phillip Starkey, John Smith of Clemente Lane and John Smith of Fetter Lane;
For Renter Warden: Robert Garlick, Ralph Trunkett and William Dawes;
For Stewards: Thomas Hamond, William Levett, Roger Baynes, Thomas Browning, John Smith of the Temple and William Rosse.

The vote took place by show of hands on 14th September, when Richard Pierce was elected as Master, William Johnson as Upper Warden, Phillip Starkey as Second Warden, and Robert Garlick as Renter Warden.[39] Richard Pierce, Yeoman of the King's Kitchen, asked to be excused from serving as Master, but when other nominated candidates also turned down the office Pierce finally accepted, becoming the first (and only) Master to have been elected directly from the Livery, without being on the Court. At the end of his year he gave the Company a large Scottish silver tankard, with his arms engraved on it and his name on the bottom of it, which unfortunately was sold, along with other items of plate, in the eighteenth century. Pierce was also a prominent victim of the Great Fire, losing all his property, amounting to some £5000. In consequence, the Company permitted him to use the Hall until he found another dwelling.

The Renter Warden chosen at this election was Robert Garlick, who was clearly sick and the Court, taking his condition into consideration, ordered that he should pay his fine of £10 pounds for the office and be allowed to stand down. Consequently, there was another election which was won by Ralph Trunkett, but he too asked to pay the fine rather than take up the post; a third election was won by William Dawes, but he also asked to be stood down; finally William Dynes was elected and agreed to serve. On the same day Humphrey Satterthwaite was chosen as Clerk and John Hurley as Beadle, both in contested elections.

Avoidance of service by payment of a fine was common. In 1667 the Court tried again to elect Robert Garlick, this time as Second Warden, but he refused *because of inability both in body and estate*; on this occasion he was successfully replaced by Ralph Trunkett. However, virtually every year one or other of the elected officers declined to serve and paid their fine accordingly.

The Company employed a number of paid servants. The most senior of these was the Clerk, first mentioned in the Ordinances of the Pastelers in 1495,[40] who was responsible for all aspects of the Company's operations. In 1567 Richard Tomson was the holder of the Company's lottery ticket and so may be presumed to have been the Clerk at that time. The office was soon to develop into an important and lucrative one and this produced its own problems. In September, 1663, Humphrey Satterthwaite was elected in place of Lawrence Bromley. However, it proved difficult to get Bromley out of his lodgings in the Hall and on 16th November he was ordered to bring the Master an inventory of the Company's goods and chattels and to hand over the Hall to his successor within a week. Only then would he get the £40 that had been agreed as his severance pay and if he did not

---

39 It may be noted that at all the annual election recorded in the seventeenth century elections only a single Master was chosen but at subsequent meetings of the Court both the Master and the Upper warden were referred to as joint Masters.

40 *That every brother of ability and power shall pay for his quarterage yearly for the priest and clerks and his dinner 4s.*

comply he would get no money at all. Satterthwaite did then take over the lodgings in the Hall, but only on condition that he paid half the rent for the water that was piped in by the New River Company, half the Poor Rate and half the assessment imposed on the Company for the services of the Scavenger [*ie*. the rubbish collector]. He was also deprived of a long established perk, since traditionally the Clerk received 4*d* for each apprentice presented to the Court – and since up to a dozen were regularly presented this was a valuable source of extra income. However, it was laid down that henceforth the money should be paid to the Renter Warden for the use of the Company.[41]

In September, 1664 the Court further laid down what expenses the Clerk could claim. These included for paper, ink and pens 7*s*; for cleaning the Hall for the whole year 10*s*; extra payments were allowed on the Grand Day (when the new Masters and Wardens took up office) and Oyster Day, up to 6*s* 8*d*; candles for the entire year 20*s*; for mops and brooms for the year 20*s*; for beer for the year 8*s*. The Court undertook to keep these perquisites under review and to increase them *according as this Company shall think fit*. There were all sorts of other incidental expenses to be met. As we have seen, the Company kept a small supply of weapons in the Hall, for use by the local Militia, and these incurred costs for cleaning and repair. In addition to the firearms there was a pike and two swords, which also needed occasional maintenance. More peaceably, a new supply of clay pipes was needed and the old ones had to be disposed of, new cooking pots were required, and a new list of the Livery had to be printed.

The Clerk's most important responsibility was to keep the records of Court and write up the Minutes. His role as archivist was taken very seriously as the Court frowned upon any unauthorized use of their records. This got Satterthwaite into trouble in 1680, when one Thomas Stone brought Mr Smith, an Attorney, to examine the Orders of the Company; unfortunately, Satterthwaite was not at home and his servant allowed Attorney Smith access to the records. This may well have been in connection with some law suit involving the Company but, whatever the reason, the Court was incensed: *it is of damage to the Company … the Court being very sensible to such inconveniences doth order that no person whatsoever shall see or peruse or have read to him any of the books, writings or laws of this company, and the Clerk shall be severely fined if he permit any such thing to be done without an order of the full Court.*

As the main legal officer for the Company, the Clerk would draw up petitions and draft reports; for example, in April 1665 he produced a *writing or instrument to be presented to the Lord Mayor and Court of Aldermen that the Company of Bakers London may be constrained to bake thrice a day*. We may presume that they were baking more often than this, to the

41 The value of swearing apprentices was emphasized in 1675 when John Dutton was fined because *he did lately bind an Apprentice at a scriveners shop and not at the Hall*, in contravention of an Order of the Court.

Figure 36. Six drinking cups, engraved with the Company's Arms that were in use up to 1612. Several other pieces of 17th century plate also use the old form of the Arms, suggesting that there was some resistance to adding the new supporters. These cups were probably used at Feasts in the Hall. Five are hall-marked 1656 and one 1659.

perceived detriment of the Cooks. The Clerk was also responsible for summoning those who had broken the Company rules to appear before the Court. The Minutes are full of such offences: in 1665 George Thorpe, a member of the Company, was fined £5 for teaching a maid to make pies and raise pastry, which was contrary to the Ordinances. Thorpe paid up, but *the Court taking notice of his good acknowledgment and submission, looking more to his obedience than punishment, did return unto him £4 10s and delivered the other 10s to Mr Warden Dawes for the use of this Company.* Fines were commonly reduced in this way, provided the offender acknowledged his fault and paid promptly. At the same Court, John Marshall was fined 13*s* 4*d* for dressing of a dinner at Merchant Taylors Hall using four workmen but no Assistant man; as he willingly admitted the error, 10*s* of the fine was returned to him. John Smith of the Temple owned up to dressing of a dinner in the Temple using five workmen and only one Assistant man and was treated in the same manner. Another Cook, Lewis White, was fined 2*s* 4*d* for employing two foreigners to work with him.

Working for more than the permitted two Companies at any one time, or not giving notice of dressing a dinner were the most common offences. In 1666 William Levitt, who was Cook to the Carpenters' Company, was fined £20 for dressing two dinners at

Haberdashers Hall without informing the Company. Levitt also worked for Samuel Pepys, and he seems to have got away with doing so, but in 1668 he was again summoned by the Court and charged with working for three Halls and employing foreigners and other men's servants. He was fined again and ordered to resign as Cook at the Bricklayers Hall, so that some other member of the Company should be free to petition for the post. Strangely, such continual rule-breaking does not seem to have been a bar to progress within the Company, since Levitt became Renter Warden in 1673, Second Warden in 1677, and Second Master in 1679, dying in office that year.

It was not just Cooks to other Livery Companies who were not supposed to work outside their main employment. In 1673 Thomas Lumber, Cook to Alderman Pritchard and to the Sheriffs of the City, was fined £5 for working *out of his Master's house and service*. Another consequence of the growing size of the Company was that there were increasing numbers of apprentices and the Court ordered that no more than three apprentices at one

Figure 37. The head of the current Beadle's Staff which replaced the staff destroyed in the Second World War.

time could be in the service of a Master, the penalty being set at £10. Mr Richard Pierce, shortly before he was elected Master, fell victim to this rule and was fined.

Returning to the Clerk's duties, he arranged the transfer into the Company of those who were changing profession. In 1606 the Common Council of London ordered that any members of the Grocers' Company who practised as Cooks should be translated to the Cooks' Company within one month. Such general proclamations were not necessarily effective and it was mostly individuals, such as John Reynolds, Citizen and Longbow Stringmaker of London who, in 1664, requested translation to the Art and Mistery of the Cooks. Mr Heatherly also translated at the same time from the Carpenters' Company.

The Clerk was generally responsible for the security of the Hall, although after each annual election the main keys were distributed amongst the new Officers; these included the key of the Till, the key to the main lock, and the keys to the great and small padlocks. Another of his jobs was to arrange for Court meetings and in 1665 he *caused a ream of paper to be printed into tickets for summoning the Company against quarter days*. An annual dinner with the Lord Mayor was held in Guildhall in February and attended by the Court and Livery. The cost seems to have been borne by the Company, and the Clerk made all the arrangements, including the gratuities that went to the staff, such as the sword bearer, the porter, the carver, the butler, the yeomen, the running porter, and the labourers in the dry and wet larders and the kitchen. Another task was organising the Searches which the Company carried out annually, to discover improper or illegal practices such as selling rotten or stolen meat. The Clerk had to get the warrant from the Recorder of London, and summon those undertaking the Searches, which usually took place over two days. Miscreants who were caught were fined and the money paid into the company accounts.

Finally, the Clerk looked after various domestic duties relating to the Company's affairs. The funerals of Members often involved a procession of the Livery, who were entertained afterwards in the Hall. In 1664 Mrs Dorothy Johnson, widow of William Johnson, Second Master who died in office, paid £5 *for the Company attending her said late husband's corpse to the grave*. This seems to have been the standard charge for funerals, but exceptionally that of Mr Acton in 1666 cost £20; £15 of which went to the Clerk and £5 to the Beadle. The hire of the Hall for a single meeting or similar purpose attracted a charge of 20*s*, with a further 6*s* going to the Clerk for cleaning the premises.

The Company also employed the Beadle, who is first recorded in 1665, when John Hurley held the post. He was replaced in December by Robert Browne, who was clearly a somewhat difficult character. In April 1667 the Court heard that he *hath lately affronted and abused several of his Masters…with unhandsome language and misbehaving himself towards them*. It was proposed that he should be dismissed but *when he himself acknowledged his offences and miscarriages and promising faithfully to reform and mind the business of this Company more carefully for the future, it was fully consented and agreed at this court that he should continue in the place of Beadle until next election day…* In fact he remained in post until his death in 1676, when Henry Watson, a Member of the Company, replaced him.

The Beadle was responsible for many minor administrative matters and for much of the ceremonial in the Company, processing before the Master on formal occasions. In 1671 a staff and gown was provided for the Beadle at the Company's expense *for the better grace of the Company when they go to the Guild Hall or any other place of public meeting*. The gilded brass head of this staff is preserved and is currently on loan to the Museum of London. A few years later, in 1679 the Court ordered *a longer Brazell staff for the Company's Arms which is carried before them by the Beadle.*[42] Proper dress was also important and in 1689 it was ordered that if any member of the Court should appear without his Gown or tried to borrow a Gown from any other member of the Court he must pay a fine of 1*s* to the Beadle.

There were other employees. In 1670 William Corbold *the present Butler to this Company* was charged to serve at all funerals organised from the Hall, at a fee of 2*s* 6*d* for every 20*s* spent. Another servant of the Company was the Carver and in 1664 Samuel Wilson, one of the Lord Mayor's officers, and a member of the Company was reappointed to the post at a salary of 40*s*, *provided & always & upon this condition that the said Samuel Wilson do and shall from time to time behave himself civilly to the said company and faithfully manage, perform and do all such lawful business as the said company shall at any time imply or command him to do*. There was also a *Scowring Woman*, who was named in 1675 as Dinah Lowden, employed for washing, cleaning and looking after the plate, pewter, and linen belonging to the Company. Her salary was 20*s* a quarter, but when she complained that she could not live on this she was awarded a rise of 5*s*.

Three important and interrelated aspects of the Company's activities came to increasing prominence in the course of the seventeenth century. The first was the holding of property, the second was the making of gifts and benefactions to the Company and the third was charitable giving. If we go back to the Charter of 1616 one of the Assistants listed was John Shield, who became one of the most significant benefactors of the Company. Shield was also a member of the Clothworkers' Company, to which he presented *A Fair French Bowl of White Silver* in 1618. Two years earlier he had been granted an annuity of £28 by the Clothworkers, in return for a loan or gift of £500 to the Company, and in 1617 he made an agreement with the Cooks' Company to the effect that they should receive this annuity forever, on condition that the sum should go to various church charities and the poor, including:

To 2 poor maids upon their marriages, either of the 20s the piece	*£2*
To the poor of the Company of Cooks	*£1*
To the Company of Cooks for their pains, yearly	*£1*

42 On 10th October 1765 the Court Ordered that the Beadle's staff be repaired in a proper manner and the following January Samuel Meriton was paid £7 12*s* 6*d* for repairing it.

Figure 38. The Bartholomew Brombley Cup, hall-marked 1656 engraved with the Company's Arms that were in use up to 1612.

This was the start of the regular charitable support for the poor of the Company, widows of Cooks and distressed Members and widows of clergymen, which was to become a characteristic feature of the Court's activities over the coming years. At almost every meeting there is a record of such a distribution, usually of a few shillings to those who had fallen on hard times, such as the 5*s* that was given to Thomas Hitchcox in 1673, a Member of the Company and now a prisoner in Ludgate.[43] Charity was one of the original purposes of the Cooks' Guild in the middle ages, but it is only from the seventeenth century that we have evidence of regular distributions. To be able to maintain this practice the Company needed an adequate income and, although the payment of quarterage and the levying of fines helped to provide this, the gifts from benefactors and the rents from property were essential for the maintenance of the Company's charitable works.

43 Unusually, in 1689, after reading a petition sent by Nathaniel Russell, then a prisoner in Ludgate, the Court ordered him to be sent £3 from Mr Corbett's gift to the poor of the Company. We must assume he had a convincing case.

The first property to come to the Company was Marsh Manor in 1482; the second was the result of a bequest in 1585 of *all that tenement or brewhouse called the Lillypot and also ten other small tenements next adjoining on the north side thereof in the parish of Steyning*. This was close to the Hall and in the conveyance to the Cooks in 1603 it is described as the Great Messuage in the tenure of Ralph Betts and three other tenements in several tenures in Steyning Lane and Lillypot Lane (the seven others had been disposed of). These buildings were destroyed in the Great Fire of 1666 and on 11th May 1674 a committee was set up with *full power to demise, let, or sell the ground in Lillypott Land to any person or persons for the best and most benefit and advantage that they can and for such time and term of years as they shall think fit for the use of this Corporation.* Consequently, in 1675 the land was leased to John Blowes of London, Carpenter, for sixty-one years, at a rent of one peppercorn for the first year (in which he could develop property on the site) and for the remaining sixty at £18 a year, which was a useful income.

Other seventeenth century benefactors included Leonard Peade, who in his will of 4th November 1663 left £10 and £100 to the Company on condition that they would pay £5 yearly to the Churchwardens of Warfield in Berkshire; another Member of the Company, Matthew Gunnell, gave two silver flagons dated 1687 and 1690, engraved with the Arms of the Company, to the neighbouring church of Easthampstead – the reason for these gifts is unclear and the Company does not appear to have held lands in these parishes.

Edward Corbett, Master 1663, was one of the most generous benefactors of the Company. He died in 1676 and there must have been considerable nervousness when the Court learned that his will was likely to be contested by a Mr Spooner and others. A committee was established to deal with this and Mr Spooner's claim was successfully paid off. Consequently, the Company inherited the considerable number of properties which Corbett had amassed. He was copyholder of the Manor of Walthamstow and owned various lands on the Surrey-Sussex border, notably Oldlands Farm and Ladyland Farm. All of these he left to the Company, together with £10 to buy a piece of plate in his memory (to go with two silver cups he had presented previously), £5 annually to the poor of the Company and a further £5 to the Company for their care and management, £2 annually to the Clerk and £1 to the Beadle. There were other general bequests, including two to the Parish of St Martin Ludgate, where the communion plate already included a silver dish presented by him. For this reason it is assumed that his London home and business were in that parish.

Although the two farms were eventually sold in the twentieth century, Oldlands estate becoming part of Gatwick Airport, the properties played a significant role in the history of the Company.[44] They were leased to tenants, but, in accordance with Corbett's

44 The history of both farms is given in detail in *A History of the Worshipful Company of Cooks, London* (published for the Quincentenary of the Incorporation of the Company in 1982) by Past Master Peter Herbage, 141–151. This volume is for the most part a re-publication of Taverner Phillips's earlier *History*, but the chapter on the Company properties is entirely new.

will, they were visited annually by the Officers of the Company. In 1687 we find that £2 was paid to hire a coach and four horses *to carry the Master and Wardens and some of the Ancient Masters into Surrey to view the Farms and to receive the rent there.* The income from the farms gave the Company a stable financial base and allowed it to develop its charitable and educational activities over the coming two centuries.

Another benefactor was John Phillips, who died in 1674 leaving land in West Ham to Christ's Hospital School to provide for the education of two children of poor Members of the Company;[45] he also left the Company his property in Crooked Lane in the Parish of St Michael Crooked Lane to pay annually for the apprenticeships of two children of poor Cooks. The first children to benefit from schooling at Christ's Hospital were presented to the Court in 1683. This was part of a family tradition of support for the Company and Phillipps's father-in-law, Thomas Payne, Master in 1666 had left £5 *to be spent for a collation*. James Ellis, who had been a Cook to Charles I, left £10 to the Company for a dinner when he died in 1677, but for some reason his wishes were not carried out. The link with Christ's Hospital survives to this day and the Company still presents boys and girls to the School.

There was also a Poor Box kept in the Hall, which was opened regularly and added to the charitable funds. One such box survives, presented by the Master, Thomas Wareham, in 1722 and with the words *Pray Remember your Oath* painted on it. It is a small but stout wooden coffer, bound in iron and with a slot at the top for coins.

Benefactors often gave pieces of plate to the Company and the seventeenth century was especially rich in such gifts. We have seen that silver spoons were traditionally presented by new Freemen and Liverymen, but affluent Members often gave more significant items. The Company's collection of plate is still a notable one but it is not as rich as it was. In the eighteenth century, when funds were needed, some of the plate was sold off, including several significant pieces.[46] What remains includes seven chalice-shaped cups, six dated to 1656 and the seventh 1659, engraved with the Company's Coat of Arms. The donor or donors of these cups is not recorded, but it is possible that they were gifts from Freemen who took up the Livery.

---

45 It is possible that the Company, along with other City Liveries, had responded to an appeal from Sir Richard Dobbs in 1552 to establish a charity *for the fatherless and other poor men's children*, which led to the founding of Christ's Hospital. However, there is no firm evidence of a connection between the Company and the School before John Phillips's gift.

46 In 1746 the following items were sold: One large dish; Mr Johnson's Cup (Johnson died in office as Second Master in 1664) Mr Symond's Cup (Renter Warden, 1663); three large and two small salt cellars; six small cups, one given by Mr Harris; two cups given by Mr Munday. In 1786 there was a further sale of plate (*the same being useless*) for the benefit of the Company. including 22 spoons, one tankard the gift of Mr Matthew Marriot, undated; one other tankard the gift of Mr Richard Pearce 1665, another tankard the gift of Henry and Abigail Brunhead, 1674, and a large salver with a foot, the gift of John Smith, undated. These pieces sold for £40 5*s*.

Figure 39. Oldlands Farm, West Sussex.

Figure 40. Ladyland Farm, Surrey.

Figure 41. The first Corbett Cup, inscribed *The Guift of Edward Corbett Renter Warden, 1657.*

The silver gilt Loving Cup which the Company purchased with the £10 left for that purpose by Edward Corbett is in a quite different category. It is 18 inches (46 cms) tall and weighs 47 ounces, with the hall-mark for 1676 and the maker's mark WM, richly decorated with repoussé scrolls and foliage. The cover is surmounted by the figure of a Roman soldier holding a spear. The bowl is inscribed *The Guift of Mr Edward Corbett who departed this life on the 15th day of May 1676 a member and worthy benefactor of this Company*. This was the second cup he had given, since there is a smaller plain silver one inscribed *The Guift of Edward Corbett Renter Warden 1657.*

Figure 42. The Company Arms at Ladyland Farm, cast iron.

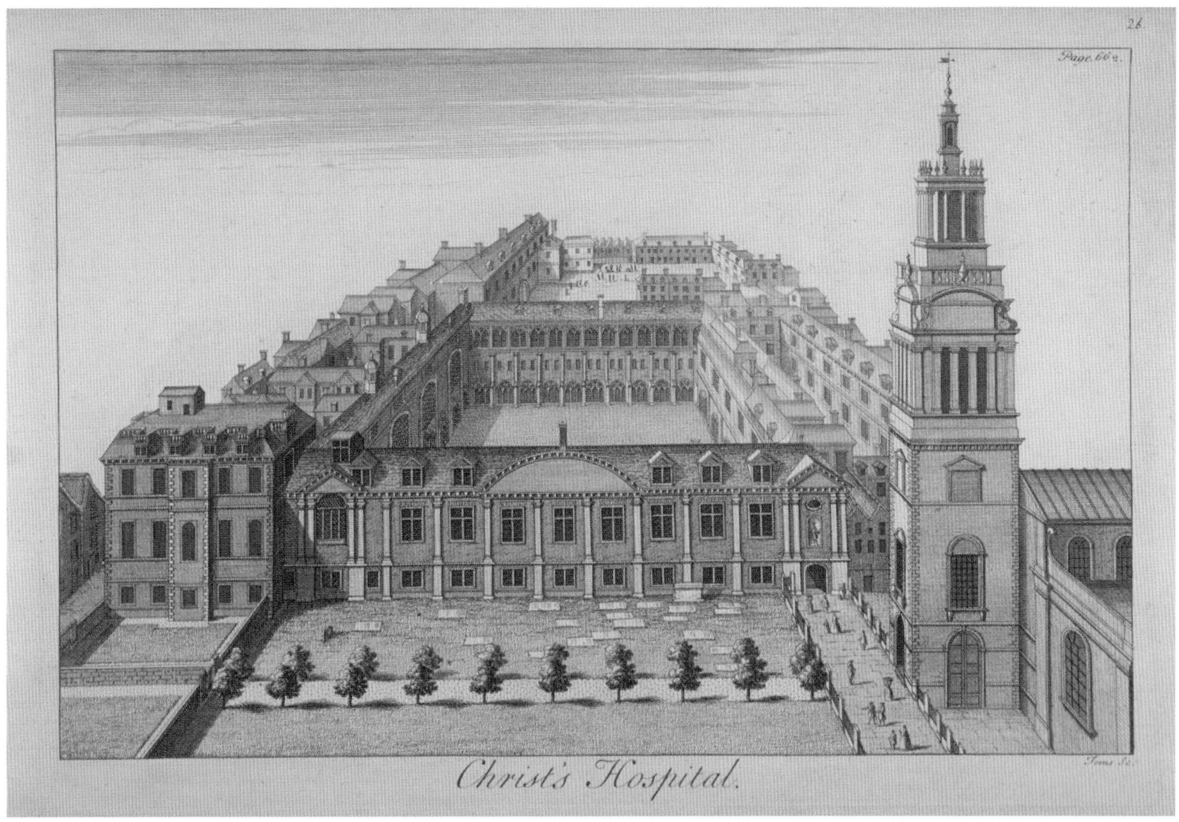

Figure 43. Perspective view of Christ's Hospital. Engraving by William Toms, c.1740.

A large cup, dated 1656 and also with the maker's mark W.M. is inscribed *The guift of Bartholomew Brombley twise Master of the Company of Cookes in London and thenafter to be presented to ye Master of ye Said Company for the tyme being at such tymes as he sits publickly in ye Hall at dinner, at his feast dinner in Remembrance of my love for the said Company for ever, 1656.* The cup is engraved with the Company Arms and the initials BB. Bromley, described as Citizen and Cook of London, is recorded in Hoxton in 1623[47] and he died in 1656, with property in Oxfordshire and Berkshire. The dates of his two Masterships are not known.

Other seventeenth century plate includes a cup given by Robert Lansdale as Renter Warden in 1663 – he went on to be Master in 1669 but no further gift is recorded. In 1664 Rice Hughes asked to be excused coming onto the Livery and when this was granted he presented a large plain cup inscribed *The thankful acknowledgement of Rice Hughes, a member of this Company Ano 1664.* In the same year John Fleming was nominated for the Livery,

47 National Archives ACC/0401/043 Deed of a Fine and Recovery. Capital messuage and mansion house, garden, orchard and appurtenances at Hoxton and in the common field of Hoxton and elsewhere in the parish, 1623.

but as his name is missing from all subsequent lists of Liverymen we can presume that he too was excused from serving. Finally another cup given to the Company through a legacy in 1672 is inscribed *The guift of John Place in his lifetime twice master of this Company of Cooks and at his death father there of.* Place is recorded as Master in 1662 but the date of his first Mastership is not known.

The range and quality of these pieces of plate, especially taking into account those items that were sold in the eighteenth century, is a good indicator of the strength and wealth of the Company in the seventeenth century. There seems little doubt that, despite the momentous events of the century including the Civil War, the Protectorate, the Restoration, the Plague and the Fire, the Company emerged in a strong and powerful position. Indeed, the seventeenth century saw the apogee of the Company's power and influence. The next century was to bring something of a decline from this high point.

Figure 44. The Corbett Loving Cup and Cover with the Arms of the Company and those of the donor engraved on the bowl, inscribed *The Guift of Mr Edward Corbett who departed this life on the 15th day of May 1676 a member and a worthy benefactor of this Company.*

CHAPTER FIVE

The Company in Transition

By the year 1700 the Cooks' Company had been the accepted regulatory body for the catering trade in London for more than two centuries. However, although they were well established, the Cooks remained a medium-sized Livery which could not compete with the Great Twelve in wealth or prestige. For example, in 1799 the gross income of the Cooks was £550, while that of the Goldsmiths was £8,208. This meant that resources were especially important to the Cooks and they were vulnerable to any sudden downturn in their income. The main sources of that income were the fees paid for binding the apprentices, fees paid by those taking up the Freedom or the Livery and for coming on the Court. There were also the fines paid by those who declined to serve in office, and the payment of quarterage by all members of the Company. One other important source of income was rent paid by the tenants of the Company's properties and here the Surrey farms and the Walthamstow estates were particularly valuable. However, although rents were to rise over time, they were still comparatively low and other sources of income, notably the sale of timber from the farms and renting out the Hall for events, became increasingly significant.[1]

The expenses to set against this income were many and varied, but comprised the day to day running of the Company, including the provision of Court dinners and the payment of salaries to the Beadle, Clerk and other Company servants. Further calls on income were for the payment of taxes and legal fees and the occasional need to respond to

1 The economic situation of the Company during this period was analysed by William Kahl, 'The Cooks' Company in the Eighteenth Century' in *The Guildhall Miscellany*, Vol II, 1961, pp. 71–81.

special demands from the King or the Lord Mayor to contribute to exceptional national or civic expenditure.

One constant and considerable drain on funds was the upkeep of the Hall, but this was also a source of income. The undercroft space below the New Hall was known as the Cloisters and was rented by Arthur Betsworth, Stationer, in 1730, for use as a book store. There were also vaults for wine. In 1738 Mr Henshaw, the Clerk was permitted, at his own expense, to erect a new office under the Hall, next to the existing office there, so that he could carry on his business as an attorney. However, while carrying out this work it was revealed that *the Hall and premises are very much out of repair and several more repairs are necessary to be done than did at first appear*, which caused unplanned expenditure of some £428 – almost the equivalent of a whole year's income. The work also involved the former Beadle, Samuel Freebody, moving out of the kitchen and larder that he occupied, so that it could be repaired and beautified for the accommodation of the Clerk and his family. The Court Minutes reveal that further repairs were needed on a regular basis in the following years, while in 1765 it was decided that a Muniment Room for the storage of documents should be added to the Hall. Perhaps on account of all this work, the Renter Warden was instructed to obtain two dozen leather fire buckets for the Hall and, to buy a gown for the Clerk and his successors to wear, showing the seniority of the position.

In the circumstances it is hardly surprising that there are several indications of cash shortages during the eighteenth century. The 1740s seem to have been a particularly difficult decade for the Company and, presumably to save money, the Court began to meet from time to time outside the Hall, with *The George* in Ironmonger Lane, the property of Thomas Savage (Master 1742) being a favourite location. There are other signs that money was short and in July, 1741, it was ordained that there would be no Stewards Feast that year and no dinner would be provided at the Company's expense. Instead the Master and Wardens should, at their joint expense, entertain the Court of Assistants, their ladies and friends in lieu of a Company dinner. This was enshrined as a standing order in 1746, when the Court ordered that for the future there would be no quarterly dinners held at the Company's expense. At the same time it was agreed that the members of the Court should be paid half a crown for their attendance, which suggests that there was little enthusiasm for conducting Company business.

Although dinners at the expense of the Company were to return, it became standard practice for the Officers to provide entertainment during their year. In September 1743 it was agreed that the usual dinner would be given by the Master and Wardens and it was also laid down that the Clerk should sit at the lower end of the table on all occasions. Nonetheless, the Company's traditions of hospitality were maintained, although *it being found inconvenient for the friends of the Court of Assistants to sit at the Court of Assistants table*, in future only Assistants and their wives *or such person as shall represent the wife of each assistant* were permitted to sit there and their friends sat at a separate table on the right hand of the Hall.

In 1746 the Clerk was ordered to make a schedule of the Company's *goods, implements, and things and of all their plate, pewter and linen* and a copy of this would be given to every Renter Warden in future. In 1759, he was asked to provide *a book called a ledger with an alphabet wherein to enter the lands and tenements belonging to the Company, the names of the tenants and the sums derived from each*. Then, in 1746 a substantial quantity of the Company's silver was sold[2] and renewed efforts were made to rent out the Hall. This had of course been common in the years after the Great Fire of 1666, when Cooks' Hall was one of the few left standing, but such rentals came to an end in 1674, when the Hall was damaged by fire. The new Hall was available for hire as soon as it was completed in 1676 and lettings resumed. In 1699 it is recorded that the Gloucestershire Feast was held there and tickets for this were sold at several taverns.[3] The Upholders started to use the Hall on the day of the Lord Mayor's Show and this arrangement continued for several years. More surprisingly, there was clearly a demand to use the buildings for dancing. Balls were held there, some organised by the Company itself for its Members, others by outsiders. On 14th March, 1738 Mr Paul Reynolds was permitted to hold a *Baul*, paying two guineas to the Company and half a guinea to the Clerk for *making good anything that shall be broke or spoilt*. A few weeks later, Mr Lowe, the dancing master, took the Hall for a Ball on the same terms.[4] But then the Court ordered that *for the future that no Ward Motes or other Parish Ward Assemblies be held at the Hall neither shall be any balls public or other dancing be had for the future unless such dancing be had by Order of this Court for the entertainment of this Company.*

Despite the need for belt-tightening, it is clear that the Livery was determined to enjoy the annual cycle of Company events, especially the Confirmation Dinner in October, when the new Officers were sworn in for the forthcoming year and all the Members danced. In the long run this proved very extravagant and stored up problems for the future, but the Court clearly attached great importance to the provision of such entertainment for the Members and their friends at this, the high point of the Company's year.

The cost of maintaining the Hall was only one of the causes of the financial difficulties the Company encountered in these years. An underlying problem was the serious decline in the numbers of boys presented as Apprentices and a consequent decline in the number of Freemen entering the Company. Between 1710 and 1745 the numbers of new Freemen fell by seventy-five percent, reflecting a similar decrease in Apprentices.

---

2 See Ch 4 p. 100.

3 This was reported in the *Post Man and Historical Account*, 6th February, 1700.

4 This was presumably the father or grandfather of the famous Joseph Lowe who taught Queen Victoria and the Royal family to dance reels at Balmoral and at Windsor Castle.

The financial consequences of this were serious, but equally worrying was that the decline indicated the Company's ability to control the trade was slipping away. It was not that there were fewer cooks working in the City (in fact there were more than ever, as we shall see), but that fewer of them thought it necessary to join the Company. To combat this, the Court obtained an Act of Common Council in 1753 which confirmed their legal right to compel the enrolment of apprentices and the translation of cooks who were Freemen of other Companies to the Cooks' Company (see Appendix 8).

The Clerk was much involved in negotiations that resulted in the 1753 Act, while in the following year he asked a Counsel, Mr Williams, to give his opinion of the Company's charters and bye-laws. Williams concluded that there were many things in the Charters that the Company could not comply with and the Court could not act safely under them. The opinion was read to the Court but curiously the Company decided to take no further action, perhaps putting their trust in the efficacy of the 1753 Act. It was under the provisions of this Act that the Clerk regularly sent out *caveats* (warnings) to apprentice cooks, reminding them of the requirement to join the Company; this was in an attempt to at least prevent them joining other companies, but these letters had little effect. Another of the Clerk's tasks was to write regularly to Freemen of the Company who had been chosen and called upon to take up the Livery and pay their fines. Many refused to do so, either on the grounds that the Company had no power to coerce them or because they lived more than four miles from the City and were outside the Company's remit. At every Court meeting the lists of those written to in the previous quarter are given, but it was clearly a losing battle.

The 1753 Act does seem to have stemmed the decline in numbers for a while, thanks to the vigorous campaign of enforcement by the Company. The clauses of the Act were published three times in the *Daily Advertiser* in 1753 and 250 copies of the Act were printed. The following year a further 2,000 copies were printed and distributed by the Beadle, but this only resulted in seven new Freemen joining the Company. The Clerk also wrote regularly to freemen of other companies who were known to be working as cooks, threatening them with legal action if they did not comply. Some then capitulated and joined, but many others did not.

It was becoming apparent that the control the Company had formerly exercised was no longer unassailable and in the first half of the nineteenth century all attempts to maintain a monopoly were abandoned, with the Clerk, David Towse, advising the Court in 1829 that they should avoid any legal proceedings that attempted to compel Freemen of other Companies to switch to the Cooks.

A related problem was the increasing number of foreigners who were attracted to come to London to work in all trades, including that of the Cooks. Such foreigners were regarded as interlopers who did not belong here and they were, for the most part, excluded from the Livery Companies. In 1739 the Clerk was instructed *to conduct, carry on, and bring to trial [the] action now pending in the Mayor's court against several foreign cooks working in the liberty of the city* but nothing actually happened. In the second half of the eighteenth century the issue became so serious that the Companies changed their stance and adopted a system of licensing foreign workmen, in an attempt to regain the Liveries' traditional control of their trades. The Cooks participated in this scheme but many of the foreign cooks continued to work without a licence from the Company. In 1773 this provoked an *Injured Freeman* to write to the Master, on behalf of himself and others, complaining about the situation: *Several of us being at this time out of employ, whereas it need not be, for there is room enough in the City for us, but the places are occupied by foreigners, some of whom never served any time at all.* These foreigners were frequently paid higher wages than those laid down by the Company for its members, but, even though the Freemen had made representations to the employers, they were refused work. The letter (the full text of which is given in Appendix 10) had no effect, but two Freemen, William Fawlkener and Thomas Massingham, did complain to the Court *of their want of business by reason of several members of the company employing foreigners*; they were advised to petition the Court of Aldermen for redress, at the Court's expense. In 1775 it was reported that the Company intended to take legal action against the *French Cooks Club*, under the Statute of Combinations.[5] Once again, nothing seems to have come of these initiatives and in truth once licensing was adopted it was inevitable that a two-tier system of employment should operate.

The fashionable craze for all things French, especially in terms of food and cooking, met with considerable opposition. The English dislike of fancy French cooking was deep-seated and clearly expressed by Richard Warner in 1791: *Notwithstanding the partiality of our countrymen to French cookery, yet that mode of disguising meat in this kingdom (except perhaps in the hottest part of the hottest season of the year) is an absurdity. It is here the art of spoiling good meat.*[6] The Anti-Gallican Society was founded around 1745 to resist the influx of French goods, and the pervasive cultural influence of France. In 1748 Hogarth painted *The Roast Beef of Old England*, a highly political picture, showing the French as a rabble of scrawny soldiers accompanied by a fat Friar, surrounding the English cook bearing a huge joint of beef. This clearly implies that in England roast beef rather than *soupe maigre* (watery soup) was the normal fare. Satirical prints were published showing French cooks displaying a marked lack of hygiene or as fashionable *Macaronis*, in sharp contrast to honest English cooks, such as Edward Heardson, a former pugilist who became cook to the Sublime Society of Beefsteaks, founded in 1735 by John Rich, general manager of the Theatre Royal, Covent Garden, as an intensely patriotic club.

---

5 *The Public Advertizer*, 28th April 1775.
6 *Antiquitates Culinariae*, 1791.

Figure 45. A satirical print by Thomas Rowlandson, 1804 entitled *A French Ordinary*, showing a filthy cook emptying the scrapings of a plate into a large pot. On the wall hang further ingredients for the pot, including a frog, a cat and a dog.

In terms of diet, the English passion for meat, especially beef, is well recorded. An anonymous Frenchman wrote in 1789 that *the dinners of the English, like all their domestic customs, have something peculiar to themselves. By supposing everything to be entirely opposite to what it is in Paris one may form a just idea of these houses in London, where the old fashions are still kept up. The French eat a great deal of bread, and very little meat; the English much meat and little bread. Joints in France are either roasted or boiled to rags; they eat them almost raw in England…the English are for what is simple and natural…the entertainments consist of two or three large pieces of meat, or of prodigious pies, in which some hundreds of birds are entombed.*[7] A rather more jaundiced view was expressed by Francois de la Rochefoucauld, who visited England in 1784: *Dinner is one of the most wearisome of English experiences, lasting as it does, for four or five hours. The first two are spent in eating and you are compelled to exercise your stomach to the full in order to please your host. He asks you the whole time whether you like the food and presses you to eat more, with the result that, out of pure politeness, I do nothing but eat from the time I sit down until the time when I get up from the table. The courses are much the same as in France except that the use of sauce is unknown in the English kitchen and that one seldom sees a ragout. All the dishes consist of various meats either boiled or roasted and of joints weighing about twenty or thirty pounds. After the sweets, you are given water in small bowls of very clean glass in order to rinse out your mouth – a custom which strikes me as extremely unfortunate.*[8] A Swedish visitor to London in 1748 also managed to damn English cuisine with faint praise: *The Englishmen understand almost better than any other people the art of properly roasting a joint, which is not to be wondered at, because the art of cooking as practiced by most Englishmen does not extend beyond roast beef and plum pudding.*[9]

Despite the British devotion to beef, the tide of French influence could not be resisted and in 1757 a satirical print entitled *The Imports of Great Britain from France* depicted a group of *high liv'd epicures*, who cannot stomach good English food, disloyally waiting on the dockside for their new French *chef*, while the ships disgorge their cargoes of cheeses and wine.

One of the effects of this slavish following of continental fashions was the dilution of the close links between the Company and the Royal Court. The Company had provided Master Cooks for the King since the middle ages. By the eighteenth century both the King and the Queen had their own privy kitchens and there was a household kitchen, with a staff of clerks to keep track of the provisions, all comprising a large section of the Royal Household. The kitchens employed Master Cooks, who were assisted by yeomen, grooms and servants.[10] Originally there had been only one Master Cook at a time, but a second

---

7 *A picture of England*, London 1789, vol II, p. 108.

8 *A Frenchman in England, 1784, being the Mélanges of Francois de la Rochefoucauld*, trans S C Roberts, London, 1995, p. 29.

9 *Kalm's account of his visit to England in 1748*, trans Joseph Lucas, London 1892, pp. 14–15.

10 See 'Introduction: Administrative structure and work', *Office-Holders in Modern Britain: Volume 11 (revised): Court Officers, 1660–1837* (2006), pp. XX-XXXVII.

Figure 46. *The Imports of Great Britain from France*, print by Louis Boitard, 1757, showing Custom House Quay with a ship unloading stereotypical people and goods from France, including a cook, a dancer, crates of perfume and wine barrels.

was appointed in 1683, a third served 1698–1718 and 1737–61 and a fourth 1702–9. If all the Master Cooks who served successive Royal Households during the eighteenth century had been members of the Company they would have brought to it both money and prestige, but, with fashionable dining increasingly modelled on the glittering French court, many of the Master Cooks and their assistants in the British Royal Kitchens were now foreigners, especially Frenchmen, with names like Centlivre, Fourmont, and Tegetmeyer. To make things worse, the influx of continental cooks increased greatly during the French Revolution, when royal and aristocratic kitchens all but disappeared throughout France.

There seemed to be no end to the problems faced by the Company. Another difficulty was caused by the fact that the catering business in London had expanded rapidly and changed considerably in the course of the eighteenth century. This was partly a result of the growth of Coffee Houses, which became the most fashionable and popular places for people to gather. Coffee Houses had first appeared in the seventeenth century and the earliest one in London opened in 1652,[11] initially providing nothing but coffee and tea. These Coffee Houses soon spread throughout the kingdom and by the end of the eighteenth century over two thousand are recorded in London alone.[12] They were often referred to as Penny Universities, since, instead of paying for drinks, clients were charged a penny and, once inside, could drink coffee and engage in discussions on every sort of topic. They also attracted business customers, with some becoming the headquarters of a particular trade, such as Lloyds', which specialised in insurance. However, in the course of the eighteenth century Coffee Houses developed as general food outlets as well and they were the places where many of the unregulated cooks were to be found. *A Guide for Foreigners*, published in 1793, observed that *the custom of giving dinners and suppers in coffee-houses has been universally adopted,[and] there is scarcely a street in the metropolis where the hungry passenger of moderate fortune may not live with convenience and elegance; and in several, not only eat and drink, but sleep, upon the most reasonable terms.*

A MACARONI FRENCH COOK.

Figure 47. *A Macaroni French Cook.* A caricature of a French cook by Matthew Darly, 1772.

Coffee Houses that served food were also known as Chop Houses and one of the best known of these was Bellamy's, close to the House of Commons. *Nothing is more common than to adjourn upon occasions of triumphs in the Committee Rooms to 'Bellamy's,' where some of the best wine that can be drank in London, and some of the best chops and steaks that were ever sought to be cooked, almost console even a country member or a stranger for an hour or two's imprisonment in a close room or crowded gallery. A man with eyes to see and a nose to smell, or a tongue to taste, perforce acknowledges that not even the houris in Paradise could serve up a better steak to the most devout Mohammedan that finds his way thither. . . . . The steaks are so hot, and*

11 In 1652, Pasqua Rosee opened a coffee-house in St. Michael's Alley, Cornhill, London. A native of Smyrna, Rosee had been brought to London by a merchant named Daniel Edwards.

12 Bryant Lillywhite, *London Coffee Houses – a reference book*, London 1963, which lists a total of 2033 Coffee Houses in the 17th and 18th centuries.

WILLIAM HOGAR

Figure 48. A cookshop drawn by William Hogarth, 1746–7. Probably intended for his Industry and Idleness series but never used.

so tender, and so accurately dressed, the old Nankin China is so inviting, and the port, the sherry, and the madeira so unexceptionable, and so excellently bodied for an Englishman's palate, that really now and then a man would rather dine at 'Bellamy's' than at home.[13] Such was the fame of Bellamy's that the last words attributed to Prime Minister William Pitt, the Younger (who died in 1806) are recorded as being *Oh, my country! How I love my country* or alternatively *I think I could eat one of Bellamy's veal pies* and the latter has the ring of truth about it! [14] Another noted Chop House was Dolly's in Paternoster Row, where Dr. George Fordyce, a noted epicurean, dined every day for over twenty years, eating steaks and drinking a jug of strong ale, a quarter of a pint of brandy, and a bottle of port. He then walked back to his house, and gave a lecture to his pupils.[15]

13 *Old and New London*, Volume 3 (1878), pp. 491–502.

14 The first is given in Stanhope's *Life of the Rt. Hon. William Pitt* (1862), vol. iv, p. 391, the second is attributed.

15 *Old and New London*, Volume 3 (1878), pp. 63–64.

Figure 49. A Cook Shop from Fable V, The Beau and the Beggar, by I. Smith, c.1770. The scene is Pottage Island, an area behind St Martin-in the-Fields then inhabited by cooks.

The traditional cookshops continued to serve the lower end of the market, but again many of these operated outside the Company's control. Women had been debarred from becoming Apprentices and joining the Company since 1694, so the fact that many cookshops were served by female cooks obviously weakened the Cooks' attempts to regulate the trade. There is a drawing of a cookshop by Hogarth in an unused sketch for his series entitled *Industry and Idleness* (1747),[16] which shows the idle apprentice stealing from his mother, the cook, who stands at the door of the shop embracing her son. He kneels before her and passes behind his back a large tankard, inscribed *Fowlers Cooke Shop*, to an accomplice. In the shop itself we can see various meats, a pie, and a smoking pot.

There is also a vivid description of a cookshop in Tobias Smollett's first novel, *Roderick Random*, published in 1780, which again indicates that the cook was a woman.[17] Newly arrived in London and having taken rooms near St Martin's-in-the-Fields, the landlord tells Roderick *there are two ways of eating in this town for people of your condition — the one more creditable and expensive than the other: the first is to dine at an eating-house frequented by well-dressed people only; and the other is called diving, practised by those who are either obliged or inclined to live frugally.* Roderick chooses the latter and is led *to a certain lane, where stopping, he* [the landlord] *bade us observe him, and do as he did, and, walking a few paces, dived into a cellar and disappeared in an instant. I followed his example, and descending very successfully, found myself in the middle of a cook's shop, almost suffocated with the steams of boiled beef, and surrounded by a company of hackney coachmen, chairmen, draymen, and a few footmen out of place or on board-wages; who sat eating shin of beef, tripe, cow-heel, or sausages, at separate boards, covered with cloths which turned my stomach. While I stood in amaze, undetermined whether to sit down or walk upwards again, Strap, in his descent, missing one of the steps, tumbled headlong into this infernal ordinary, and overturned the cook as she carried a porringer of soup to one of the guests. In her fall, she dashed the whole mess against the legs of a drummer belonging to the foot-guards, who happened to be in her way, and scalded him so miserably, that he started up, and danced up and down, uttering a volley of execrations that made my hair stand on end.* This incident takes some time to sort out, but in the end *we sat down at a board, and dined upon shin of beef most deliciously; our reckoning amounting to twopence halfpenny each, bread and small beer included.*

There is an illustration of about the same date (1780) of above ground cookshops near to Roderick's lodgings, in what was known as Pottage Island, behind the church of St Martin's-in-the-Fields. In a broadsheet entitled *The Beau and the Beggar*, two such shops are illustrated, one bearing the sign *Hot Roast and Boild every day*. Once again, the shop is occupied by a woman who is presumably the cook. The purpose of the broadsheet was to publish a crude satirical verse pointing up the plight of the poor:

16 British Museum, Department of Prints & Drawings, No 1896, 0710.29.
17 *The Adventures of Roderick Random*, Chapter 13.

Figure 50. Portrait of Edward Heardson, Cook to the Sublime Society of Beefsteaks, 1756–86 and British bare-knuckle boxing champion. Mezzotint by John Smith after painting by John Barry.

Thro Pottage Island came a mawkish Beau
Whode Green Tea Stomach at ye strong Hautgout
Heav'd Sickly up: Cursing He hastes away
A half-starv'd Beggar comes, he longs to stay,
Ling'ring, he snuffs the Salutary smell –
Thinks in that Place, tis Luxury to dwell –
Hence it is plain, the Proverb is compleat
That one Man's Poison is anothers Meat.[18]

The eighteenth century also saw the development of other venues for eating and drinking in congenial surroundings. Among these were the Pleasure Gardens, the most famous of which was Vauxhall Gardens under their enterprising proprietor, Jonathan Tyers. Although Vauxhall Gardens had opened as the New Spring Gardens shortly after the Restoration in 1660 their fame and popularity dates from the re-opening under Tyers in 1732. One of the main reasons for going to Vauxhall was to dine amidst the rural surroundings in the painted Supper Boxes. Here patrons were served with a ham, famously carved so thinly you could see through it, and with chicken, salads, fruit, wine and punch. On special occasions dinners were served in large tents erected for the purpose, as in 1799 when the birthday feast for the Prince of Wales was attended by twelve thousand people, who consumed one hundred dozen chickens, a hundred and forty dozen bottles of port wine and much else besides. There were numerous other pleasure gardens in the capital, including Ranelagh, Marylebone, and Cuper's, all serving food for their clientele, but as they were outside the limits of the City of London they could claim to be outside the jurisdiction of the Cooks' Company.

On top of all the other problems, in 1764 a major fire occurred at the Company's Hall. This was widely reported in the press, including a detailed account in the *London Chronicle* of 27th November: *On Saturday night about 10, a fire broke out in the workshop of Mr Laiden, snuff-maker, at the back of the Castle and Falcon Inn, Aldersgate Street, and burnt furiously till four o'clock yesterday morning; which consumed several small houses in the same court. Cooks Hall was reduced to ashes. The flames reached Mr Brown's timber yard, and consumed a great quantity of mahogany and other wood, to the amount of several thousand pounds in value. Two houses in the front of Aldersgate Street were damaged; the Castle and Falcon Inn received but little damage. Several persons were much hurt in endeavouring to save their goods. A guard of soldiers attended to prevent the people from being plundered. Mr Alderman Harley, assisted by the officers, gave such directions to the firemen, guards etc.. as will, we hope, not only prevent any future bad effects from this terrible accident but hinder those worst of thieves who take advantage of so*

18 Guildhall Library Print Room, Catalogue No p5430840.

calamitous a misfortune, from pilfering the few remaining effects of the already too much distressed; three of whom were detected in secreting goods during the fire and committed to prison.[19]

The *Gazetteer & New Daily Advertizer* reported on 1st December that the fire had damaged Cooks' Hall so much, *that it is imagined it must be entirely rebuilt; in which case, we are informed, the company will not rebuild there, but let the ground out on building leases.*

The damage caused had been considered by the Court of Assistants on 29th November, and the initial decision was not to rebuild. However, on further consideration, it was decided to rebuild as the fire was confined to the Great or New Hall built in 1674, provided the Insurance Company met the claim.[20] It was also realised that there was an opportunity for the Company to resolve the problem of maintaining the Hall by letting it to a tenant. The reconstruction took some two years to complete and on 18th October 1766 it was reported that *The Hall and apartments belonging to the Cooks Company, which were greatly damaged by the late fire, have been all repaired and beautified; and the fine picture of King Edward the Fourth granting the charter of incorporation to the master and Wardens of the Company of Cooks has also been beautified and placed in the new-built entertaining room belonging to the said company.*[21]

On 3rd October, 1767, the following advertisement appeared in the press: *To be let, the Hall belonging to the Worshipful Company of Cooks, with the apartment and premises thereto belonging, situated in Aldersgate Street, London. The premises are very large and commodious, stand on much ground and would suit a merchant or tradesman who wants a great deal of room; the whole has been lately substantially repaired and may be reviewed at any time.* A few days later the Court agreed that *Thomas Dobb of St Paul's Churchyard, manufacturer of glass, have a lease of the Hall, except the Beadle's apartments, for seven years, the Company to have free liberty to meet five times in every year in the Court Room, to have their election once a year in Common Hall and also to have the free and sole use of the room called the Pantry. At the same Court resolved that the Master and Wardens be desired to secure the Company's deeds, writings, goods and utensils in a proper place of safety.* This seemed a practical solution, especially as many of the Court meetings were already held outside the Hall. Dobb was soon advertising in the press that *Messers Dobb & Tassoni having now fitted up in a most superb manner Cooks Hall…the greatest variety of fine lustres and Girondoles, and all other fine cut glass, to be seen at Cooks Hall aforesaid.*[22]

---

19 *Lloyds Evening Post* on 26th November, 1764, reported: *Yesterday a man was, by the sitting Alderman at Guildhall, committed to Wood Street Compter, for taking away from the late fire in Aldersgate Street, last Saturday, a table and cloth, the property of Mr Robert Henshaw, Clerk.*

20 The Hall was insured with the Hand in Hand Insurance Company.

21 *Gazetteer & New Daily Advertizer.* The Court minutes for 3rd July, 1766, record that *a black frame with gilt beading be forthwith provided for the charter picture belonging to this Company and the Company's Arms to be forthwith carved and placed up in the hall and that the same should be done at a price not exceeding 12 guineas; and frames made for the names of the Benefactors with such like gilt beading as is ordered for the frame of the picture.*

22 *Public Advertizer.*

Figure 51. The interior of Dolly's Chop House, Ludgate Hill, by Henry Bunbury, 1781.

Unfortunately, the Company had not acquired the ideal tenant and in January 1769 the Renter Warden informed the Court that Dobb owed £25 for half a year's rent due at Christmas, despite being *applied to several times for the same to no purpose*, and so the Clerk was ordered to take legal measures against the him. This obviously did not work and on 11th July, 1771, the Court Minutes again record that *Mr Dobb the Company tenant, not attending to pay his rent pursuant to the notice, ordered that the Renter Warden do take forthwith proper methods for recovering rent due.* Ironically, this turned out to be the last entry in the Minutes for the very last meeting of the Court that was ever held in the Hall. Less than a month later, on 8th August, 1771, another fire occurred which this time completely destroyed all the buildings, save for the two houses in front of the Hall, which were only slightly damaged. The blaze was reported in the press, with the account in *The London Evening Post* being the most graphic and detailed:

The terrible fire which happened yesterday in Aldersgate street, was caused, it is supposed, by leaving a candle burning in one of the outhouses belonging to Cooks Hall, which was entirely consumed, together with a large quantity of timber belonging to Mr Hatton. Several houses backwards were much damaged, and had it not been for the amazing activity and intrepidity of Mr Harley, of Little Britain, who ventured amidst the flames with an engine pipe, the melted lead pouring down on each side of him like water, and an engine playing upon him to prevent him being burnt to death, Mr Mott's new Inn would have suffered greatly, if not been totally consumed. Mr Harley's hands and legs are terribly scorched. Surely this person deserves more than bare thanks from Mr Mott and the Insurance Office. This was presumably the same Mr Harley who, as Alderman, had masterminded the fire fighting operations back in 1764. *The Middlesex Journal* added that *as many people have given out that a ball was held at Cooks Hall on Thursday night and that the fire was occasioned by leaving some candles burning, we are desired to contradict so false an assertion, as no assembly has been held in the room for near two years.*

On 12th August the circumstances of *the late dreadful fire at the Company's Hall* were considered by the Court and there seems to be some suggestion that it might have been caused by arson.[23] Two eye-witness accounts, preserved in the Company's papers, are

23 Guildhall Library Ms 9999.

tantalizingly short. The first relates that *Hatton says that this morning passing by Mr Corp's door his apprentice told him he believed he could tell how the fire happened; that Dobb's apprentice told him his Master was very uneasy and could not sleep; that the day before the fire happened, he was at Cook's Hall the whole day & did not come home to his dinner as usual. Friday morning at one was alarmed by cry of fire; that he observed the flames at the upper end of his Country House come from Cook's Hall.* The second report records that *John Porter had been with a friend in Aldersgate Street and returning home after twelve smelt smoke and burning of hay and straw. Some persons whom he informed of it called him names and would not believe him. A person brought a poker with which he knocked a padlock off the door; on opening it a considerable smoke came from the further part of the Hall; that he assisted at the fire till four in the morning.* If these do imply arson, it was Mr Dobb, the tenant, who was under suspicion, but nothing was proved. Instead, the Master, Wardens and Clerk were instructed to go to the Insurance Office to sort out the claim. To their relief, the Hand in Hand Insurance Company agreed to provide the capital sum of £1,000, with a further £12 *6s* 10*d* to cover the damage done to the two houses adjoining the Hall. Dobb was hoping to avoid any liability and asked whether the Company's goods in the Hall were insured against fire; the Beadle told him that they were not but were included in the lease granted him by the Company. A month later Dobb was held responsible for the £25 outstanding rent, together with *such sum as he shall receive from the Insurance Office for the fixtures and things belonging to the Company scheduled to his lease burnt by the late fire.* Once this bill was settled, the lease was cancelled.

The Wardens organised the disposal of the remains of the pewter, copper, lead, iron and other materials that were left in the ruins of the Hall, and these were sold for the benefit of the Company. On 15th November, Joseph Peet, a Carpenter, agreed to pull down and take away, at his own expense, all the old materials left standing after the fire, except the lead and loose iron, for which he paid £21. On 25th November, George Wyat, a Surveyor, produced a plan of the ground where the Hall had stood and the Court ordered that this be advertised as available for a building lease. Consequently, in January, 1772, an advertisement appeared in several newspapers:

To be let by the Worshipful Company of Cooks, on a building lease for 61 years, a piece of ground about 100 feet by 40 feet (on which lately stood Cooks Hall) situated on the east side of Aldersgate Street, London; underneath part of which are wine vaults; together with one timber messuage in front of the said street and adjoining northward on the passage leading to the said piece of ground.[24]

Nathaniel Wright of Lothbury, a Carpenter, agreed to take the lease for five years and to spend at least £1500 *in erecting good substantial buildings on the same.* He also agreed to insure these new buildings in the names of the Masters or Governors of the Company for at least the same sum of £1500.

---

24 *Daily Advertizer*, 10th January, 1772.

So a troublesome saga ended and since this time the Company has operated without a Hall of its own. After the fire there must have been discussions about the desirability of rebuilding the Hall, but the cost of maintaining such a large property, together with the benefit of rents received from the new buildings on the Aldersgate Street site, convinced the Court that there were few advantages for the Company in having their own premises. It was a pragmatic judgement, leading to other than purely financial benefits, as it inaugurated a regular cycle of meetings and dinners in different taverns belonging to Liverymen, allowing the Members of the Company to sample the wares of their fellows. There were a number of favourite venues, including *The George* in Ironmonger Lane, *The Mitre* in Fleet Street, *The Plough* in Leadenhall Street, *The London Tavern* in Bishopsgate and, in summer, *The George and Vulture* in Tottenham, which made a popular outing to the country. These were all well known venues and in 1781 Willam Hickey reported that *The London, Bishopsgate Street, in my opinion surpassed every other tavern we went to. The dinner was allowed to be excellent and served in a style of magnificence peculiar to that house, wines all of the best. Here everybody was so well pleased that several of us remained at table until seven o'clock in the morning.*[25]

Meetings of the Court were held in Guildhall, and in April, 1772, it was ordered that every Liveryman should receive, at the Company's expense, a silver medal for admission to such meetings. This was to be worn on the breast of the coat and on the death of a Liveryman his medal was to be returned to the Company. These medals (or badges) were still something of a novelty and the Cooks seem to have got the idea from the Vintners; the actual delivery of the medals to the Livery in May was clearly thought to be a matter of public interest and it was widely reported in the press.[26]

The principal meeting of the year was Confirmation Day in October, when there was also a Dinner and a Ball. The practice of having a grand dinner on this day seems to have started in the first half of the eighteenth century although it was initially provided by the new Master and Wardens. On 14th September 1751 it was agreed that the Court of Assistants should be allowed to bring their friends to the next dance on the 22nd October, when three musicians would be hired for the occasion. In 1760, when the Confirmation Dinner was held *the ladies made their usual appearance, but there was neither music at dinner, nor ball in the evening on account of his late Majesty's death.*[27] The fire which caused the loss of the Hall did not stop the Company dancing and a variety of different inns and taverns were used for the balls.

---

25 Alfred Spencer (Ed.) *The Memoirs of William Hickey* (London: Hurst & Blackett) 1913–25, II, p. 315. See also Dictionary of the Principal London Taverns since the Restoration, compiled by J Paul de Castro, c1930, 4 vols, in the Guildhall Library, Ms 3110A.

26 *London Evening Post*, 11th April.

27 *London Evening Post*, 3rd November. George II had died on 25th October.

In subsequent years detailed instructions were issued for the Confirmation Dinner. The Masters and Wardens were given five dinner tickets and two ball tickets, to allow them to be accompanied by their wives and friends, while each member of the Court also received two Ball tickets.[28] Liverymen had to wear their silver medals to the event and anyone lending his medal to another would be fined a guinea. Dancing was not the only diversion, since packs of cards could be hired from the Renter Warden for two shillings deposit, refundable on their return, and a special card room was set up off the Ball room.

A number of further details of the Confirmation Dinners are recorded. They were normally attended by around 220 people and started at four o'clock, followed by the Ball at eight o'clock. The menu was fairly standard and the two courses of the 1806 Dinner were typical:

First Course
15 dishes of Fish, with sauces
22 dishes of Fowl, 2 in each
11 Hams each around 22 lbs
17 dishes of Greens and Roots
8 dishes of Salads
11 Stands of Fruit
11 Jellies

Second course
14 Dishes of Ducks, 2 in each
14 Easterlings, 2 in each
8 Pigeon pies
8 Marrow puddings
14 Dishes of Mince Pies, 6 in each

For the first time in 1782 there is a record of the various Toasts that were proposed (see Appendix 9) and these are little different from the ones in use today. The detailed arrangements for the Crowning ceremonies are recorded from 1809. We also learn that a room was provided for the ladies with their cloaks and another for the gentlemen with their hats. At dinner, when the food was removed from the tables it was taken immediately to the room used by the Livery for drinking after dinner; every dish was covered when served and remained so until the lids were ordered to be taken off; the sauces were served in separate plates and not in any of the other dishes. In 1805 Mr Joseph, Pewterer of New Street, provided the necessary pewter dishes and only Port and Lisbon wines were served.

28 A packet of miscellaneous papers relating to the Company (Guildhall Ms 9997) includes a Ticket to the Ball in 1809. Printed in red, this has the Arms of the Company at the top and the words *This ticket will admit one person to the Ball of the Worshipful Company of Cooks at the Bishopsgate Tavern, Bishopsgate Street, on Friday October 20, 1809 (signed) Tho Butler, Master; no admittance before half past seven o'clock.*

After the 1794 Confirmation Dinner the Company was charged for several items which had been ordered after hours, so the Court laid down that in future anyone taking tea or coffee after eight o'clock in the evening or anything else after three in the morning must pay for it out of their own pockets. Since the Dinner began at four in the afternoon these timings give some impression of the lavish nature and extreme length of the entertainment! The dancing was supposed to stop at two in the morning although the musicians sometimes played on.

In 1796 it was laid down that there would be no Madeira or Wine provided for the Dinner at the Company's expense – a clear sign that another financial crisis was looming. In 1798 the Dinner was initially cancelled, but then reinstated, while in March, 1799, it was recommended that the Court should find ways of reducing the expenses of the Company, since these were exceeding the income. This followed a major review of all the Company's properties, examining the income they provided and the costs they incurred, which led the Renter Warden to present a gloomy report to the September meeting of the Court. He stated that receipts for the year would be about £707, including £151 4*s* from the sale of timber, which was set aside to pay the Land Tax; this left gross receipts of only £555 16*s*. Expenditure would be about £550, including £25 tax on the Company's income; there were also extra charges outstanding from the enquiry into the Estates. Annual receipts over the last five years had averaged £500 while annual expenditure was running at around £531. This expenditure was made up in part of fixed costs, amounting to £232 10*s*, but a very large element was the Confirmation Dinner, which cost £178 and the residue comprised the annual Court Dinners. In the light of this stark assessment, the Court had no hesitation in recommending that the Confirmation Dinner be suspended until the Company's finances were in a better state. Other economies included abolishing the refreshments served at Court meetings, *being unnecessary and a waste of time*. In future, the newly elected Masters and Wardens would be sworn in as the last business of the quarterly Court and then after dinner the new Master would take the chair. At the October Court in 1799 this procedure was employed for the first time.

In fact, the traditional Confirmation Dinner and Ball were soon reinstated and in January 1808 there was a motion before the Court to prevent the Members of the Company selling the tickets sent them as Liverymen for the Dinner, suggesting it was a coveted event in the London social season. The favoured venue for the Ball was now *The London Tavern* in Bishopsgate, a large inn noted for its fine dining facilities. John Farley, the author of *The London Art of Cookery* (1792) was the Principal Cook and the landlord was Samuel Hale, an active member of the Company. However, there was a disastrous Confirmation Dinner there in 1809 and immediately afterwards a Committee of the Company met at Fishmongers Hall to investigate this.[29] They requested that *Mr Hale be informed that the*

29 There is a detailed report in the Court Minutes for 3 November, 1809.

Committee as well as the Company around them were and are very dissatisfied with the [Confirmation] dinner put on the table, as being scanty in quantity and not liberally provided as to quality. The long list of complaints included:

That the Fruit Riders at eight shillings being very small in appearance and stuffed with paper shavings were disgraceful to the Company and caused many unpleasant remarks;

That the Dining Room being let to another Company when engaged by and for the Cooks Company;

That the Pink Room being totally neglected till the Company nearly prepared the Room themselves;

That the North and South Venetian Rooms being left unprepared are serious infringements on the Agreement and call for animadversion and suitable deduction;

That there are vouchers only for three hundred and eighty four bottles of wine and that no more be paid for;

That the price of £7 – 16s for thirteen bowls of sugar is beyond what should be charged;

That the keeping back of the rooms which were engaged for the Company threw the entertainment into disorder and was productive of very great inconvenience;

Figure 52. Interior of an eating house, etching by Thomas Rowlandson, c.1800.

That such inconvenience reflects upon the Company and that the Accommodations were not equal to the liberal price paid for them.

It was resolved that the Renter Warden would pay Samuel Hale £200 on account, full settlement pending an interview with him by the Committee. When they met again the explanations offered by Hale (which are not recorded) were judged unsatisfactory but nonetheless the Committee authorised payment of the balance of the account, £74 16*s*.

Figure 53. The Livery badge belonging to Robert Baxter, 1779 (Master 1819).

In the following year, 1810, it was noted by the Court that that over the past decade the Company income had averaged £780, but the expenditure had regularly exceeded this and unless some retrenchment took place the Company would again go into debt. It was therefore suggested once more that the Confirmation dinner should be discontinued *(which it is not the practice of the majority of public companies to give)* and replaced by an annual dinner for the Livery at one of the Quarterly Court Dinners. This was agreed and a Livery Dinner was held instead in the *Crown & Anchor Tavern*. These measures did not resolve the problems and in 1811 the Audit Committee pointed to *the great expenses incurred in entertainments of the Court and Livery which from Michelmas 1810 to Michelmas 1811 amount to the sum of £281 – 14s – 5d. The Committee therefore submit to the consideration of the Court the necessity of retrenching the Company's expenses ... and recommend that at no future entertainments no water, cyder, perry or spruce beer be allowed or paid for by the Company... no wax lights be used ... the venison dinner be regulated so as to be less expensive (the committee observing that the expense of the venison dinner this year amounts to near £54).* The Court should revert to the ancient custom of allowing Members to invite only two friends, instead of four, and the custom of presenting each Liveryman with a silver medal should be discontinued. The Renter Warden was asked to do everything in his power to promote economy and lessen the expenditure of the Company. The Court agreed these proposals, except the abolition of the silver medals.

It is clear that bankruptcy had been narrowly avoided. This, combined with the problems of exercising their traditional control of the trade, indicated that the Company's function, purpose and position were all undergoing fundamental change. In the future, the role of the Company would be less that of a regulatory body and more that of a symbolic and honorific association, representing the highest standards in the profession but without the power to enforce them on the trade as a whole. The Cooks were not alone in

Figure 54. The Livery badge belonging to Lucas Birch, 1787

experiencing such changes and most of the other livery companies evolved in a similar way in the course of the eighteenth and early nineteenth centuries. In the case of the Cooks, the economic problems, exacerbated by the fires in the Hall, give us an exceptionally vivid picture of how these changes occurred.

It is easy to forget, against this background, that business had to go on as usual, but the Court records reveal the Company carrying out its regular functions, punctuated by occasional dramas. One of these occurred on 24th November, 1703, when a fierce windstorm struck the British Isles and did not die down until 2nd December. Even today, it is considered one of the greatest storms ever recorded in Britain and it caused a huge amount of damage. It was described by Daniel Defoe in *The Storm*, which was his first published work (1704) and the destructive force even reached the Cooks' Company. At the Court on 5th April, 1704, it was ordered that John Hall, Master, and William Cleaver, Past Master, should *take the trouble to go to the Company's Farms in Surrey and dispose of the Timber that is blown down by the late great Storm of wind to the best advantage they can the use of this Company*. This no doubt provided a boost, albeit an unplanned one, to the Company's funds and the trees on the farms continued to provide one of the most significant sources of income in the coming years. In 1708 the Court requested tenders from *any friend of any Member of this Company* for cutting timber on the farms and this may have still been part of the clearing-up after the great storm. When, in 1770, an advertisement appeared in the *Daily Advertiser* inviting bids from *such persons as may be desirous of purchasing timber* Mr William Allen offered the huge sum of £650 and his detailed proposal is recorded in full in the minutes, showing the prices paid for the various trees. This was an exceptional amount from a very large sale, but it is no exaggeration to say that the trees from the Surrey farms kept the Company financially afloat throughout the eighteenth century.

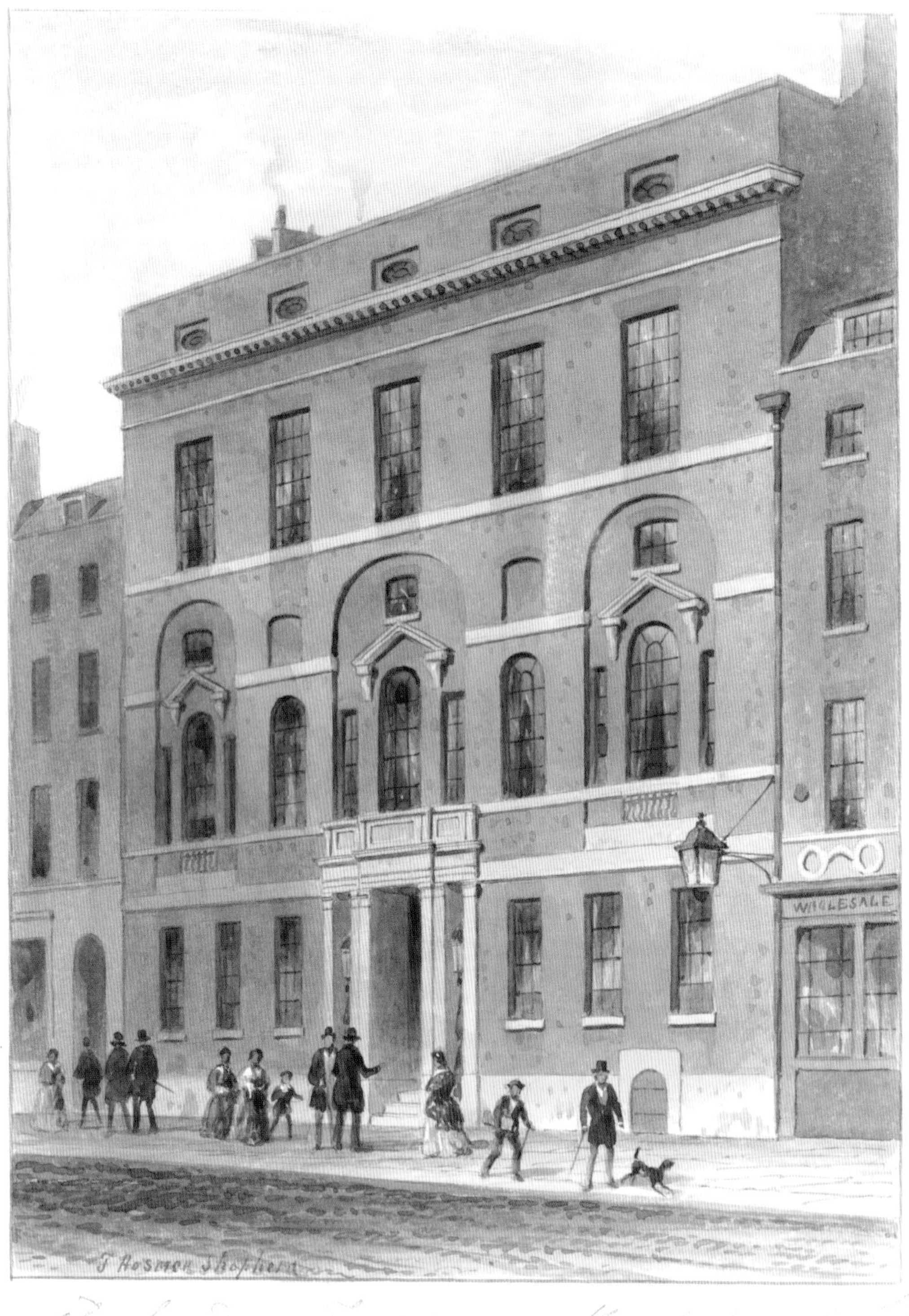

Figure 55. The London Tavern, watercolour by Thomas Shepherd, 1848.

Domestic problems also occupied the Court. In July, 1742, Mr Burding, the Beadle, and his family were reported to have behaved in a very disorderly manner and they were told to quit their apartment in the Hall and find themselves lodgings elsewhere. In September the Court reproved him for his behaviour but, following his humble petition, confirmed him in post, provided that neither he, nor his wife and daughter came into the Hall, except to their own lodgings. He was also told not to *intermeddle in the Hall or the Company's affairs* and ordered not to let anyone, other than his immediate family, have use of his apartments in the Hall. Burding was given a copy of this order, so that he could not claim ignorance of it as an excuse in the future. This seems to have worked for some six years, but in January 1747 he was again ordered to quit his lodgings and move himself and his furniture elsewhere. In September he appeared before the Court to hear several charges against him, including neglecting his duties and being often *disguised in liquor* when attending the Court. The Company had had enough and he was discharged and replaced by Richard Peacock.

Peacock seems to have managed better than his predecessor and when his wife was sick in 1751 the Company sent him 20*s in consideration of the expenses he has been at during his wife's illness*. This is just one example of the way in which the Court took care of its Members and servants. In 1753 the Renter Warden was instructed to pay the disgraced Beadle, John Burding, a guinea so that he could buy himself a coat. In May, 1775, John Tovey, a Freeman since 1765, was reported to be very ill in Saint Bartholomew's Hospital, having had his leg amputated, *by reason whereof his wife and family are reduced to great want.* The Court immediately awarded them 7*s* 6*d* a week and in October Mr Tovey was sufficiently recovered to come and return thanks to the Company for their generous support. As he was still unable to work, the Court awarded him 2s 6d a week till further notice, but he died six months later and his widow, Elizabeth, was granted three guineas and admitted as a quarterly pensioner at 10*s* 6*d* for the future. Another interesting act of charity took place in 1788, when Sir Alexander Kennedy, a Past Master, reported that he had redeemed from pawn the silver medal belonging to William Hibbert, Liveryman, for 8*s*.The Court reimbursed him and confirmed that the medal was considered to be the property of the Company, but, since it was clear that Hibbert had fallen on hard times, the sum of £5 was given to Sir Alexander to be distributed to the distressed Liveryman at the rate of 5*s* per week.

The Court continued its regular charitable donations to the widows of Members of the Company and the widows of clergymen, even in the midst of the financial crisis, as these were largely funded from Edward Corbett's benefaction of 1674. Before the economic situation became critical, gifts were also made to national causes, notably in 1757 when £50 was presented to the Marine Society for the placing of men and boys in the Sea Service. A few years later the financial position prevented such philanthropy and a subsequent request from the Marine Society was turned down (1794), as were appeals on behalf of British forces serving in Europe, for the relief of the suffering caused by the hurricane in Jamaica (1781) and for the construction of a Naval Pillar commemorating British naval victories over the French. In September, 1780, a letter was received from the Town Clerk stating that *very large expenses had been incurred in maintaining the troops sent into the city for the protection of public and private property during the late tumults, and in the past the liveries had contributed to such expenses, request they do so again*. This is a reference to the anti-Catholic Gordon Riots which caused much damage in London, but after some consideration the Company decided it was not able to help.

In June, 1754, there was a burglary in the Hall. Mr Henshaw, the Clerk, informed the Court that, between two and three on the morning of 1st June, persons unknown did *feloniously break into the parlour belonging to this company's Hall and thereout steal a large blue cloth belonging to this company and force and break open the lock of the said parlour and steal several goods belonging to him*. Two women were arrested and committed to Newgate for offering for sale some of the stolen goods. The Court ordered the Clerk to prosecute them and any others who may have been involved and on 10th January, 1747 the *London Evening Post* reported that *Yesterday Deborah Herod was committed to Newgate by Alderman Davis, charged on the oath of John Burding and her own confession, with feloniously stealing a Piece of Plate, whereon was engraved the Arms of the Cooks Company*. This was not the only break-in at the Hall and in 1771 the Renter Warden was instructed to pay Henry Bayly, the Beadle, £20 to compensate him for the losses sustained in the burglary of his apartment. Perhaps it was this break-in that led the Court to provide a proper iron chest in which to deposit the company's plate in January, 1773.

In the late eighteenth century and into the first decades of the nineteenth century the members of the Worshipful Company must have felt somewhat bruised by adversity and surrounded by problems. Nonetheless, they had come through a turbulent and difficult period with some success and the Livery could celebrate their survival and look forward to better times in the future. It is hardly surprising that gifts of pieces of silver, which had been common in the seventeenth century, had dried up entirely in the eighteenth – indeed, two sales of silver had helped to keep the Company solvent. However, a spirit of optimism was demonstrated by one spectacular gift made in 1799 by Samuel Hale, Landlord of the *London Tavern*, to the Master, Phillip Sewell. This was a pair of Chinese export porcelain punch bowls, inscribed with the arms of the Company. It is not known why Samuel Hale made his gift, but he was obviously a man of substance, since the punch bowls would have been very expensive. He is recorded as being a Vintner who had translated to the Cooks' Company in 1790, under the Act of Common Council. He went on to hold all the high offices in the Company, culminating as Master in 1817, despite his dispute with the Court over the Confirmation Dinner in 1809, described above. His gift, made right at the end of the eighteenth century, was clear proof that the Company still flourished, despite the troubles of the preceding decades.

The bowls are decorated with trophies of game (heron, pheasant, fish, swan, and duck). Enamelled inside each bowl is a turtle, which was a new and much sought-after delicacy. Turtles were captured in the West Indies and brought live back to Britain. They were eaten as the centrepiece of many great banquets and a particularly popular dish was Turtle Soup. This was expensive, so enterprising cooks made Mock Turtle Soup from a calf's head stewed in Madeira and flavoured with herbs. To obtain the real thing you needed to visit the most renowned manufacturer, Samuel Birch, proprietor of the firm of Birch & Birch, whose career in the Company and the City is chronicled in the next Chapter. Birch was Master of the Company in succession to Phillip Sewell, to whom Samuel Hale had presented his bowls and no doubt they were used on great occasions to serve the Livery with the very best Turtle Soup from Birch's *Little Green Shop*. The Company motto, *Vulnerati non victi*, inscribed on the bowls, could never have seemed more appropriate.

Figure 56. One of a pair of Chinese export porcelain punch bowls, given by Samuel Hale, Landlord of the *London Tavern*, to the Master, Phillip Sewell, 1799. On loan to the Museum of London.

CHAPTER SIX

The Development of the Modern Company

The clouds that hung over the Company in the early years of the nineteenth century were lifted in 1814 when Samuel Birch became the first (and so far only) Cook to hold the office of Lord Mayor of London. This provided a real cause for celebration and the Company set out to enjoy the limelight.

Samuel Birch was an unusual man, who achieved fame in his three spheres of activity, as a Politician, a Playwright and a Pastrycook.[1] Born in London on 8th November, 1757, he was the son of Lucas Birch, Pastrycook and Confectioner of 15 Cornhill, where Mr Horton had established the premises in the late seventeenth century. The shop was known as Horton & Birch and is said to have been in existence by 1690, when the King went there to purchase Horton's Invalid Jellies for Nell Gwyn when she was ill.[2] Apprenticed to his father Lucas in 1772 and admitted to the Freedom of the Company in 1779, Samuel was elected Master in 1799, following his father who had held the office in 1770, and preceding his brother (another Lucas) who was Master in 1805. In 1778 he had married the daughter of Dr John Fordyce,[3] by whom he had thirteen children.

Birch took a close interest in the family firm, now known as Birch & Birch or, more colloquially, as *Birch's Little Green Shop* and Samuel was nicknamed *Mr Pattypan* by the popular press. In addition, from an early age Birch was involved in both political and

1 See *Dictionary of National Biography*, Oxford University Press, 2004, article by G F R Barker, revised by Gail Baylis and *The Lord Mayors of London, Old and New London*: Vol 1 (1878), pp. 396–416.
2 These details are given in Herbage, *History*, 1982, p. 215.
3 Presumably the surgeon of that name who practised in Uppingham and was the uncle of the distinguished Scottish physician George Fordyce.

literary affairs. He became a member of the Common Council in 1781 and, from 1807, Alderman of the Candlewick Ward. A strong Tory and Anti-Gallican, he proposed the formation of volunteer defence units at the outbreak of the French Revolution and when the idea was adopted he became Colonel Commandant of the 1st Regiment of Loyal London Volunteers. In 1805 he spoke strongly against the Catholic Petition for Emancipation in Ireland, taking a stand for the Protestant cause which twice earned him the freedom of the city of Dublin.

In 1811 he was elected a Sheriff of London and the Company provided carriages for the sixteen members of the Court to attend his installation, while a banner bearing the Arms of the Company was carried in the procession. Then, on 8 November, 1815, the Court attended his swearing in as Lord Mayor and the next day the Company provided a barge, hired from Mr Searle of Westminster Bridge and manned by forty members of the Livery, as part of his procession. Later that day all the Livery dined with the Court at *The London Tavern*, when musical entertainment was provided, making it quite like the old days of the Confirmation Balls. Everything went smoothly and at the next meeting of the Court the Clerk, David Towse was thanked for his care in making the arrangements and given a gratuity of £10. During his year, Birch dined with the Company and presented them with his mayoral banner.

Birch's tenure of office saw him oppose the Corn Bill of 1815, prohibiting the free importation of foreign corn, and when the Bill became law he had to deal with serious rioting in London. These events were commemorated by a medal struck in the Mayor's honour and bearing his bust, with a wheat sheaf on the reverse and the inscription *Free Importation, Peace and Plenty*. He also installed in the Guildhall a statue of King George III by Sir Francis Chantrey and wrote the lengthy patriotic inscription carved on the base of the figure. The Battle of Waterloo took place during Birch's year and a splendid Feast was held in Guildhall, the catering provided by his family firm.

Birch's other interest was in the theatre and he wrote several operettas, one of which, *The Adopted Child*, was very successful, receiving numerous performances in the 1790s. He also had plays performed in West End theatres, including Drury Lane, the Haymarket and Covent Garden. Indeed, such was his prominence in all his chosen fields that a comic poem was published relating the journey of a Frenchman to London, where he found that Birch seemed to be responsible for everything:

Monsieur grown tired of fricassee,
Resolved Old England now to see,
The country where their roasted beef
And puddings large pass all belief.

Figure 57. Portrait of Samuel Birch as Lord Mayor, 1814, by Mary Pearson.

[a later verse]

Guildhall at length in sight appears,
An orator is hailed with cheers.
'Zat orator, vat is hees name?'
'Birch the pastry-cook—the very same.'

The visitor goes on to observe Birch as Colonel of the Militia, as poet and as playwright and returning to France he swears he has met the Emperor of London.[4]

Despite such public prominence, Birch remained close to and a great supporter of the Company, while running his very successful catering business. Birch's Turtle Soup was especially celebrated – it was said that *Tea is no tea if not Twinings, Turtle merely the scrapings of a broth pot if not Birch's*, and it seems to have been his father Lucas who first cooked Turtle for a Civic Banquet in 1761. The delicacy was normally served with Birch's Punch, a rum based potion with several secret added ingredients. His sweetmeats were also renowned and his vast and elaborately decorated Twelfth Cakes (for Twelfth Night) were much prized.

The Birch premises in Cornhill survived into the 20th century, in time for there to be a photograph of the 18th century shop-front. In 1836 Samuel disposed of the business to his nephew (by marriage) and former apprentice, John Ring. He was joined in the enterprise by Mr Brymer, a clockmaker by trade and together they formed the firm of Ring and Brymer, which was to dominate civic entertainment in London for many years. Pearse Morrison wrote in his autobiography that one Lord Mayor *thought, when his time came round that he could do without the famous City caterers, Ring & Brymer. So he made arrangements on his own account, quite overlooking the fact that the one firm had made a study for years and years of providing civic banquets; that they had the appliances, the service, the capacity in every way to do as no other house could hope to. This Lord Mayor found that his year of office cost him thirty thousand pounds out of his own pocket, and since then few Mayors have disputed the claims or capacity of the famous City house. I have not heard of a more expensive Mayoralty, from Alderman Cotton's time down to 1894, twenty years Ring & Brymer ruled.*[5] The firm of Ring and Brymer was acquired by Trusthouse Forte in 1962, ending over a century of service to the City. Alderman Birch died in 1841,[6] aged 84 and Father of the Company. In 1839 he had given £500 towards the relief of the poor brethren of the Company and in his will he left a further £500 for the relief of the widows and orphans of the poor members.

---

4 Quoted in 'The Lord Mayors of London', *Old and New London: Volume 1* (1878), pp. 396–416, where it is attributed to Theodore Hook or some other clever versifier, but the original has not been found.

5 *Rambling Recollections of Pearse Morrison, Member of the Corporation of the City of London*, London 1905, p. 126.

6 The City were supporters of Princess Caroline, the estranged wife of the Prince Regent, and as a demonstration of royal disapproval several Lord Mayors, including Birch, were not awarded the knighthood usually bestowed on the holders of this office.

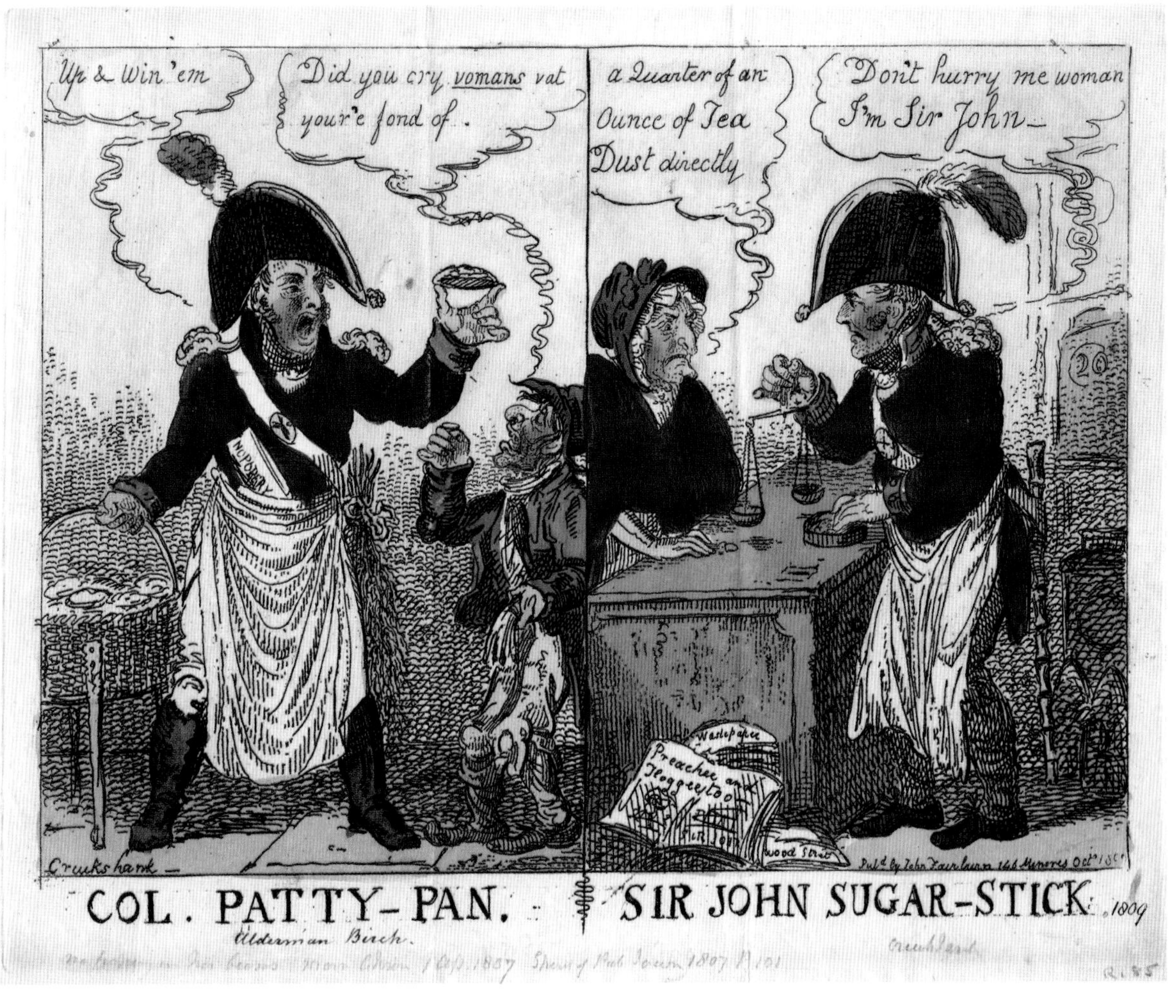

Figure 58. Satirical print of Col. Patty-Pan and Sir John Sugar-Stick (Alderman Samuel Birch and Alderman Earner) by Isaac Cruikshank, 1809.

Throughout his life Birch had played a very active role in the affairs of the Company and he would certainly have been involved in the continuing efforts to exercise some measure of control over the trade. In January, 1813, the Clerk presented a case to the Court to show that the sellers of hams and tongues were indeed cooks: *There are many persons in this City of London who keep shops for the sale of Hams, Tongues, Bacon, German Sausages, dried Pigs heads and such like articles, some of which articles, as Hams and Tongues, are cooked by such persons and cut out for sale by the pound or such other quantities larger or smaller as their customers may desire. These shopkeepers do not sell either bread, vegetables, or any other kind of victuals, nor do they provide their customers with a room to eat in. They merely cook their hams and tongues and cut them up as above mentioned and the buyers take them to their houses or elsewhere to eat it.* This reflects the growth of specialised food outlets, especially Ham Shops and Tongue Shops and the Cooks' case was taken to the Common Sergeant, who accepted the argument, but it does not seem to have got any further.

Figure 59. Photograph of Samuel Birch's premises in Cornhill, c.1910.

Another sign of the declining influence of the Company was the rapidly increasing numbers of foreign cooks, soon to be referred to as *chefs*, coming mostly from France. There had, of course been foreign cooks working in Britain since Perot le Doulce was *cook pro ore* to Henry VII and Henry VIII, but the real invasion came with the French Revolution, when many cooks to the King and to the Nobility fled abroad. Louis Eustache Ude had served as an apprentice in the kitchens of King Louis XVI, where his father was a *chef*, and he came to England to work for the second Earl of Sefton at Croxteth Hall, Liverpool. During the twenty years he cooked for the Earl he wrote and published (in 1813) *The French Cook, Or, The Art of Cookery: Developed in All Its Branches*, a manual of French cooking that was to influence generations of British cooks. As might be expected, the book was hardly complimentary to native English traditions: *It is very remarkable that in France, where there is but one religion, the sauces are infinitely varied, whilst in England, where the different sects are innumerable, there is, we may say, but one single sauce. Melted butter, in English cooking, plays nearly the same part as the Lord Mayor's coach in civic ceremonies, calomel in modern medicine, or silver forks in fashionable novels. Melted butter with anchovies, melted butter and capers, melted butter and parsley, melted butter and eggs, melted butter for ever: this is a sample of the national cookery of this country.*

Figure 60. Portrait of Louis Eustache Ude, frontispiece to *The French Cook, Or, The Art of Cookery*, 1813.

Ude moved to London to work for Frederick, Duke of York and on the Prince's death in 1827, he became the first *chef* at a new gambling club called Crockfords in St James's Street. Paid the astronomical salary of one thousand guineas a year, he soon gained the club a reputation for outstanding food. In 1839, after a dispute about the level of his salary, he moved to the United Service Club House on Albermarle Street, remaining there until he died, aged 77, in 1846.

Figure 61. Portrait of Alexis Soyer, frontispiece to *The Pantropheon, or the History of Food and its Preparation*, 1853.

Ude's natural successor was Alexis Soyer, who also arrived in Britain as the result of a revolution, this time the July Revolution of 1848 that led to the deposition of King Charles X. He was appointed *chef de cuisine* at the new Reform Club in Pall Mall and designed the kitchens with the architect Sir Charles Barry. A great believer in modern technology, he introduced gas for cooking, refrigerators cooled by cold water and ovens with temperature controls. Guided tours of the Reform Club kitchens were organised and Soyer soon became the most famous cook in Victorian England, renowned not only for great dishes (his Lamb Cutlets Reform are still served in the Club) but also for his philanthropic activities – he set up soup kitchens in Ireland during the 1847 Potato Famine and assisted the training of army cooks during the Crimean War. He also wrote many cookery books, including *Soyer's Shilling Cookery for the People* (1854) and *The Pantropheon, or the History of Food and its Preparation* (1853).

These *chefs* not only introduced French food to the British public but they also promoted new ways of dining. In London Gentleman's Clubs became the centre of fashionable eating for both aristocrats and professional men, while for family outings there were the new *restaurants* and *hotels* – both words imported from across the channel.

In these circumstances it was hardly surprising that, in 1829, the Clerk to the Cooks' Company reported that they no longer had the power to enforce *persons exercising the trade of cook to take up their Freedom in this Company*; this was in the light of a famous case brought by the Painter-Stainers' Company in 1824 against James Le Cren, a member of the Curriers' Company who was carrying on a trade in commercial painting. He was summoned to show why he was painting in the City when not a Freeman of the Painters' Company, but he fiercely contested the action. The case was eventually concluded in Le Cren's favour in 1827, after three years of litigation and at considerable cost to the Company. This led the Cooks' Clerk, David Towse, to conclude that he was *decidedly of the opinion that it would not be prudent in this Company at present to adopt any legal proceedings to compel any persons exercising the Trade of Cook within the City of London, especially those who are Freemen of other Companies, to take up their Freedom and become members of this Company, but I think the Company may with propriety continue as heretofore to summons persons carrying on the Trade and who are not Freemen of other Companies to attend this Company and take up their Freedoms.*

In 1842 a Committee was appointed by the Court to define what exactly was meant by *carrying on the trade as a cook*. This reported that *we are of the opinion that every person who dresses provisions of fish, flesh, poultry, game, or vegetables, or a mixture or compound of any of the said articles, or in pies or patties and sells the same for a profit is a Cook. Also that every person who makes pies, puddings, or tarts or other articles composed of paste with fruit or preserves or without either of raised or other crust and sells the same for profit is a Cook. That as to other articles, such as cakes, sweet biscuits etc we are not able (from any documents we have searched) to form a decided opinion.*

This was almost the last attempt by the Company to enforce its historical rights to control the trade. There were occasional cases of individual Cooks seeking to maintain their traditional claim to sell beer and ale with food, as in 1868 when Henry Holt was summonsed for doing this without a licence. He decided to take out a temporary licence for six months, to avoid a fine, but appealed to the Company for help and the Clerk was instructed to give him all possible assistance. However, the Courts ruled that Cooks were not above the law in such matters. This was all part of a general trend towards opening up the City and its institutions to a wider constituency. In 1838 the Court of Common Council had reduced the fees for admission to the Freedom of the City from £25 to £5 and removed the requirement that a Freeman must be a member of a Livery Company. Finally, in 1859, the rule that anyone engaged in retail within the City must be a Freeman was abolished by a further Act of Common Council, effectively ending any possibility that a Livery Company could exercise a monopoly, or even play a significant role in the development of trade. Evidence of this is provided in the Cooks' Company by the gradual decline in apprenticeships, which occur only infrequently after 1850.

There were, in addition, a series of government initiatives designed to make the City and its Companies more transparent. In these circumstances it was useful to have friends in Parliament and a letter from Alderman Shaw MP in 1808 shows that the Company was not slow to cultivate such contacts:

Dear Sirs

Parliament having again met for the dispatch of business, I seize the opportunity to reassure you of the high sense of gratitude which animates my breast for the kind and friendly patronage I have invariably received at your hands and to add that should you have occasion to transact any business in the House of Commons, I hope and expect you will honour me by freely commanding my services in all matters in which I can in any manner be useful to you.

In 1834 Sir Francis Palgrave led a Municipal Inquiry into the State of the Livery Companies, with a view to recommending how they might be reformed. John Towse, Clerk, gave evidence to this Inquiry and described the history of the Company, its Charters and other legal instruments. We learn that the Company then comprised 189 Members, of whom 120 were practising Cooks, including 14 Members of the Court of 26. Numbers continued to grow throughout the nineteenth century and this serves as a reminder that historically the Cooks were one of the larger Liveries. It was only in the second half of the twentieth century that a reduction in numbers took place, culminating in the current restriction to a maximun of seventy-five Liverymen, which makes the Cooks now the smallest of the City Liveries.

The Commissioners heard that *The Company have control by their Charter and Bye-laws to search and inspect the several shops within the Cities of London and Westminster and the liberties thereof and four miles compass thereof round about, and places where the art or trade of a Cook is carried on; and to fine such persons as they shall find in default and to make distresses for the same. Such control has not been exercised during the present Clerk's time, nor for many years prior; but the Company have not abandoned it.*

Towse told the Inquiry that there might once have been more than one class of Freemen, with a separate group known as Yeomen, but they no longer existed and had not done so for a vast number of years. This is of some interest, since Yeomen are recorded in several other Livery Companies but there do not appear to be surviving records of a Yeomanry of Cooks. It is possible that Towse may have been drawing upon archival material that has since been lost. The Clerk refused to permit the Commissioners to inspect any of the Company accounts – a common response from Livery Clerks that led to one of the recommendations of the Inquiry being that the Accounts of Livery Companies should be freely available for public inspection.[7] A Second Commission of Inquiry took place in 1884 and once again the Clerk drew up and presented extensive evidence.[8] This reveals that there were then two-hundred-and-fifty-nine who were Free of the Company, of whom ninety-eight were Liverymen, but the most telling statistic was that from 1870 to 1880 the total number of apprentices bound was a mere ten. On the plus side, the Commissioners did praise the role the Company had taken in the provision of educational courses, and these were to play a major role in the future.

One result of the increasingly limited control which the Company exercised over the trade was that the meetings of the Court took on a different character; in the past and until the close of the eighteenth century Court business was dominated by matters relating to the practice of cookery, especially the taking of apprentices, the election of Freemen

7 *Second Report of the Commissioners appointed to inquire into Municipal Corporations*, 1837, 180–6.
8 *Reports from Commissioners, Inspectors and others; 23:III London Livery Companies*, 1884, Cooks Company pp. 259–271.

and Liverymen, and with cases of individuals or companies that had infringed the Cooks' ancient rights. In the nineteenth century the Minute Books might be almost be mistaken for those of a property company which also operated a number of charities for the benefit of poor cooks, since references to the trade and practice of cookery are few and far between. On the other hand, rents, which had remained low in the eighteenth century, now rose substantially and the Company's property portfolio became the major source of income. Day to day business was now handled by the General Committee, first established in 1839 and made up of two Past Masters and the Current Master, assisted by the Clerk. One of their main duties was to oversee all land transactions and leases, and to make regular visits to inspect the various properties. They made detailed and lengthy reports, which specify in minute detail such things as the height of fencing, the depth of ditches, and necessary repairs to buildings. Some problems consumed inordinate amounts of time, such as the application in 1836 from the Directors of *Sir John Rennie's Brighton Line of Railway* to cross one of the fields at Oldlands Farm. Agreement was not reached until 1839, when the land was compulsorily purchased for £465 and the railway also had to pay an additional £60 compensation for damage done to the ground during construction work. The Company had previously faced a compulsory purchase order in 1829, when its property in Crooked Lane was subject to the *Act of Parliament Regarding* the *Improvement of the Approaches to London Bridge*. In this case the initial valuation was considered much too low and an independent assessment demanded. This valued the property at £1086, considerably more than was originally offered and the sum was gratefully agreed by the Company.

Figure 62. Lord Mayor's Banquet 1828, lithograph by George Scharf, 1829.

There were also occasional dramas, including a destructive fire in 1856 at the Company's premises in Aldersgate Street, leased to Solomon Maw, which led to a long wrangle between the Company, the tenant and Union Insurance. This was settled when most but not all of the claim was met and the Company received a lump sum of £1739 – enough for Union Insurance to retain their business. But, despite such setbacks, the careful stewardship of the Company properties now generated sufficient income to make the Livery relatively stable financially, after years of near insolvency. In 1857 the income was a respectable £1848 – 19*s* – 3*d*, of which £435 was from timber felled on the Sussex farms.

This new-found security also allowed the Company to extend its charitable activities. It still enjoyed the substantial legacies of Edward Corbett, John Shields, John Phillips and others from the seventeenth century and in the eighteenth century new benefactors included Thomas Hope (£200), John Davis (£200), and Sir Alexander Kennedy (£100), but it was in the nineteenth century that the most substantial gifts were made. Samuel Birch's gift and legacy amounted to £1000 for the benefit of the Poor of the Company, while Robert Miller, Master in 1882, made many gifts during his lifetime and bequeathed a further £1,000. Charles Silverside, Master in 1887, also bequeathed £1,000, and a similar sum was left by Miss Elizabeth Baxter in 1882, as a mark of her gratitude to the Company for their frequent invitations to attend the Summer Entertainments held at the *Star and Garter* in Richmond.[9] There were several other smaller gifts, of which the most practical was £20 from W S Angell, Master in 1843, to provide *good black tea* for the use of the widowed pensioners of the Company and this gift was distributed regularly for many years.

In July, 1827, the Renter Warden reported that one of the Company's pensioners, Ann Blunden, had admitted that she had sufficient income to maintain herself. Consequently, in order to prevent false claims in the future, the Beadle was ordered to undertake an annual investigation of existing pensioners to ensure they were all still deserving of support. These reports were then included in the Court Minutes, giving a regular glimpse into the lives of poor Cooks and their relatives. There is no doubt that, as in every profession in London, there were many cases of real hardship, in an age when private charity was all that was available to the sick and indigent. A random selection from the year 1832 is typical of all: John Wilson, Cook aged 66, is very infirm and has not been able to feed himself for seven years; John Mason, Cook aged 68, is in Bishopsgate Workhouse, with a rupture and bad sight and is unable to get employment. Elizabeth Flower, widow of 88, is very infirm, with no income but the pension from the Company; Mary Branson, widow of 56, has seven children, three of whom are under nine years of age. She works as an *ornamental confectioner has but very little employ*; Agnes Tucker, widow of 55 with two children, sells oysters and fruit in the street, and receives 2*s* a week from the parish. For such people a modest pension from the Company of a guinea or half a guinea per quarter was literally a lifeline. With this sort of help a pensioner was occasionally able to climb out of total poverty; Sarah Wallis wrote to the Court in 1858 to say that her circumstances had now improved and she was no longer in need of a pension

9 She was presumably the daughter of Robert Baxter who was twice Master, in 1819 and 1844.

from the Company, but sent her thanks and hoped that someone else might now benefit as she had done. Sadly, such cases are extremely rare.

The Company's involvement with charity schools continued and from time to time, as vacancies arose, two sons of poor Cooks were presented to Christ's Hospital for education there, according to John Phillips's will of 1674. A sign of the close links between the Company and the Hospital was that the Cooks' Arms were painted on a window of the new Hall in the Hospital in 1830. Similar support was shown for the public school at Londonderry, part of the Irish Plantation, and £20 was paid regularly to the Bishop of Derry as the Company's subscription towards its continuance and enlargement. It is also in the nineteenth century that the custom developed for the Masters and Wardens of the Associated Companies to dine together during the year.

The improved financial position allowed the Company to respond on occasion to national charitable appeals. In 1811, £21 was subscribed to the Fund for the Relief of the Sufferings of our Brave Allies the Portuguese; the Master had proposed making a contribution of £50, but the lower sum was voted on an amendment. In 1820s, £20 was contributed to a Floating Chapel for Seamen and the same sum was voted to the Orphan Asylum (1823). In 1836 the Lord Mayor proposed erecting a statue of the Duke of Wellington and £10 was subscribed, while £21 was contributed to the City Committee of the Patriotic Fund in 1855, presumably to support the Crimean War. But the majority of appeals were rejected, including some which held a potential benefit to Company. In 1850 a request to become a subscribing member of the Committee for the 1851 Exhibition was turned down, although this might have provided a valuable showcase for the culinary arts of Britain. Also turned down was the request in 1865 from the London Rifle Brigade for a cup to present as a prize in their annual shooting competition. This was followed by a letter from Colonel Walmsley of the London Artillery Brigade to say that he had heard that the Company was to give money for prizes to the London Rifle Brigade and could the Artillery Brigade also be considered? The Clerk was instructed to reply that this was the first the Company knew of such an intention, but should they decide to help the London Rifle Brigade they would also consider the claims of the Artillery. In fact, it was not until the middle of the twentieth century that the Company forged a link with the army, in the form of the 625th Light Anti-Aircraft Regiment.

In the nineteenth century there was a general trend amongst the Livery Companies towards the development of educational programmes. As the ability to control trade waned, more and more Liveries saw education as a positive way in which they could continue to provide a useful service to their Members and to society at large. For the Cooks, education allowed the Company to recover its sense of purpose, which had all but evaporated in the first decades of the century. In 1869 the Company was invited to attend a meeting with the Lord Mayor to discuss *the promotion by the Livery Companies of a general system of technical education* but nothing really developed from this. However, in July 1874 a letter was received from the National Training School for Cookery requesting support. This was a new institution that had grown out of the Third International Exhibition held in London in 1873. It was first proposed by Henry Cole, Chairman of the Exhibition Commissioners, at a meeting held at Grosvenor House in July. Cole stated that one aim of the International Exhibitions, beginning with the Great Exhibition of 1851, was to provide technical education and *having this year to deal principally with food, determined to make a humble experiment in cookery, and with that view formed classes at which practical instruction was given to the public. Their main object in doing so was to draw prominent attention to the great need of improvement in cooking which prevailed among the middle and lower classes and he felt that if the result of their effort was to produce such an improvement, they had performed a great national work.* These classes had indeed been a success and consequently it was now proposed to establish a National School of Cookery. The aim would be to teach *the best methods of cooking articles of food in general consumption among all classes, and an association should be formed with the intention of making it self-supporting.*

The School was duly set up and began giving classes for girls. This emphasis on female students reflected one of the major changes that had taken place in a profession which had been dominated by men for centuries. By the mid-nineteenth century the great majority of professional cooks were women, employed as domestic servants in the households of the aristocracy and the burgeoning middle classes. While the City catering firms, hotels, clubs and taverns continued to use mainly male cooks, the domestic market was almost exclusively female.

The Company was inclined to support the new School, but, after inspecting the premises in Exhibition Road, Kensington, they expressed concern that the courses seemed to be *for the upper classes who can afford to pay for good cooks and expensive provisions and certainly not for the benefit of the poorer classes.* However, it was realised that there was an opportunity here to develop cookery for the working classes, in the way that Henry Cole had intended. The Court proposed that there should be a Special Committee *to consider the best means of extending the knowledge of cookery both in theory and practice* and how this might be achieved working with the National School of Cookery. This motion was only just passed on a vote of 10 to 9, but it signalled a fundamental change in the Company's approach to the promotion of the art of cookery. The scheme was immediately championed by Liveryman Robert Miller (Master 1881) who was to become one of the Company's most generous benefactors.

The Special Committee on Cookery reported in October, 1876, that it had again visited the National Training School where they found two sorts of classes were offered: firstly *The Practice Kitchen for Middle Class Cookery was in full work, there being some 16 or 18 persons engaged, some giving instructions, the remainder doing the work.* The second course was

The Artisan Kitchen [which] is also in good work from 12 to 14 being engaged; we considered the cookery a little in advance of the artisans' requirements but the cookery was of a lower scale than the middle class cooking.[10] Nonetheless, it was this artisan cooking that the Company decided to promote. They proposed sending girls from the City Ward Schools to the National Training School for instruction and in January, 1877, Mrs Edith Clarke, the Lady Superintendent of the National Training School for Cookery submitted the list of dishes that she thought should be taught to these children, so that *each girl will learn plain cooking thoroughly*. This marked the formal establishment of the programme.

Twelve girls were selected from the local Ward Schools and given an intensive eight week course under the tuition of Miss Maude Gardner. The Master and several members of the Court paid frequent visits to the lessons and the Special Committee was of *the opinion that so far as the experiment has gone it has been successful and if carried out on a comprehensive scale would fulfil the terms of the reference to us 'as the means of improving the practical knowledge of cookery of the working classes'*. In March all the girls went to the *Albion Tavern* to demonstrate their skills to the Masters and Wardens and to be examined on what they had learned. Each girl was given a cookery book by Robert Miller and the party was entertained with cakes and wine.

The courses became a regular event and by the time of the fourth series they had developed a standard pattern, with the examination now taking place at the National School attended by members of the Company, together with some sixty visitors and press. The girls were smartly dressed and wore handsome favours in the colours of the Company. All participants received a copy of Tegetmeyer's *Handbook of Cookery*[11] and the three best were presented with leather bound cookery books by Robert Miller. One of these occasions was reported in *The Times*:

In a quiet and unpretentious way the Cooks' Company have been during the past seven years providing for the instruction of the girls attending the City of London Ward Schools in the art of cookery, and on Saturday an examination of a class of these children was held at the National Training School of Cookery at South Kensington. Many ladies were present to witness the demonstration of proficiency on the part of the little cooks. The pupils, of from 12 to 14 years of age, were from the Bishopsgate Ward, Breadstreet Ward, and Bridge. Candlewick and Dowgate Ward Schools. They have received 16 lessons, two each week, and form the 13th group of children from the City Ward schools who have been taught in the National School of Cookery at the expense of the Company of Cooks. The dishes to be prepared were such as might form the dinner of the artisan class, and the girls were set to prepare soup, fry liver and bacon, fish etc.. cook vegetables and make

10 *The Times*, 18 July, 1874.

11 Subsequently replaced by *Popular Lessons in Cookery* by Miss A Maude Gardner, the teacher.

pastry and cakes, no reference books being allowed. The productions of the young artists were handed round, and the visitors formed themselves into a jury of taste.[12]

This work had received royal recognition in 1882, during the celebrations marking the 400th anniversary of the foundation of the Company. This was commemorated by a service at St Botolph's Aldersgate Street followed by a dinner given by the Master, Robert Miller, in the Crystal Palace. In his speech at dinner the Master traced the history of the Company and said *the art of the Mystery was still preserved and being carried out in a vigorous manner by the lessons the Company had for several years past and were continuing to give to girls from the Ward Schools of the City in practical Cookery. These had done an immense amount of good among the lower classes...being an important means of stemming the desire for strong drink, which unfortunately has been a curse in this country.* Mr Miller also produced and paid for commemorative ceramic plaques of the Company's Arms which were presented to every Liveryman and, in view of the work done by the Company in progressing technical education, Her Majesty the Queen agreed to accept one.[13] The Company also agreed to purchase a splendid Ivy Leaf Cup from Messers Thomas & Co of Bond St, costing £126 19*s* 0*d*, as a permanent record of the anniversary.

Shortly after this, in April, 1883, a letter arrived from the Reverend JW Sharpe, HM Inspector of Schools in the Education Department in Whitehall, referring to the fact that as *the Cooks' Company has for some years past done such good work to the Ward schools of the City* it had been suggested that there should be a much larger scheme set up in London for all eligible girls over the age of twelve to undertake cookery classes. The Government would provide a grant of 4*s* to each girl, enabling them to take up the offer. Furthermore, *all interested in the work have agreed with me in the feeling that the Company should be invited to take the initiative in the matter*. This was undoubtedly a feather in the Company's cap, but when the Committee considered the proposal they realised that there would be around 1300 eligible pupils and consequently the task of rolling out the scheme for all London schools and the cost of doing so was too great for them to undertake. Reluctantly, the proposal was rejected. It was probably the right decision, as in the next few years increasing taxes and decreasing rents caused a serious problem for the Company's economy and once more income fell below expenditure. In 1886 the Cookery Classes at the National Training School had to be suspended, after nine successful years. Two years later, in 1888, the School contacted the Company because they needed a new site on which to erect a permanent building and they had identified a plot in Buckingham Palace Road. £10,000 was required

12 *The Times*, 14 July, 1884. The National Training School of Cookery (NTSC) was set up in 1873 to promote knowledge of cookery, and became a limited company in 1888. The College broadened its syllabus to include other aspects of domestic economy and, in 1902, this was recognised in a change of title when it became the National Training School of Cookery and Other Branches of Domestic Economy, and finally the National Training College of Domestic Science (NTCDS) between 1931 and the College's closure in 1962.

13 *The Times*, 23 August, 1882.

Figure 63. The Quater-Centenary Commemoration Vase, presented by the Masters, Wardens, and Father of the Company in 1882.

but the Company responded that at the present time they did not have sufficient funds available to make a donation. They did, however, make modest donations to charities concerned with food and nutrition, such as *The Universal Cookery & Food Association* to whom they gave annual prizes worth £15; another such charity was *The Ragged School*, where they provided an annual banquet and this was probably how the Company became involved with the *National Refuges for Homeless and Destitute Children*, which in turn were to become the *Shaftesbury Homes and Arethusa* charity, which still exists today.

In April, 1893, the Court agreed to appoint a Special Committee *to consider the best way to advance and promote the profession of Cookery and to obtain any technical advice they may deem necessary*. The Committee reported that the state of the Company's funds did not allow for any major new expenditure, but given the success of the previous courses in cookery for the girls of the Ward Schools they recommended a similar initiative now. Inquiries had revealed that cookery was not taught in the various Homes which existed for fatherless and orphaned girls and here the Company's advice, guidance and help would be welcomed.

The actual proposal was for a course of twenty lessons for thirty six girls, which should not cost the Company more than £30. The Committee arranged for two courses, with eighteen girls in each course, to be run under the auspices of *The National Refuges for Homeless and Destitute Children* in their homes at Ealing and at Sudbury near Harrow. These duly took place and the outcome was reported to the Court in July 1894. The format was a demonstration lesson, given by a staff teacher from the National Training School for Cookery, at which the girls took notes and then they made the same dish from memory the following week. Members of the Court attended nearly every lesson and found the standards of cleanliness and preparation exemplary. Six prizes were offered, with first prize of Warne's *Model Cookery*, with coloured illustrations, awarded to Martha Vaun at Sudbury and Rose Beasley at Ealing. Every girl who took part was presented with a copy of *Practical Household Cookery* as a reward for their diligence.

Figure 64. The Shakespeare Coconut Cup, bequeathed to the Company by Past Master Robert Miller in 1898. According to tradition, the stem of the cup is made from the wood of a mulberry tree planted by William Shakespeare at Stratford-on-Avon in 1609 and cut down in 1756.

The success of this venture, not to mention its modest cost, persuaded the Company to sponsor these lessons on a continuing basis. A third venue, the Ladies' Charity School, Notting Hill, was added in 1895 and these three hosted the lessons for more than fifty years. The annual report to the Company stated *The girls passing through this course of lessons are afterwards most useful in the Kitchens of the various homes and when they enter service gratifying letters are frequently received from Mistresses confirming this experience of their usefulness and steadiness....your committee are convinced that greater good could hardly be done in any other direction in promoting technical education with an equal expenditure of money.*

Throughout this period the life of the Company continued as it had done in the past and from 1819 the Confirmation Dinner was reinstated, but without the traditional Ball. The same formula was used each time: the dinner, with a main course of venison, was normally for around one hundred people, including guests, and was served at 5.00pm. The Company's bowls and plate were used and only port, sherry and Portuguese Bucellas wines were served in the Company's special Black Bottles. A spiced hot port and lemon, known as Negus, was also made up for the occasion. The location of the Confirmation and Court dinners varied from year to year and the landlords of various large taverns, who were normally members of the Company, would write to the Court at the beginning of each year promoting their house as a suitable venue for Company entertainments. Only one location seemed not to change, for the Ladies Summer Entertainment was held each July at the *Star and Garter Hotel*, Richmond.[14] Members and guests arrived in carriages, hired at the expense of the Company, and champagne was drunk. After dinner the company retired to the Ballroom, where there was a piano installed and comic vocalists entertained the assembly. The appropriately named Mr Jolley asked whether the words of his songs for the 1851 entertainment should be printed and was told they should, which suggests that that there was an element of audience participation.

In 1870 the *Star and Garter* was destroyed by fire, and the Ladies Entertainment was moved to a variety of different taverns and to the Crystal Palace, while a new hotel was constructed on the same site. In 1883 the Company took a barge, the *Maria Wood*, for the occasion, starting from Kew in the morning and going to Pope's Grotto at Twickenham. The assembled company returned to Kew at 8pm, making a day of it. Provision was made for both breakfast and dinner, with around one hundred people onboard, Members of the Company and their lady guests, listening to the military band that was engaged to play on the barge all day. The new *Star and Garter* at Richmond was used occasionally, but it never gained the popularity of its predecessor and in the early twentieth century the Ladies Entertainment was moved to Nuthall's Restaurant in Kingston, where dinner usually followed a cruise on the River Thames.

The Court dinners could be lavish affairs and provided good business for the taverns that hosted them, since much wine was drunk. Not surprisingly, things sometimes got out of hand, as in 1810 when it was found necessary to ban Benjamin Deacon, *on account of his conduct*,[15] from all future entertainments of the Company. To guard against gate-crashers, it was laid down that Livery badges must be worn at all Company events. The quarterly meetings of the Court now normally took place in the Guildhall, while other dinners were held in *The London Tavern* or other appropriate hostelry. Committee meetings were often held in the Fishmongers' Hall, although taverns and coffee houses were also used. In the

14 This became the *Star and Garter Home* for Ex-Servicemen and Women in 1916.

15 These words appear in the rough notes for the Minutes, but are omitted in the final version.

second half of the century, committees met in the Clerk's offices at 24 Laurence Poultney Street and, after *The London Tavern* closed, *The Albion* in Aldersgate Street became the preferred venue for Court dinners. It remained so until 1907, when the manager of *The Albion* died and the premises were closed. *De Keyser's Royal Hotel* on the Victoria Embankment now became the favoured location for dinners and for committee meetings.[16] It was here, on 18 July, 1911, that a dinner was held to celebrate the Coronation of King George V, following the pattern of a previous Coronation Dinner, for King Edward VII, on 15th July, 1902, which took place in the Whitehall Rooms of the *Hotel Metropole* on Northumberland Avenue.

There was a proposal in 1877 for a Central Hall to be acquired specifically for the use of Livery Companies without their own Halls.[17] This suggestion was reported in *The Standard Newspaper* , which argued that the need for such a Hall had arisen in part because the old *London Tavern*, which had been used for entertaining by several companies, was closed and had been pulled down. The idea received a fair amount of support and the Cooks were interested because the Clerk's offices in Laurence Pountney Street, leased from the Merchant Taylors, were also scheduled for demolition. So when the plans for a new Central Livery Hall stalled, the Company advertised for suitable premises in the *City Press* and new offices were found on the upper floor of Metropolitan Buildings, 63 Queen Victoria Street, at a rent of £170 per annum. At the same time it was decided to move the Company Archives from the Fishmongers' Hall, where they had been since the destruction of Cooks' Hall, and space was taken with the National Safe Deposit Company, also in Queen Victoria Street. However, the move was not immediately successful and the following year the Clerk had to draw the attention of the Court to the *serious mischief* being caused to the Company records in the Safe Deposit in Victoria Street; after the intervention of the General Committee, the storage conditions were improved to an acceptable level, although the Company flags were found to be worn beyond repair and had to be replaced, at a cost of £37.

The move to Queen Victoria Street also provided an opportunity to examine and list all the archives and other items that had been stored at the Fishmongers. One of the wooden boxes contained four crimson silk caps and these were presumably the original Crowns used in the recently abandoned Crowning Ceremony. From 1809 the Masters and Wardens had been sworn into office during the sitting of the October Court, instead of at

---

16 Sir Polydore De Keyser was born on 13 December 1832 at Termonde, near Antwerp in was the son of Joost Constant Fidel Keyser and of Catharina Rosalie Troch, the daughter of a respected surgeon of Termonde. His father established the Royal Hotel in London, which by 1882 had become the largest hotel in the city. De Keyser joined his father in running the business, and he also became active in City affairs. He was elected Alderman for the ward of Farringdon Without in 1882, and was elected Sheriff later the same year.

17 This idea was revived from time to time and the Clerk attended meetings on the subject in 1914 and 1932.

Figure 65. The Master's Badge, with the Arms of the Company, dating from 1872.

the Confirmation Dinner and this was probably when the tradition of the Crowning ceremony was dropped.

In the course of the nineteenth century the Cooks sometimes showed themselves reluctant to join in the ceremonial occasions staged by the City. In 1837, shortly after succeeding to the throne, Queen Victoria agreed to preside over the Lord Mayor's procession and to make this a really special event all the Companies were invited to attend in their barges, but the Cooks decided not to do so. The Company did attend Her Majesty's next visit to the city on 28th October 1844, when they processed with their banners and afterwards repaired to the *King's Head Tavern* in Poultry. However, their most elaborate show was for the arrival in the City of Princess Alexandra of Denmark, betrothed to the Prince of Wales, on 10th March 1863.

At the time this was first proposed the initial response from the Company was somewhat lukewarm and when offered the chance to take part and to have seats in St Paul's Churchyard to view the procession they turned it down. It was thought there would be too

Figure 66. Wager Cup, given by Ralton Gardner Hammond, Master 1917 and 1933. It is a copy of a late 17th century Wager Cup. The challenge is to drink a toast from the larger cup and then from the smaller one, without spilling a drop. Anyone who wagers they can do it is likely to lose.

much waiting around, because the City would be closed off from early in the morning, although the Princess was not expected till late in the afternoon. Moreover, the weather in March could well be inclement. However, the Court did agree to celebrate the forthcoming nuptials with wedding cakes, costing 12*s* 6*d* each and decorated with a Coventry Ribbon Wedding Favour,[18] which would be sent to every member of the Court. Mr Ring of Ring and Brymer reported that he was making similar cakes for other Livery Companies and suggested that the Clerk go and inspect these in order to garner ideas for the design and ornament of the Company cakes.

However, it was pointed out that the Grocers, the Goldsmiths, and the Salters had all agreed to join the procession and it was decided that the Cooks should not be left out. The meeting of the Court in April, after the event, received a detailed report of the proceedings. The Master and Wardens had processed in an open carriage, accompanied by four young Watermen bearing banners. The coach itself was an elegant open Landau, with a Rumble[19] but without a driving seat, drawn by four fine young grey horses, with black harnesses and silver plated appointments, rosettes and streamers in the Company's colours. The two postillions wore blue cloth jackets with white buttons, buckskin breeches, top boots, white gloves and black hats with silver bands laced with ribbons. The Beadle's gown and cap were renovated and cleaned for the occasion and the Master and

18 The Coventry ribbon weaving trade developed in the first half of the 19th century.

19 An open rear seat.

Wardens had new gowns and carried bouquets of red and white flowers arranged in the form of the Danish flag.

Other Royal occasions were marked in different ways: in 1887 Queen Victoria's Golden Jubilee was celebrated when Warden McQueen presented each member of the Court with a handsome engraving of the Queen aged eighteen, after the portrait by Winterhalter.[20] The Master and Clerk also went to the Jubilee Service at St Paul's, and with their Ladies attended the Jubilee Ball in Guildhall. More practically, the ever generous Past Master Robert Miller arranged for each of the Company's pensioners to receive an extra two guineas in celebration of the event.

The Clerk to the Company for much of this period was John B Towse. With his brother, William B Towse, Clerk to the Fishmongers' Company, the pair served their two Companies faithfully for many years and it must have been William who arranged for the Cooks to hold Committee meetings in Fishmongers' Hall and to store many of their documents there too. In recognition of his care and attention in assisting the Company William Towse was presented with a piece of plate valued at £25 and when he died in 1889 the news was reported to the Cooks by his brother John, saying that he was *so well known to the members of this Court*. The Towse family were devoted to the City and its institutions and they provided the Clerks to the Cooks' Company for an unbroken period of 116 years. There had been long-serving Clerks before – Thomas Freebody was in post in 1693, the date of the first surviving Minute Book, and served for at least 45 years until 1738, when he ceded his position, unwillingly it seems, to Robert Henshaw, who held the office for a further 36 years. In 1779 John Towse was elected to the post, holding office for 22 years before handing over to his son John David Towse in 1801. When he retired, after 38 years, he was presented with a silver salver and the Court ruled that he should be invited to all Company entertainments. John David recommended his eldest son, John Beckwith Towse, and he was duly elected; he proceeded to set the record by serving as Clerk to the Company for a remarkable 56 years. In 1889, on completion of his fiftieth year as Clerk, the Court gave him a banquet at *The Albion*, to which all his numerous family were invited, and he was presented with a silver dish and a purse containing the substantial sum of £112, contributed by the Members of the Livery. After serving for a further five years, he was knocked down by a Hansom Cab on Christmas Eve, 1894, and taken unconscious to St Bartholomew's Hospital by two policemen. Sent home and apparently recovering from his injuries, he wrote to the Court apologising for the fact that he was unable to attend the January meeting, especially as this was his first absence in upwards of 50 years. Nonetheless, he had been able to give instructions to Past Master Woodbridge, who was appointed Temporary Clerk, for preparation of the Court's business. Sadly, John Towse did not

20 The original oil portrait is in the National Galleries of Scotland.

recover his health and he died on 14th May, 1895. He was to have received a pension of £150 *per annum*, instead his widow was granted a pension of £80.

John Towse was succeeded as Clerk by George Clifton Sherrard, who nearly matched his predecessor's length of service, holding office until his death in 1945, a period of exactly fifty years. He was succeeded by his nephew, George Sherrard, who died in 1963, giving the family dynasty a total of 67 years, the second longest in the history of the Company.

John Towse's death in 1895 was followed little more than a month later by that of the Beadle, John Huggins. Although he had served for only eleven years, it must have caused quite an upheaval for the Company to lose its two key professional officers in so short a period. Just before Huggins was appointed in 1884, Past Master Robert Miller made another of his frequent and generous donations to the Company, presenting a new Beadle's Staff with a silver gilt head, to replace the old brass one.[21] This new Staff was feared lost when the Clerk's office was destroyed by fire in 1941, but the Staff head was found in the ruins and renovated. It remains in use today.

Figure 67. The *Star & Garter Hotel*, Richmond c.1900 and which the Company regularly used for the Ladies' Summer Entertainment.

21 The old staff head is preserved and on loan to the Museum of London.

On the whole, Beadles did not serve for as long as Clerks – the longest in office was Gideon Print, who held the post for thirty years from 1779–1809, despite being *very infirm* in 1799, when an Assistant Beadle had to be appointed. The first recorded Beadle was John Hurley in 1665 and he, like all his successors, seems to have been well looked after by the Company. New hats and gowns were issued when required, a Christmas Box was presented every Christmas, and a pension was paid on retirement. When Beadle Hummerston died in 1816 the post was advertised and the duties set out as follows: the Beadle should write summonses to all meetings and entertainments, and attend them in his gown and with his Staff of Office. He must carry out all orders given by the Master, Wardens and Clerk and deliver all letters from the Clerk relating to Company business. He was responsible for the smooth operation of the Court and for summoning the Company's pensioners to attend the meetings when alms were distributed. He had to give notice to the Hallkeeper at Guildhall to provide a room for the Court to use and to arrange for the Robemaker to deliver the gowns for the Wardens on Court days, to see these were in good condition and to return them to store afterwards. He also had to bring the Company's books from the Clerk's house to Guildhall on Court days. The Beadle must take care to keep the Company's clock going, setting the time by the Clock on St Paul's Cathedral. More significantly, he was responsible for collecting outstanding Quarterage from the Livery and for discovering the names of all who practised cookery in the City without being Free of the Company. Finally, it was laid down that the Beadle *shall on no account solicit any member of the Company on their transacting business with the Company for any gratuity or other money, beyond the fees allotted to him* – on pain of dismissal.

In the closing years of the nineteenth century there was a growing interest in the history of the Company and the preservation of its archives and artefacts. In 1898 John Phillips presented his *History of the Company*, a manuscript *all in his own hand*, which is now in the Guildhall Library. In the same year the Court agreed to contribute ten guineas for the purchase of cookery books to add to collection presented to the same Library by Past Master Thomas Staples, proprietor of *The Albion* tavern. Again in 1898 Past Master Miller died and left in his will £1000 to the Company, together with his album in three volumes of portraits of Members of the Company, presented to him in 1882,[22] his Shakespeare cup and other items. Finally, in 1901 the Samuel Hale Punchbowls were loaned to the Museum of London, where they remain.

At the very turn of the century, on 12th January, 1900, the Company granted the sum of a hundred guineas to help equip the City of London Imperial Volunteers for service in the Boer War. This led in 1901 to the award to the Company of the South African War Medal, in commemoration of their *spontaneous and patriotic liberality* in helping to raise and

22 Destroyed in the fire in the Clerk's office in 1941.

equip the Volunteers. It was to prove a foretaste of what was to come in the violent and unpredictable twentieth century. Britain declared war on Germany on 4th August 1914 and the repercussions of this were soon felt throughout the country. The Cooks' Company, in common with most other Liveries, resolved that *during the continuance of the War all the Company's dinners be abandoned* and immediately agreed that seventy-five guineas would be sent to the Prince of Wales's Fund for the relief of those in distress as a result of the War. Nonetheless, the Company was determined to try and carry on as normally as possible, and so throughout the period 1914–1918 they continued to organise and promote cookery classes and to distribute pensions to poor cooks and their families. These included the usual regular allocations of good black tea, although in 1918 and 1919 coffee was substituted for tea, presumably because tea was scarce.

The effects of the war could not be ignored and from 1915 we find the Clerk writing regularly to the Company's tenants to inquire whether they had taken out insurance against bomb damage by enemy aircraft. In 1916 the Master reported that he had given instructions for pipes and tobacco to the value of three guineas to be sent to Lieutenant Wallinger Goodinge, a Liveryman of the Company, who was on active service with Queen Victoria's Rifles, for distribution to his men, while in 1918 a donation of ten guineas was made to the *Soldiers and Sailors Free Buffet* at London Bridge Railway Station. The Court continued to meet regularly and the Minute Books make no reference to wider world events; the end of the War, like its beginning, is hardly mentioned. However, in 1919 a case of port was purchased so that Members of the Court might have a glass after their meetings, while in June the Master suggested that after the peace terms were signed there should be a dinner for the Court, the Livery and their Ladies in celebration. The Treaty of Versailles was duly signed on 28th June and the dinner took place.

It was in this same year, 1919 that the Company began to make regular use of the Innholders' Hall in College Street, between Cannon Street and Upper Thames Street. As early as 1891 it had been suggested that the Company should rent the Innholders' Hall for their meetings and the Court had agreed to view the premises, but at that time it was decided not to pursue the matter. It is not clear what changed their mind, but from 1919 to the present day the Innholders' Hall has been the main home of the Company.[23]

During the War the Company had subscribed to a variety of War Loan Bonds; these had proved good investments and the financial position was once again sound. This made it possible for the series of cookery classes to be continued, although the pupils now attended in the evening and the courses were run by the Shaftesbury Homes charity. It was also proposed that the Court should revert *in some degree* to its former practice of dining after meetings. Soon the traditional round of Court Dinners and the Ladies' Entertainments

23 In 1988 the Innholders Hall was closed for two years for renovation and the Cooks used mainly Cutlers' Hall, returning to the Innholders in 1990.

were re-instated, with all events held normally at Innholders' Hall. Wines and cigars were ordered annually and the Company's wine order for 1926 was typical of many:
12 dozen Pol Roger 1915 Vintage Brut Champagne
9 dozen and 10 bottles Cockburns 1908 Vintage Port
12 dozen Cockburn's 1912 Vintage Port
2 dozen Ducasse 1878 Vintage Liqueur Cognac
4 dozen Oloroso sherry
12 dozen Chateau Mont Brun Goutte D'Or Sauterne
2 dozen Cavendish Special Dietetic Whisky
Total Cost .... £339 – 4s – 10d

In 1930 the ceremony of Crowning the New Masters and Wardens was reintroduced, when John Herbert Bishop was crowned Master, using the original crowns which were repaired by the firm of Ede and Ravenscroft for the sum of £4 – *2s* – *6d*. In 1995 new crowns were made by Jane Arkwright, thanks to the generous bequest to the Company of Past Master Sidney Bishop, although the original crowns remain in store.

Then, in 1932, the Company celebrated the 450th anniversary of its First Charter, with a grand dinner at which a silver cup, subscribed by the Livery, was formally received.

By this time the Company, as a whole, no longer had any direct involvement with the regulation of the profession, although a good number of Liverymen were still drawn from the world of catering. Nonetheless, the Court continued to defend its corporate identity, and in July 1923 they learned that the famous City firm of Ring and Brymer was using the Company Arms on their bill heads, apparently without permission. The Clerk was instructed to inquire on what authority they did so and was informed that the firm had used the Arms since Samuel Birch's time, but, despite such a precedent, the practice was stopped.

During these years the Company increasingly developed its social and leisure activities, demonstrated by its involvement in the City Livery Golfing Society that was formed in 1927, with the aim of holding an annual competition open to all Livery, Companies. A splendid trophy was presented by the Coach and Coach Harness Makers Company to commemorate the admission of HRH Prince Arthur of Connaught to their Court – hence the competition was for the Prince Arthur Cup. The Cooks' Company sent a team to the first such contest in 1927 and formed their own Golfing Society the following year. This held regular spring and autumn meetings, which included an annual match against the Painter Stainers' Company as well as the Prince Arthur Cup. Meetings were abandoned at the outbreak of war in 1939 and it was not until 1957 that Past Master Sidney Herbage circulated members in an attempt to revive the Society and a team was entered for the Prince Arthur Cup. It was only in the 1970's that the Society was firmly

Figure 68. The Innholders' Hall, dating from 1670, which has been used by the Company since 1919.

re-established, with an annual match against the Army Catering Corps. The revival has continued and the Society remains an active component of the modern Company.

With the outbreak of the Second World War the Livery had inevitably reverted to a more austere wartime regime, abandoning all dinners and entertainments. Then, on 29th December 1940, the Company became a victim of the London *Blitz* and the Clerk reported that his offices at 34 and 36 Gresham St had been totally destroyed by fire during an enemy raid on the City. All his papers, books and archives (including many original documents), together with the Poor Box and its contents, the Ballot Box, the Beadle's Staff and the Master's ivory mallet were lost in the fire – indeed it was going to take some time before it was possible to say exactly what had been lost. The Master, B.B.Tarring presented a new oak ballot box and a gavel made from the wooden piles underneath Winchester Cathedral, to replace those destroyed in the fire. Fortunately, the bulk of the Company's historic papers, many of which had themselves been damaged in the fires of 1764 and 1771, were lodged in the Guildhall Library and so the historical record was not totally lost. However, in another bombing raid, the Company's property in Staining Lane was totally demolished.

In other respects, the Company attempted to carry on as usual, as they had done in the First World War, and the cookery classes with the Shaftesbury Homes continued. Meetings took place whenever possible, although the difficulties are vividly apparent from a note in the Minutes of the Court held on 19th July, 1944:

The Meeting was held in the Hall of the Innholders' Company on a site surrounding which all immediately adjoining buildings have been destroyed in the course of the present War. Further, that during the course of the Meeting the City of London was under further bombardment from the enemy by flying bombs, as a result of which many more buildings in the City had this day been destroyed or damaged.

With the end of the war in 1945 it was possible to return to the regular cycle of meetings and dinners, but post-war austerity and continued rationing meant that entertainments were on a relatively modest scale. Nonetheless, the Company's standards were preserved and the tradition of dining in full evening dress was maintained at a time when many Liveries adopted dinner jackets as the norm. In 1951 there was a special Coronation Banquet on 13th May, attended by the Lord Mayor (Denys Lowson) and held in the Apothecaries' Hall.[24] There was also an outstanding anniversary to be celebrated, the Quincentenary of the Foundation of the Company which occurred in 1982, and the Court began thinking about this as early as 1971. As was the case for the Quater-centenary in 1882, a special Committee was set up and this planned all the events. The central feature

24 The Company has used a variety of venues for dining on special occasions, including Guildhall, Goldsmiths' Hall and Plaisterers' Hall, since Ironmongers' Hall is only large enough for the normal Livery dinners.

was a Thanksgiving Service, held in the church of St Vedast-alias-Foster in Foster Lane, as St Botolph's, Aldersgate, the church most closely associated with the Company, was closed and under threat of being made redundant.[25] The service was followed by a Banquet in Goldsmiths' Hall, which could accommodate larger numbers than Innholders' Hall. It was a splendid and glittering occasion, again attended by the Lord Mayor (Christopher Leaver) and, in a way that demonstrated the family loyalty which has been a feature of the Company over the centuries. The response for the Ladies and Guests was given by Mrs Beryl Sherrard, widow of the late Clerk George Sherrard, whose father had been Clerk before him, taking up his post in 1895, eighty-seven years earlier. A special enamel badge depicting the arms of the Company was commissioned to mark the occasion and presented to all who were Members of the Company during the Quincentennial year. An equally splendid Banquet was given in Plaisterers' Hall on 2nd February, 2000, to mark the new Millennium, when the Principal Guest was the Bishop of London, Richard Chartres, preceded by a service of Evensong in the Church of St Anne and St Agnes.[26] Later in the year the old custom of taking a cruise on the River Thames was revived, when some one-hundred-and-eighty Members and guests sailed from Tower Bridge to the Dome and back to the London Eye, recalling the river cruises held on Ladies' Day in the nineteenth century.

One topic that came up again for discussion in the early 1970s was the possibility of building a new Hall. The building on the Aldersgate Street site was out of date and needed to be rebuilt. It was suggested that the redevelopment might include a Livery Hall for the Company, perhaps in the basement of the new building. Plans were drawn up by the architects Thomas Saunders & Associates for construction of a new Hall and the costs came out at around £200,000. In June 1974 these plans were put before the Court and were debated at length. There were strongly held views both for and against, but in view of the expense, the loss of potential rental income, and uncertainty about the future, the motion *That the Company should take no further action with regard to a Livery Hall* was finally passed by a large majority. This did not end the efforts to acquire a suitable property. In 2002 the Company came close to buying premises at 19/20 College Hill, to provide permanent office space and to act as an investment, but there was insufficient space for a full Hall and the proposal was abandoned early in 2003. The subsequent economic downturn in the first decade of the new century, combined with the rapid developments in communications technology which made the need for physical office space in the City less pressing, have discouraged for the time being further thoughts of acquiring more property.

---

25 The threat of redundancy was lifted in 1989 and the Company's annual service on Candlemas Day (2 February) was revived.

26 St Botolph's, Aldersgate, was on this occasion under restoration.

Figure 69. The Innholders' Company Dining Hall.

However, the question of the redevelopment of the Aldersgate site remained, especially after a fire in the building in 1977. The Sussex farms, Old Lands and Ladyland, had passed out of the Company's control. The former was the subject of a series of compulsory purchase orders by the Civil Airports Authority from the 1930's onwards, while the sale of Ladyland was completed in 1980, following long discussions and negotiations. Many regretted the loss of this property, which had been in the Company's possession since it was bequeathed by Edward Corbett in 1676, but the buildings were in need of repair and it was probably only a matter of time before the land would also be subject to compulsory purchase. The area comprising both farms today occupy much of the site of Gatwick Airport, although the original farmhouses survive. The Walthamstow properties were also gradually sold off after the Second World War, with the last plot going in 1994 in accordance with the provisions of the Leasehold Reform Act of the previous year. The London property in Staining Lane had been destroyed in the war and the site sold on to the Goldsmiths' Company in 1948 and the few other freeholds owned by the Company were also sold in subsequent years. This left only Aldersgate Street, which was undoubtedly a valuable though not a straightforward asset.

The site of the Company's Hall, destroyed in 1771, had been leased for many years to the firm of J & S Maw, who had extended the boundaries of the property by building on the adjoining plot, owned by St Bartholomew's Hospital. After the Second World War this property was leased to a mail order company, W. Williams Ltd, with the Cooks owning seventy-two percent of the site and St Bartholomew's holding the remaining twenty-eight percent.[27] Any new development would have to be undertaken by a property company and would involve negotiations with the freeholders and agreements regarding the subsequent division of rental income. Discussions started in 1978 and involved long and complex negotiations between the parties. The Company was ably represented by its surveyor, Ian Kennard, and after various false starts the developer appointed was Arlington Securiities Ltd.[28] The agreement was signed and sealed in December 1982 and the process of demolition and rebuilding was put in hand, although the work was not finished until 1986. There was then a suggestion that the Company might sell their freehold for a substantial sum (£10 million was proposed) but this was rejected. The property was leased to H Schroeder Wagg and subsequently sub-let to Deutsche Bank and the rental income received has provided the main source of the Company's income since this time.

The Company was now financially secure and this allowed the collection of quarterage to be abandoned, although fines for not wearing the Company medal on all appropriate occasions are still levied. In the post-war years the Company continued to support the development of the catering profession, through annual prizes and training qualifications awarded through the City and Guilds. In 1959 a Special Committee was set up to consider further ways in which the Company could assist cookery. This proposed that the Company should provide assistance to a training scheme for cooks, run by the London and South Eastern Regional Committee of the Cookery and Food Association. The Company has assisted the Association from its foundation in 1885 and continues to do so today. The Craft Guild of Chefs was established in 1965 as a Guild of the Cookery and Food Association and this soon developed into one of the leading bodies representing the profession in Britain, as well as having many members worldwide. The Company agreed present prizes to the value of £500 to members of the Craft Guild at *Hotelympia*, the trade fair for the industry, and this donation was used mainly to develop the Chef of the Year Contest.

27 Part of the Hospital's freehold was assigned to the Wellcome Foundation in the year 2000.
28 The firm was subsequently taken over by Rush and Tompkins.

In 1968 the Special Committee, now called the Catering Trade Liaison Committee, supported a proposal for a competition to be called *The Worshipful Company of Cooks City of London Cookery Contest*. This was open to all chefs and cooks in restaurants, inns, clubs and other catering establishments in the City and entrants had to produce a main course dish of any type. The competition was to be held every two years and the first prize was to be £25. This was agreed and the first contest was organised. There were twenty entries from ten firms and the prizes were presented by the Lord Mayor. However, although this was considered a success, there was a demand for a simpler competition aimed specifically at those who were starting out in the trade. This led in the 1970's to proposals to work with the newly formed University of Surrey and which offered courses in catering management. Another initiative was the Graduate Awards scheme, launched in 2003 by the Guild of Chefs, with the aim of creating formal recognition for young working cooks. This scheme tests the knowledge and skills of cooks aged twenty-three or under in a series of challenging culinary examinations. As well as gaining new skills and an industry recognised qualification on their CV, graduates achieving the eighty-five percent pass rate or above, enjoyed prizes including study tours to Luxembourg with Villeroy and Boch and Scotland with James Knight of Mayfair, as well as a grand prize for the highest achiever in the final exam.

This was only part of the wide-ranging support for young cooks that the Company now provides. In 1975 the Company had reviewed its prize schemes to establish a common policy and standardisation of awards. As the training of apprentices, one of the Company's original functions, had fallen into disuse, it was decided that current awards should be directed at encouraging young people in their training. As a founder member of the City and Guilds of London Institute, the Company gives prizes to students obtaining the highest results in the NVQ in Catering and Hospitality which the Institute awards.

Although the Company's general charitable activities continued in this way after the War and the distribution of tea was even revived for a short period, the *poor and decayed cooks and widows* who had been the traditional recipients of Company charity were now comparatively rare and supported by the Welfare State. Consequently, the various charitable legacies were amalgamated into a single Fund in 1987, administered by a new Charity Committee under the Chairmanship of Past Master Michael Kenyon. The broad charitable fields supported by the Company now include academic research and development in the area of catering, working with the Academy of Culinary Arts to promote education in cookery, and giving to culinary education at the Community College Hackney. Among many notable disbursements, the Company has supported research into nutrition at the Centre for Culinary Research at Bournemouth University, the provision of two *Bronze Teapot* catering units for St. John Ambulance, and the publication by Cancerbacup of a menu book for people suffering from cancer. The Company also sponsors *The Hoxton Apprentice* restaurant, where the cooks and waiting staff are drawn exclusively

Figure 70. The Quincentenary Loving Cup, made by C.J. Vander for Asprey and Company, 1969. It was presented by Past Master Peter Sherrard, Father of the Company, to mark the Quincentenary on 11th July 1982.

from disadvantaged young people from the East End of London who are training in the catering profession.

Other initiatives include a two-year bursary scheme at the Lakefield Centre for the training of young cooks in Hampstead and sponsorship of the *FutureChef* competition, run by Springboard UK. This is a four staged nationwide culinary programme helping young people aged between twelve and sixteen to learn to cook. The William Heptinstall Award is given annually to enable a young person to widen his or her culinary experience whilst travelling outside the UK and is worth a total of £3,500 to the recipient.

The Company is also linked with the Associated Companies (the Mercers, the Broderers, and the Masons) in a scheme in which each donates a sum to a central fund every year, allowing a substantial donation to be made to a particular charity annually. The recipient is designated by each of the Companies involved in rotation – thus, in 2002 the Cooks chose the St Ethelburga Centre for Peace and Reconciliation, to provide a kitchen for the Centre.

Since 2001 an annual lecture has been held at the Guildhall, London, in order to discuss modern food issues and the City as a centre for the food trade. Seven Livery Companies which have close associations with the sector, namely the Cooks, Bakers, Butchers, Farmers, Fishmongers, Fruiterers, and Poulters promote the event. The format usually includes a welcome address by the Lord Mayor, a key lecture, and a panel session comprising a range of leading specialists from the food industry. In 2008, the seven Livery Companies took on the organisation of the event themselves, in conjunction with the City of London Corporation.

In 1956 the War Office had moved to disband the 625th Light Anti-Aircraft Regiment, leaving the Company for the time being without a direct link to the armed forces. It was not until September 1975 that Brigadier E J Faulkner of the Army Catering Corps proposed a link between the Company and the Corps and this was formally agreed in the following month. This was the logical unit for the Cooks to support and a flourishing and mutually beneficial link developed. The Army Catering Corps had been formed in 1941 with the express orders *to feed the troops* but in 1993 the Corps was subsumed into the Royal Logistic Corps, which assigns cooks to the various regiments and corps of the British Army. The new arrangements inevitably blurred the individual identity which the Catering Corps had developed, but the Company continues to give active support for the training and development of cooks serving with all the forces of the Crown. One aspect of this is sponsorship for the Combined Services Culinary Arts Team which was formed in November 1997 to represent the three Services in world-class national and international culinary competitions. A series of awards are also given to young cooks from each of the armed services. These include a Combined Services competition, culminating in awards for the Young Chef of the Year for each of the services, from which an overall winner, Combined Services Young Chef of the Year, is chosen. There are separate competitions for RAF Young and Senior Chef of the Year and for the Royal Navy. An award is also made annually to the Outstanding Military Caterer. The winners of these awards are invited to a Prize-Winners lunch given by the Court in February of each year.

Given all these wide-ranging activities, there can be no doubt that the Company continues to play an active and valuable role in the promotion of cookery, both in the City and on a wider national scale. That role has of course changed greatly since the Company was first formed to act as the regulatory body for the profession, but the work currently undertaken remains very much in the spirit of the original Guild.

In the modern world, food in general, and the culinary arts in particular, play an even more prominent role than in the past. Television has brought *celebrity chefs* into the living room, with seemingly endless cookery programmes and competitions. More people eat out than ever before and restaurants offering dishes from every corner of the world can easily be found, especially in London. Few people now employ domestic cooks, but in many families cooking is one of the main leisure activities. At the same time there has been a huge expansion of fast-food outlets, offering quick and cheap meals not so far removed from those described by William FitzStephen in the twelfth century. What is new is the growth of opposition to a number of fast food restaurants and hamburger chains, which have been accused of selling 'junk food' which is unhealthy and wasteful. The relatively recent development of universal school meals has also attracted the attention of campaigners for wholesome food. In a reaction against the very widespread use of pesticides and intensive farming methods in the twentieth century, organically grown food is widely promoted, along with meat from animals that have been raised organically and allowed to range freely. Ironically, this is to return to the standards that existed in the past, when pesticides and battery farms were unknown.

Faced with such complexity and an endless range of choice, it has become increasingly difficult to judge quality and to maintain standards. In some ways this offers new opportunities for the Cooks' Company to influence our food choices in a way that is not totally dissimilar to its historical role. The Company helps to help maintain standards through its educational programmes, influences future developments by its support of research projects, and stimulates debate through the City Food Lectures. Like other Livery Companies, the Cooks today primarily enjoy a fellowship and a social organisation, but they also retain a close interest in the development of their profession, as they have done for more than half a millennium.

The publication of this volume coincides with the five hundred and fiftieth anniversary of the Grant of Arms to the Guild of Cooks by John Wrexworth, Guyenne King of Arms on 31st May, 1461. This, one of the most significant indications that the Company was emerging from the medieval Guild, was to be *a sign and a cognisance in form of arms for them and their successors to bear and use for perpetual memory*. So they have been, and today the Worshipful Company of Cooks still proudly bear these arms and their accompanying motto:

VULNERATI NON VICTI

Figure 71. The Cooks' Trophy, commemorating the Silver Jubilee of Queen Elizabeth II in 1977, presented annually to the Inter-Services Chef of the Year.

APPENDIX ONE

The Roll of the Company before 1662

List of Cooks receiving the Freedom of the City of London, 1309–12

Calendar of letter-books of the city of London: D (1905)

1309	November	30	Thomas de Godeshelle, cook,	admitted	13*s* 4*d*
	December	6	Henry de Wylynghale, cook,	admitted	20*s* 0*d*
			Henry de Bramptone, cook,	admitted	10*s*
1310	January	13	Simon Burgeys, cook of the Friars Minors,	admitted	1 mark
	September	14	Nicholas de Oxford, cook,	admitted	10*s* 0*d*
1311	July	25	Hervey, late cook to Sir William de Carleton,	admitted	22*s* 6*d*
	September	15	Master John De Laxfeld, cook to the Sheriffs Of London	admitted*	
	December	21	Solomon, the cook of Breadstreet,	admitted	20*s* 0*d*
	December	25	Laurence Shail, cook,	admitted	12*s* 6*d*
			Walter de Shardeburgh, cook,	admitted	1 mark
			Robert de Bykerwyk, cook,	admitted	15*s* 10*d*
			Henry Basset, cook,	admitted	1 mark

* He gives nothing being pardoned by the Mayor for that he has stood with divers Sheriffs of the City and had served them well and faithfully.

1312	January	13	Robert Sailleben, cook,	admitted	half a mark
			William Waledene, cook,	admitted	half a mark
			Geoffrey de Dynyngtone, cook,	admitted	half a mark
	January	14	Richard de Bartona, cook,	admitted	10*s* 0*d*
			Ralph de Thorntone, cook,	admitted	10*s* 0*d*
			Henry de Teukesbery, cook,	admitted	half a mark
			John de Gildeford, cook,	admitted	half a mark
			Simon de Berdefeld, cook,	admitted	10*s* 0*d*
			Richard de Brehille, cook,	admitted	half a mark
			John de Dynesle, cook,	admitted	half a mark
			Adam de Kirkeby, cook,	admitted	half a mark
			John de Wycombe, cook,	admitted	half a mark
	January	25	John Cosyn, cook,	admitted	half a mark
			Nicholas le Hurlere, cook,	admitted	half a mark
			Ralph de Cordwanerstreet, cook,	admitted	half a mark
			John Knyght, cook,	admitted	half a mark
	February	2	John de Courtone, cook,	admitted	10*s* 0*d*
	February	24	Stephen le Keu, residing at the end of the bridge,	admitted	half a mark
	May	14	John le Warener, cook,	admitted	10*s* 0*d*
	May	21	John de Flete, cook, valet to Sir John De Gisors, the Mayor	admitted at the instance of the said Mayor. He gives nothing.	
	June	3	Peter de St Ives, cook,	admitted	10*s* 0*d*
	June	7	William de Preston, cook,	admitted	half a mark
	August	10	Martin de Droenesford, cook,	admitted	half a mark
	October	28	John de Hodestone, cook,	admitted	half a mark

The names of Cooks recorded in miscellaneous medieval documents

1279 Jordan de Turri, Cook, left to his sons *all his houses, pensions, and rents.*

1279 Johanna Travers, widow, left her Cook, Roger, her best shop.

1300 Cooks charged with forestalling: John de Kent, John de Paris, Agnes Godman, Laurence Schail, Richard le Barber, William Gorre, Peter le Blunt, William Crel, Hugelyn of St Magnus, John de Reigat, Edmund Sket, John Bussard, Nicholas Sket, Robert the cook of Foxle, William de Waledon, John de Mardenheth and many other cooks.

1313 John de Wolwich, Cook, bequeathed to his wife and daughter a house in the parish of S. Magnus for life and *a house and shops* in Southwalk.

1351 Henry Pecche bought two rotten capons baked in pastry from a cook called Henry de Passelewe. The subsequent case heard by Philip le Keu, JohnWynge, William Bisshop, Walter Colman, Peter le Keu, and William Miles, cooks, of Breadstreet, John Chapman, cook, of Milkstreet, and Richard le Keu, of Ismongerelane [Ironmongerlane].

1353 Henry, Cook to John Preston, is left by his Master his second-best robe and 10*s*.

1355 Henry de Walmesford, Cook, was charged with selling bad meat. The Jury consisted of Thomas Maluele, John Wenge and Geoffrey Colman, Cooks of Breadstrete, and John de Ware and John de Stoke, Cooks of Ironmonger Lane.

1365 John Russelle of Abyndone, Poulterer, prosecuted for putrid pigeons, before a jury of John Vygerous, Thomas de Wynchestre, Pyebakers, and John Wenge, Geoffrey Coleman, John Lowe, Thos Coleman and Richard de Daventre, Cooks.

1372/3 Roger de Ware, Cook of London, was charged with being a common nightwalker.

1373 Geoffrey Colman and Thomas Ballard, Cooks of Breadstreet, and Edmund Cadent and William Longe, Cooks of Eastcheap, sworn to make *scrutinies*.

1374 The jury in a case against butchers accused of selling bad meat included Thomas, Geoffrey and John Colman, Robert Multone, John Heurl and Thomas Ballard, all Cooks of Breadstret, and Henry atte Boure, John Bernes, Adam Hermyte, John Birlyngham, James Scot, and John Aubrey, all City Cooks.

1374 John West, Cook, to the pillory for selling bullock's flesh unfit for human consumption.

1382 Reynald atte Chaumbre charged with bringing into the City a boatload of corrupt fish. Case considered by a jury of Cooks, John Lowe, Geoffrey Coleman, John Westerham, Reynald Coleman, and Robert Multone.

1422 Gilbert Page, Cook and William Audley, Cook, issued mutual bonds of £20 to John Bederenden, chamberlain, swearing good behaviour towards each other and towards the Masters and Goodmen of the Mistery of Cooks and Pastelers.

The names of Masters of Misteries recorded in the Letter Books of the City of London

Piebakers

1377	William Claretone, John Vigerous, Andrew Smythe, and John Pyjoun elected and sworn masters of Piebakers.
1392	William Pigeoun, John Fox, William Kirkeby, Walter Spencer sworn 6 November.

Pastelers

1377	John Pygeon, Reginald Swetbone, Thomas Lyle, William Radclyve
1379	Thomas Clayman, John del Hege, William Radeclyve, Reginald Swetebon sworn Masters of the Mistery, 15th November.
1421	Robert Marcheford, John Powlyn, Walter Maungeard, William Birchenham sworn 19th November.

Cooks and Pastelers

1418	John Hardy, William Orkesle, John Wottone, Robert Fynche sworn 19th December.
1438	John Stockwell, Ralph Chapman, John Bekke, Henry Nour, sworn 20th December.

Cooks

1416	John Fouler, Thomas Radclyff, Thomas Broun, Gilbert Page sworn 2nd December.
1425	Robert King, Thomas Gerard, John Hardyng, John Waderove sworn 23rd December.
1428	John Beke, Robert Vyns, John Stokwell, John Rychemond, sworn 16th December.

Cooks of Eastcheap

1393	William Baldeswelle, Edward Brydde sworn 21st June.

Cooks of Breadstreet

1393	John Wyldbournham, William Goldynge sworn the same day.

List of the Pastelers 1538

National Archives Ms E 36/93. This is a list of City Liverymen by Company. The list of the Pastelers is divided into three groups, presumably representing the Court, Livery and Freemen. There is no separate list of Cooks, since they were also known as Pastelers.

John Stephenson
John ffludd
Rogar Playfote
Richard Nyeson
Thomas Nashe
Robert Bryde
Raffe Iswell
Richard Wilkinson
Roger Bettes
John Laurence
Richard Parker
William Spinke
Richard Towneshend
William Anderson
John Mirfyn
Rogier Brushe
John Cooke

John Armestrong
Thomas Baytman
John Mathews
Mathew White
Stephen God
Richard Husband
Ariane Hanbusche
Thomas Samond
Christopher Smythe
John Chamberlayn
John Wilcokes
Barnard Garrat
Richard jemson
John Aleyn
George Briges

John Poope
Robert Cotyngham
John grove
Richard Monke
Richard fflynthurste
William Harward
Thomas Lorkyn
Andrew Rive
William Palmer
John Mynstrelsey
William Robynson
John Hodges
William Pogehorne
John Holte
John Creswell

Masters and Wardens of the Cooks' Company recorded before 1662, the date of the first surviving Court Minute Books

1500 John Woodall and Thomas Nelson, Masters
(named in the Deed Poll of 21st May granting the site of the Hall to the Company)

1552 John Sturtle, Citizen and Cook, receives a bequest in the will of John Armestrong

1604	John Harte,	Master
	Richard Scarlet	Warden
	Arthur Harte	Warden
	(Mentioned in the Charter of 2 James I)	

1610 Owen Semper — Warden
(Imprisoned for refusing to pay the Company's contribution to the Ulster Plantation)

1615	Thomas Norman	Master
	John Stokes	Master
	Nicholas Pinfold	Warden
	Robert Wood	Warden
	(Mentioned in the Charter of 13 James I)	

From various sources:

1618	Nicholas Pinfold	Master
	Thomas Norman	Master
1619	Robert Wood	Master
1620	John Smith	Master
1621	Thomas Hardwen	Master
1622	Robert Parker	Master
1623	John Toyle	2nd Master
1624	John Toyle	Master
1625	John Emyn	Master
1626	John Simpson	Master
1627	John Bartram	2nd Master
1628	James Ashley	2nd Master
1629	John Bartram	Master
	Richard Pierce	Master

Renter Wardens from 1630–1661

From the Renter Wardens' Accounts

1630 Symon Haman
1631 Edwin Eales
1632 Robert Hardinge
1633 William Greene
1634 William Russell
1635 Thomas Smithe
1636 Richard Marshall
1637 James Waters
1638 David Webb
1639 William Hammond
1640 John Skinner
1641 William Jones
1642 John Place
1643 James Ellis
1644 Leonard Pead
1645 Stephen Warman
1646 John Johnson
1647 George Thorpe
1648 Oswald Metcalf
1649 Richard Roche
1650 John Jones
1651 Abell Gurney
1652 Francis Duke
1653 Robert Fitkin
1654 John Jackson
1655 John Smith
1656 Edward Corbett
1657 Richard Gaye
1658 William Johnson
1659 Richard Smith
1660 Thomas Paine
1661 Philip Starkey

APPENDIX TWO

List of Masters and Wardens from 1662

Date	Master	Second Master	Warden	Renter Warden
1662	J Place	R Gay	W Johnson	R Lansdale
1663	E Corbett	J Knowles	T Payne	J Symons
1664	E Peirce	W Johnson [died]	P Starkey	W Dynes
1665	R Gay	T Payne	R Lansdale	T Carpenter
1666	T Payne	P Starkey	W Harman	W Watts
1667	T Payne	R Lansdale	R Trunkett	J Marshall
1668	P Starkey	R Russell	W Dawes	J Reynolds
1669	R Lansdale	W Harman	W Dynes	W Whitingham
1670	R Russell	R Trunkett	T Carpenter	S Maw
1671	W Harman	W Dawes	W Watts	T Hager
1672	R Trunkett	W Dynes	J Marshall	T Stone
1673	W Dawes	T Carpenter	J Reynolds	W Levitt
1674	W Dynes	W Watts	W Whitingham	T Browning
1675	T Carpenter	J Marshall	S Maw	M Sellers
1676	W Watts	J Reynolds	T Hager	J Webb
1677	W Dynes	W Whittingham	W Levitt	A Spencer
1678	J Reynolds	T Hager	T Browning	E Woodward
1679	W Whittingham	W Levitt (died)	M Sellers	J Weston
1680	T Hager	T Stone/ W Dynes	T Humphreys	E Oldham/A Spencer
1681	T Carpenter	M Sellers	J Carter (d)/J Webb	M Marriot/A Spencer
1682	J Marshall	T Humphreys	A Spencer	J Smith
1683	M Sellers	J Webb	J Weston	S Freebody
1684	T Humphreys	A Spencer	J Smith	J Pether

1685	J Webb	J Smith	S Freebody	J Annison
1686	A Spencer	S Freebody	J Pether	E Jones
1687	S Freebody	J Weston	E Jones	J Sargeant
1688	J Weston	J Pether	J Sargenat	W Lodge
1689	J Smith	J Sargeant	J Annison	T Nutt
1690	J Pether	E Jones	W Lodge	W Cleaver
1691	J Sargeant	J Annison	T Nutt	A Tuck
1692	E Jones	T Nutt	D Catekite	M Lucas
1693	J Annison	D Catekite	W Cleaver	J Baines/W Sturt
1694	T Nutt	W Cleaver	A Tuck	R Baynes
1695	D Catekite	A Tuck	M Lucas	J Ramsey
1696	W Cleaver	M Lucas	W Sturt	R Moseley
1697	A Tuck	W Sturt	R Baynes	J Davis
1698	M Lucas	R Baynes	J Ramsey/R Moseley	J Hall
1699	W Sturt	R Moseley	J Davis	T Hope
1700	R Baynes	J Davis	J Hall	T Dance
1701	R Moseley	J Hall	T Hope	E Wilkinson
1702	J Davis	T Hope	T Dance	R Warman
1703	J Hall	T Dance	E Walter	J Cartwright
1704	T Hope	E Walter	E Wilkinson	H North
1705	T Dance	E Wilkinson	J Cartwright	T Walker
1706	E Walter	J Cartwright	H North	L Renant
1707	E Wilkinson	H North	T Walker	T Diston
1708	J Cartwright	T Walker	L Renant	R Curd
1709	H North	L Renant	T Diston	G Fox
1710	T Walker	T Diston	R Curd	T Ayliffe
1711	L Renant	R Curd	T Ayliffe	S Russell
1712	T Diston	T Ayliffe	S Russell	L Pead
1713	R Curd	S Russell	L Pead	J Bird
1714	T Ayliffe	L Pead	S Roe	C Eeles
1715	S Russell	S Roe (d)/ J Bird	J Bird/ T Rudduck	H Constable
1716	L Pead	T Rudduck	C Eeles	J Hacket
1717	J Bird	C Eeles	H Constable	R Savage
1718	T Rudduck	H Constable	J Hacket	T Wareham
1719	C Eeles	J Hacket	R Savage	Cpt E Hanshaw
1720	J Hacket	R Savage	T Wareham	B Cole
1721	R Savage	T Wareham	Cpt E Hanshaw	J Piercy/T Martin
1722	T Wareham	Cpt E Hanshaw	B Cole	J West
1723	Cpt E Hanshaw	B Cole/T Martin	T Martin/J West	J Newbury
1724	T Martin	J West	J Newbury	J Hakes
1725	J West	J Newbury	J Hakes	I Windsor/H Bunn

1726	J Newbury	J Hakes	H Bunn	S Freebody
1727	J Hakes	H Bunn	S Freebody	T Lane
1728	H Bunn	T Lane	T Warner	J Moseley
1729	T Lane	T Warner	J Moseley	R Beale
1730	T Warner	C Corffield	A Moreing	W Child
1731	S Russell	J West	W Child	J Davis
1732	C Corffield	A Moreing	J Davis	N Ball
1733	A Moreing	J Davis	N Ball	R Clarke
1734	J Davis	N Ball	R Clarke	P Morris
1735	BN Ball	R Clarke	P Morris	B Miller
1736	R Clarke	P Morris	B Miller	E Howard
1737	P Mossis	B Miller	E Howard	W Hasleham
1738	B Miller	E Howard	W Hasleham	L Pead
1739	E Howard	W Hasleham	L Pead	T Savage
1740	W Hasleham	L Pead	T Savage	T Davis
1741	L Pead	T Savage	T Davis	R Masey
1742	T Savage	T Davis	R Masey	R Walter
1743	T Davis	R Masey	R Walter	W West
1744	R Masey	R Walter	W West	WBodycott/WLafosse
1745	R Walter	W West	W Lafosse	N Johnson
1746	W West	W Lafosse	N Johnson	A Cole
1747	W Lafosse	N Johnson	A Cole	W Sellers
1748	N Johnson	A Cole	W Sellers	B Hancock
1749	A Cole	B Hancock	J Lumley	R Horton
1750	B Hancock	J Lumley	R Horton	E Manlove
1751	J Lumley	R Horton	E Manlove	T Northcote
1752	R Horton	E Manlove	T Northcote	J Langton
1753	E Manlove	J Langton	R Wareham	J Pickering
1754	J Langton	R Wareham	J Pickering	J Collins
1755	R Wareham	J Collins	W Deacle	A Garnault
1756	W Deacle	A Garnault	J Johnson	T Hummerston
1757	A Garnault	J Johnson	T Hummerston	J Bayes
1758	J Johnson	T Hummerston	J Bayes	P Romilly
1759	T Hummerston	B Bayes	P Romilly	W Lafosse
1760	J Bayes	P Romilly	W Lafosse	C Runnington
1761	P Romilly	W Lafosse	C Runnington	M Miller
1762	W Lafosse	C Runnington	M Miller	T Bothell
1763	C Runnington	M Miller	T Bothell	T Lindsey
1764	M Miller	T Bothell	T Lindsey	R Wood
1765	T Bothell	T Lindsey	R Wood	P Poe
1766	T Lindsey	R Wood	P Poe	N Farmborough

1767	R Wood	P Poe	N Farmborough	L Birch
1768	P Poe	N Farmborough	L Birch	T Coward
1769	N Farmborough	L Birch	T Coward	T Webb
1770	L Birch	T Coward	T Webb	Sir A Kennedy Bt
1771	T Coward	T Webb	Sir A Kennedy Bt	S Ansell
1772	T Webb	Sir A Kennedy Bt	S Ansell	W Stiles
1773	Sir A Kennedy Bt	S Ansell	W Stiles	H Cox
1774	S Ansell	W Stiles	H Cox	R West
1775	W Stiles	H Cox	R West	T Vanhagen
1776	H Cox	R West	T Vanhagen	A Punnett
1777	R West	T Vanhagen	A Punnett	J Worgan
1778	T Vanhagen	A Punnett	J Worgan	B Simpson
1779	A Punnett	J Worgan/B Simpson	B Simpson/W Foster	W Foster/J Barrow
1780	B Simpson	W Foster	J Barrow	W Bothell
1781	W Foster	J Barrow	W Bothell	J Lindsey
1782	J Barrow	W Bothell	J Lindsey	S Tugwell
1783	W Bothell	J Lindsey	S Tugwell	W Smelt
1784	J Lindsey	S Tugwell	W Smelt	F Berry
1785	S Tugwell	W Smelt	F Berry	T Lindsey
1786	W Smelt	F Berry	T Lindsey	R Wood
1787	F Berry	T Lindsey	R Wood	S Ansell
1788	T Lindsey	R Wood	S Ansell	T Vanhagen
1789	R Wood	S Ansell/T Vanhagen	T Vanhagen/W Bothell	W Bothell/J Linsey
1790	T Vanhagen	W Bothell	J Linsey	S Tugwell
1791	W Bothell	J Linsey	S Tugwell	W Smelt
1792	J Linsey	S Tugwell	W Smelt	F Berry
1793	S Tugwell	W Smelt	F Berry	J Jeavens
1794	W Smelt	F Berry	J Jeavens	S Hannam
1795	F Berry	J Jeavens	S Hannam	P Sewell
1796	J Jeavens	S Hannam	P Sewell	S Birch
1797	S Hannam	P Sewell	S Birch	W Rich
1798	P Sewell	S Birch	W Rich	W Ellsworth
1799	S Birch	W Rich	W Ellsworth/T Farrance	T Farrance/S J Neele
1800	W Rich	T Farrance	S J Neele	T Knapp
1801	T Farrance	S J Neele	T Knapp	J B Slann
1802	S J Neele	T Knapp	J B Slann	J Davenport
1803	J B Slann	J Davenport	L Birch	T Vanhagen
1804	J Davenport	L Birch	T Vanhagen	J Bond
1805	L Birch	T Vanhagen	J Bond	T Butler
1806	T Vanhagen	J Bond	T Butler	J Stuart
1807	J Bond	T Butler	J Stuart/R H Marten	R H Marten /J Francies

1808	T Butler	R H Marten	J Francies	B Yates
1809	R H Marten	J Francies	B Yates	J Purnell
1810	J Francies	B Yates	J Purnell	T Spooner
1811	B Yates	J Purnell	T Spooner	W Cooper
1812	J Purnell	T Spooner	W Cooper	H Hart
1813	T Spooner	W Cooper	H Hart	S Hannam Jr
1814	W Cooper	H Hart	S Hannam Jr	S Hale
1815	H Hart	S Hannam Jr	S Hale	J J Debatt
1816	S Hannam Jr	S Hale	J J Debatt	R Baxter
1817	S Hale	J J Debatt	R Baxter	J T Sleap
1818	J J Debatt	R Baxter	J T Sleap	J Barker/W Akerman
1819	R Baxter	J T Sleap	W Akerman	F Oxley
1820	J T Sleap	W Akerman	F Oxley	J Danford
1821	W Akerman	F Oxley	J Danford	C Awdus
1822	F Oxley	J Danford	C Awdus	W S Angell
1823	J Danford	C Awdus	W S Angell	W Leftwich
1824	C Awdus	W S Angell	W Leftwich	W K Fostert
1825	W Leftwich	W K Foster	W Wyatt	S G Coleman
1826	W K Foster	W Wyatt	S G Coleman	R Hayward
1827	W Wyatt	S G Coleman	R Hayward	F G Wolf
1828	S G Coleman	R Hayward	F G Wolf	G Neele
1829	R Hayward	F G Wolf	G Neele	W T Flanders
1830	F G Wolf	G Neele	W T Flanders	R Stephens
1831	G Neele	W T Flanders	R Stephens	J Mollard
1832	W T Flanders	R Stephens	J Mollard	J J Cuff
1833	R Stephens	J Mollard	J J Cuff	E Fenning
1834	J Mollard	J J Cuff	E Fenning	R Sewell
1835	J J Cuff	E Fenning	R Sewell	T Farrance Jr
1836	E Fenning	R Sewell	T Farrance Jr	G Button
1837	R Sewell	T Farrance Jr	G Button	W Hine
1838	T Farrance Jr	G Button	W Hine	S E Hale
1839	G Button	W Hine	S E Hale	J Edwards
1840	W Hine	S E Hale	J Edwards	R Mollett
1841	S E Hale	J Edwards	R Mollett	J W Lockett
1842	W S Angell	R Mollett	J W Lockett	G Rich
1843	R Mollett	J W Lockett	G Rich	J C Watson
1844	R Baxter	G Rich	W Phillips	H Briant
1845	G Rich	W Phillips	H Briant	P Smith
1846	W Phillips/R Sewell	H Briant/R Chapman	P Smith	J S Phillips
1847	J Danford	P Smith	J S Phillips	W Bellamy
1848	P Smith	J S Phillips	W Bellamy	J Ody

1849	J S Phillips	W Bellamy	J Ody	J S Sedger
1850	W Bellamy/E Fenning	J Ody	J S Sedger	J T Sleap
1851	W Hines	J S Sedger	J T Sleap	G Marten
1852	J S Sedger	J T Sleap	G Marten	R Miller
1853	J T Sleap	G Marten	R Miller	J R Stevens
1854	G Marten	R Miller	J R Stevens	T Thorne
1855	G Rich	J R Stevens	T Thorne	A Pill
1856	J R Stevens	T Thorne	A Pill	G W Masters
1857	T Thorne	A Pill	G W Masters	J C Hudson
1858	A Pill	G W Masters	J C Hudson	G Webb
1859	G W Masters	J C Hudson	G Webb	C Grover
1860	J Hudson/J Phillips	G Webb	C Grover	T Thomas
1861	G Webb	C Grover/W T Phillips	T Thomas	J Matthew
1862	W T Phillips	T Thomas	J Matthew	J Mollett
1863	T Thomas	J Matthew	J Mollett	J North
1864	J Matthew	J Mollett	J North	J Ring
1865	J Mollett	J North	J Ring	W Hubbard
1866	J North	J Ring/J Phillips	W Hubbard	J Chapman/W Adcock
1867	J R Stevens	W Hubbard	W Adcock	G W Rich
1868	W Hubbard	G Marten	G W Rich	E Kitchen
1869	G Marten	W Adcock/G W Rich	E Kitchen	H C Bose
1870	G W Rich	E Kitchen	H C Bose	G A Johnson
1871	E Kitchen	H C Bose	G A Johnson	E Goddard
1872	H C Bose	G A Johnson	E Goddard	T H Staples
1873	G A Johnson	A Pill	T H Staples	S W Cawston
1874	A Pill	T H Staples	S W Cawston	W Danford
1875	T H Staples	S W Cawston	W Danford	S Brewer
1876	S W Cawston	W Danford	S Brewer	G Silverside
1877	W Danford	S Brewer	G Silverside	J Phillips
1878	S Brewer/J Matthew	G W Rich	J Phillips	R Miller
1879	G W Rich	J Phillips	R Miller	W T Brown
1880	J Phillips	R Miller	W T Brown	R Cox
1881	R Miller	W T Brown	R Cox	C Chard
1882	W T Brown	R Cox	C Chard	F Hammond
1883	R Cox	C Chard	F Hammond	J R Stevens
1884	C Chard	F Hammond	J R Stevens	C H Silverside
1885	F Hammond	J R Stevens	C H Silverside	F C McQueen
1886	J R Stevens	C H Silverside	F C McQueen	T A Woodbridge
1887	C H Silverside	F C McQueen	T A Woodbridge	A Thorne
1888	F C McQueen	T A Woodbridge	A Thorne	J W Goodinge
1889	T A Woodbridge	A Thorne	J W Goodinge	C Tyler

1890	A Thorne	J W Goodinge	C Tyler	F D Matthew
1891	J W Goodinge	C Tyler	F D Matthew	G C Sherrard
1892	C Tyler	F D Matthew	G C Sherrard	G W Rich
1893	F D Matthew	G C Sherrard	G W Rich	A R Mollett
1894	G C Sherrard	G W Rich	A R Mollett	E Carlile
1895	G W Rich	A R Mollett	E Carlile	F W Tarring
1896	A R Mollett	E Carlile	F W Tarring	S Cawston
1897	E Carlile	F W Tarring	S Cawston	G T Goodinge
1898	F W Tarring	S Cawston	G T Goodinge	C M Phillips
1899	S Cawston	G T Goodinge	C M Phillips	T J Robinson
1900	G T Goodinge	C M Phillips	T J Robinson	Sir A G Marten
1901	C M Phillips	T J Robinson	Sir A G Marten	C Thorne
1902	T J Robinson	Sir A G Marten	C Thorne	J Donne
1903	Sir A G Marten	C Thorne	J Donne	H Volckman
1904	C Thorne	J Donne	H Volckman	W Hubbard
1905	J Donne	H Volckman	W Hubbard/J Stevens	F Hammond
1906	H Volckman	J Stevens	F Hammond	B Morice
1907	J Stevens/J Phillips	F Hammond	B Morice	A Bose
1908	F Hammond	B Morice	A Bose	S Woodbridge
1909	B Morice	A Bose	S Woodbridge	A C Goodinge
1910	A Bose	S Woodbridge	A C Goodinge	W F McQueen
1911	S Woodbridge	A C Goodinge	W F McQueen	C G Algar
1912	A C Goodinge	W F McQueen	C G Algar	A Evans
1913	W F McQueen	C G Algar	A Evans	R G Hammond
1914	C G Algar	A Evans	R G Hammond	H F Pardy
1915	C G Algar	A Evans	R G Hammond	H F Pardy
1916	A Evans	R G Hammond	H F Pardy	J S Towsey
1917	R G Hammond	H F Pardy	J S Towsey	H J Kimbell
1918	H F Pardy	J S Towsey	H J Kimbell	W Downs
1919	J S Towsey	H J Kimbell	W Downs	F P Towsey
1920	H J Kimbell	W Downs	F P Towsey	H W Hiscock
1921	W Downs	F P Towsey	H W Hiscock	P G Herbage
1922	F P Towsey	H W Hiscock	P G Herbage	A D Robinson
1923	H W Hiscock	P G Herbage	A D Robinson	F Woodbridge
1924	P G Herbage	A D Robinson	A Evans	W E Kent
1925	A D Robinson	A Evans	W E Kent	D Duff
1926	A Evans	W E Kent	D Duff	J H Bishop
1927	W E Kent	D Duff	J H Bishop	G H Johnson
1928	D Duff	J H Bishop	G H Johnson	G Russell
1929	J H Bishop	G H Johnson	G Russell	D Haydon
1930	G H Johnson	G Russell	D Haydon	W Goodinge

1931	G Russell	D Haydon	W Goodinge	F T Phillips
1932	R G Hammond	W Goodinge	F T Phillips	A Jerrold-Nathan
1933	W Goodinge	F T Phillips	A Jerrold-Nathan	F W Bishop
1934	F T Phillips	A Jerrold-Nathan	F W Bishop	P T Gardner
1935	D Haydon	F W Bishop	P T Gardner	L G Russell
1936	F W Bishop	P T Gardner	L G Russell	P F Herbage
1937	P T Gardner	L G Russell	P F Herbage	C W Gardner
1938	L G Russell	P F Herbage	C W Gardner	B B Tarring
1939	P F Herbage	C W Gardner	B B Tarring	R Woodbridge
1940	C W Gardner	B B Tarring	R Woodbridge	C F Woodbridge
1941	B B Tarring	R Woodbridge	C F Woodbridge	Sir H Kenyon
1942	R Woodbridge	C F Woodbridge	Sir H Kenyon	S H Bishop
1943	C F Woodbridge	Sir H Kenyon	S H Bishop	J E Gardner
1944	Sir H Kenyon	S H Bishop	J E Gardner	G J McDonald
1945	S H Bishop	J E Gardner	G J McDonald	C R Algar
1946	J E Gardner	G J McDonald	C R Algar	G Russell
1947	R Woodbridge	C R Algar	G Russell	F J Towsey
1948	B B Tarring	G Russell	F J Towsey	S M Wade
1949	G Russell/Sir H Kenyon	F J Towsey	S M Wade	N V Kenyon
1950	F J Towsey	S M Wade	N V Kenyon	H H Powell
1951	S M Wade	N V Kenyon	H H Powell	W D Kenyon
1952	N V Kenyon	H H Powell	W D Kenyon	C E Sugden
1953	H H Powell	W D Kenyon	C E Sugden	C S Hinton
1954	W D Kenyon	C E Sugden	C S Hinton	H Marten-Smith
1955	C E Sugden	C S Hinton	H Marten-Smith	B Wilton
1956	C S Hinton	H Marten-Smith	B Wilton	J Hemsworth
1957	H Marten-Smith/J Towsey	B Wilton	J Hemsworth	L J Freeman
1958	B Wilton	J Hemsworth	F T Phillips	P Sherrard
1959	J Hemsworth	F T Phillips	P Sherrard	HH Tickler
1960	C R Algar	P Sherrard	HH Tickler	W Goodinge
1961	P Sherrard	HH Tickler	W Goodinge	A W Goodinge
1962	HH Tickler	W Goodinge	A W Goodinge	Lt-Cmdr W Russell
1963	W Goodinge	A W Goodinge	Lt-Cmdr W Russell	S J Herbage
1964	A W Goodinge	Lt-Cmdr W Russell	S J Herbage	J G Price
1965	Lt-Cmdr W Russell	S J Herbage	J G Price	B Wilton
1966	S J Herbage	J G Price	B Wilton	G G Swan
1967	J G Price	B Wilton	G G Swan	E C Horne
1968	B Wilton	G G Swan	E C Horne	J H Balls
1969	G G Swan	E C Horne	J H Balls	H J Marten-Smith
1970	E C Horne	J H Balls	H J Marten-Smith	J D Powell
1971	J H Balls	H J Marten-Smith	J D Powell	P F Herbage

1972	H J Marten-Smith	J D Powell	P F Herbage	M V Kenyon
1973	J D Powell	P F Herbage	M V Kenyon	M H Powell
1974	P F Herbage	M V Kenyon	M H Powell	C J Cleugh
1975	M V Kenyon	M H Powell	C J Cleugh	C J Algar
1976	M H Powell	C J Cleugh	C J Algar	J F Wright
1977	C J Cleugh	C J Algar	J F Wright	J C Kenyon
1978	C J Algar	J F Wright	J C Kenyon	P Sherrard
1979	J F Wright	J C Kenyon	P Sherrard	H H Tickler
1980	J C Kenyon	P Sherrard	H H Tickler	G R Young
1981	P Sherrard	H H Tickler	G R Young	H F Thornton
1982	H H Tickler	G R Young	H F Thornton	F W Hopton Scott
1983	G R Young	H F Thornton	F W Hopton Scott	A W Murdoch
1984	H F Thornton	F W Hopton Scott	A W Murdoch	Sir Lindsay Bryson
1985	F W Hopton Scott	A W Murdoch	Sir Lindsay Bryson	L C Grainger
1986	A W Murdoch	Sir Lindsay Bryson	L C Grainger	R S Anderson
1987	Sir Lindsay Bryson	L C Grainger	R S Anderson	C E Messent
1988	L C Grainger	R S Anderson	C E Messent	H E Taylor
1989	R S Anderson	C E Messent	H E Taylor	P Towsey
1990	C E Messent	H E Taylor	P Towsey	R P Horne
1991	H E Taylor	S J Herbage	R P Horne	N D Phillips
1992	S J Herbage	R P Horne	N D Phillips	J B Kane
1993	R P Horne	J H Balls	J B Kane	J K Powell
1994	J H Balls	J B Kane	J K Powell	J G Price
1995	J B Kane	J K Powell	J G Price	D Hodgson
1996	J K Powell	J G Price	D Hodgson	P D Herbage
1997	J G Price	D Hodgson	P D Herbage	P A Wright
1998	D Hodgson	P D Herbage	P A Wright	M J Messent
1999	P D Herbage	P A Wright	M J Messent	R E Hammerton
2000	P A Wright	M J Messent	R E Hammerton	O H W Goodinge
2001	M J Messent	R E Hammerton	O H W Goodinge	G A V Rees
2002	R E Hammerton	O H W Goodinge	G A V Rees	R M Grainger
2003	O H W Goodinge	G A V Rees	R M Grainger	P R Messent
2004	G A V Rees	R M Grainger	P R Messent	A G Fairbrass
2005	R M Grainger	P R Messent	A G Fairbrass	J F L Lowndes
2006	P R Messent	A G Fairbrass	H F Thornton	G A A Craddock
2007	A G Fairbrass	H F Thornton	G A A Craddock	J B Righton
2008	H F Thornton	G A A Craddock	J B Righton	G J Osborne
2009	G A A Craddock	J B Righton	G J Osborne	B E G Puxley
2010	J B Righton	G J Osborne	B E G Puxley	B F W Baughan

Fathers of the Company

Robert Wood	1639
William Russell	1657
John Place	1663
James Ellis	1669
Richard Gray	1685
Thomas Carpenter	1689
William Watts	1696
Samuel Russell	1733
Joseph West	1738
Henry Bunn	1740
Samuel Birch	1841
Robert Baxter	1843
Robert Chapman	1858
William Hine	1866
John Phillips	1871–1879
William Robinson	1879–1894
George Rich	1894–1904
John Phillips	1904–1913
Francis Hammond	1913
John Stevens	1913–1928 (January)
Thomas Woodbridge	1928
Francis Hammond	1928–1937
Ralton Hammond	1937–1951
Joseph Towsey	1951–1959
Wallinger Goodinge	1959–1973
Frank Phillips	1973–1975
Sidney Bishop	1976–1979
Peter Sherrard	1979–1982
Harry Tickler	1982–1999
Sidney Herbage	1999–

APPENDIX THREE

Clerks and Beadles of the Company

Clerks

Richard Tomson	1567
Robert Glover	1615
George Scoshe	1619
Lawrence Bromley	1663
Humphrey Satterthwaite	1663–1682
Richard Bromhall	1682–1690
Charles Tracey	1690–1693
Thomas Freebody	1693–1738
Robert Henshaw	1738–1774
James Gwyn	1774–1779
John Towse	1779–1801
John David Towse	1801–1839
John Beckwith Towse	1839–1895
George Clifton Sherrard	1895–1945
George William Sherrard	1945–1962
C E (Sam) Messent	1962–1972
Henry Lavington	1972–1988

Beadles

John Hurley	to 1665
Robert Browne	1665–1675
Henry Watson	1675–1703
George Bartholomew	1703–1707
James Smithersgill	1707–1716
Thomas Petty	1716–1732
Samuel Freebody	1732–1736
Charles Corffield	1736–1737
John Barding	1737–1749
Richard Peacock	1749–1757
William Hartshorn	1757–1768
Harry Bailey	1768–1778
Gideon Print	1778–1809
James Hummerston	1809–1816
Nathaniel Neal	1816–1817
J A Knapp	1817–1835
Thomas Sharp	1835–1860

Clerks

Sam Messent (acting Clerk)	1988
Michael Thatcher	1988–

Beadles

John Thomas Sharp	1860–1884
John Huggins	1884–1895
William Winsor	1895–1914
Frank Hudd	1915–1920
Simpson Adams	1920–1948
George Mead	1948–1963
Paul Marsh	1963–2001
Robert Fox	2001–2007
John Cash	2007–

APPENDIX FOUR

The Ordinances

Ordinances of the Cooks, 1475

From *Calendar of letter-books of the city of London: L: Edward IV-Henry VII* (1912), folios 109–110

Ordinaciones Cocorum.
26th April, 15 Edward IV. [1475]

Petition of good men of the Mistery of Cooks that certain ordinances might be approved to the following effect:

That forasmuch as divers persons of the said Craft with their hands embrowed and fowled be accustomed to draw and pluck [poultry], other Folk as well gentlemen as other common people by their selves and clothes to buy of their victuals, whereby many debates and strives often times happen against the pleas, such conduct should be forbidden, under penalty.*

That no one of the Craft sell fish and flesh together on Wednesdays.

* This clause appears to be an attempt to restrict the drawing and plucking of poultry to Cooks.

That no one of the Craft bake, roast or seethe Flesh or Fish two times and sell it, under penalty.

That no one sell any victuals to any huckster [dealer in small goods, a peddlar] that is to say Elys Tarts or Flans or any such bake meats, except to free persons of the said City; or any mould ware be made by hand or by mould to sell in their Shops or to any huckster to retail or to any other, except if it is ordered before the Feasts, under penalty.

That no one of the Craft colour or maintain any foreign person nor set him to work as long as there is any freeman to set to work that can work.

That no one of the Craft send any manner roast victuals to any place but it be paid for in money to the value of the victual without pledge or it go out of their doors or be cut off their broches [spits].

Provided always that if any of the said Fellowship sell any victual raw or unseasonable that than he satisfy the Bier of his hurts and make fine of *6s 8d*.

The ordinances to be shown to the whole of the Fellowship twice a year at a convenient place, under penalty.

The ordinances approved.

Folio 318–319 b.
Ordinances of the Pastelers, 1495
Ordinacio dez Pastelers
15th Dec., 11 Henry VII. [1495]

Came the Wardens and other good men of the Art or Mistery of Pastelers of the City before the Mayor and Aldermen, and complained that whereas in time past they had been of power to have a company of them self in one clothing and been able to bear the City's charges, they had now fallen into such poverty, owing to their being deprived of their living by vintners, brewers, innholders, and tipplers, that they could no longer appear in one clothing, nor were able to bear the City's charges, unless speedy remedy be applied. They prayed therefore that certain articles might be approved and enrolled, to the following effect:

That every brother of the Fellowship attend an appointed church on the Feast of Exaltation of Holy Cross [14 Sept.] to hear Mass, and make offering of one penny, a brother's attendance being excused for reasonable cause, but not the offering of a penny.

That he also attend on the following morning to hear a Requiem for the souls of all deceased members.

That every brother, on due warning, attend funerals, obits, &c., of Brethren and Sistern of the Fellowship.

That disputes be submitted to the Wardens before action be taken at law.

That the Wardens have authority to search and oversee all manner of dressed victuals in open shops, to see if they be wholesome and also whether the pennyworths thereof be reasonable for the common weal of the King's liege people or not.

That all persons that seethe, roast, or bake victuals for sale in the City pay henceforth such quarterage to the Wardens as freemen had been accustomed to pay in support of the Craft.

That no one thenceforth send any victuals ready dressed about the streets or lanes to be sold, under penalty of forfeiture of the same to the use of poor prisoners in Ludgate and Newgate and fine.

That no person or persons enfranchised in the said Craft of Pastelers from henceforth shall take upon him or them to make any great Feasts as the Sergeants' Feast, the Mayor's Feast, the Sheriffs' Feast and the Taylors' Feast without the advice of the Wardens to the intent that the Feasts of every one of them shall be well and worshipfully dressed for the honour of this City and also for the honour and profit of the persons that shall bear the charges thereof, under penalty prescribed.

That what person or persons of the same Craft that hereafter shall serve the Mayor for the time being or any of the Sheriffs for the year of Mayoralty or Shrievalty as their household Cook or Cooks shall neither in his own proper person nor by any of his servant or servants by Colour, Craft or otherwise that year dress or do to be dressed any Feasts, Breakfasts, Dinners or Suppers, for any Weddings, Obits, Crafts or otherwise out of the Mayor or Sheriffs' houses without such Feast, Breakfast, Dinner or Supper be made at the cost and charge of the said Mayor and Sheriffs for the time being to the intent that every man of the same Fellowship may have a competent living, under penalty prescribed.

That from henceforth there shall be but one shop occupied on the Sunday of the said Craft in Breadstreet and one in Bridgestreet to the intent that your Suppliants the good Folks of the same Craft may serve God the better on the Sunday as true Christian men should do; and the two shops to be opened by the advice of the Wardens for the time being, that is for to say one shop to be occupied on the Sunday in the one street and another shop in the other street and another person to occupy and open a shop on the next Sunday in the one street and another in the other street and so always one to occupy after another, under penalty prescribed.

That if any person or persons enfranchised in the said Craft hereafter make any bill or bills of fare and proportion for any Feast, Dinner or Supper by the desire of any person or persons or else make covenant with any to dress such Feast Dinner or Supper that then none other of the same Craft shall put any such person or persons from the making and dressing of the said Feast, Dinner or Supper, under penalty of 20*s*.

That every one enfranchised in the Craft that hereafter shall be commanded by the Wardens to bear the Corpse of any brother or sister of the same Craft to burying shall bear the same Corpse or Corpses to the Church and to burying without any resistance, grudge or gainsaying of any person or persons so commanded upon pain of 3*s*. 4*d*.

That if any foreign or stranger take upon him to make or dress any Feast, Dinner or Supper within the same City or liberties thereof that than it shall be lawful to the Wardens for the time being with a Sergeant of the Mayor's to them assigned to attach, take and arrest any such Foreign or stranger so making any Feast, Dinner or Supper and to bring the same Foreign or stranger to prison and to bide the punishment of the Mayor and Aldermen for the time being and over that to forfeit at every time so doing 10*s* to be divided in manner and form above said.

That every brother of ability and power shall pay for his quarterage yearly for the priest and clerks and his dinner 4*s*.

That no freeman of the Craft slander or revile another, under penalty.

That any brother making unreasonable complaint to the Wardens shall forfeit 20 pence.

That no one of the Craft shall from henceforth make or do to be made upon one day more than two Dinners and one Supper, under penalty of 6*s* 8*d*
Petition granted.

Confirmation of Statutes & Ordinances

From Guildhall Library Ms 9989, *Abstract of Company charters etc 1461–1735 (compiled between 1735–64 by Liveryman Wood)*
27th February, 1503, 23 Henry VII
Confirmation of the Bishop of Canterbury, Lord Chancellor and other of Statues and Ordinances made by the Cooks Company pursuant to an Act of Parliament of 19 Henry VII, whereby no Company can make acts or statutes without the approbation or admission of the Lord Chancellor and judges or others therein named.

27th November, 23 Henry VIII, 1532
The confirmation or approbation of Sir Thomas More, then Lord Chancellor, the Duke of Norfolk and others of several other laws and ordinances which were made by the Company.

APPENDIX FIVE

The Charters

The Charter of King Edward IV, 11th July, 1482

National Archives, C 66/549, membrane 1,
Translated from the Latin original.

The King to all to whom etc.. greeting. Know you that We bearing in mind how our well beloved honest and freemen of the Mistery of Cooks of our City of London have for a long time outside the aforesaid City, personally taken and borne, and to this day do not cease to take and bear, great and manifold pains and labour as well at our great feast of St George as at others according to our command, and whilst they in their own persons have thus employed themselves about our affairs, they have oftentimes been impanelled and summoned on Assizes, Juries and other inquisitions within the same City and by reason of their personal labours of this sort they have been the least able to appear, so that they have hitherto had and sustained many evils and losses by reason of losing important business and of amerements. We proposing that grievances of this sort be hereafter removed from the said honest and freemen of the mistery aforesaid for the reasons aforesaid and other considerations, us specially moving have granted to them, according to their supplication, that the same mistery and all men of the same mistery of the aforesaid City may be in substance and name one Body and one Commonalty perpetual, and that two principal men of the same Commonalty with unanimous assent of twelve or eight persons at the least of the same Commonalty in the Mistery aforesaid most expert every year may be able to choose and make of the Commonalty aforesaid two Masters or Governors in the same Mistery most expert to superintend rule and govern the Mistery and Commonalty aforesaid and all men of the same Mistery and the business of the same for ever. And that the same Masters or Governors and Commonalty may have perpetual succession and a Common Seal to be used in the affairs of the same Commonalty for ever. And that they and their successors for ever may be persons fit and able to purchase and possess in fee and for ever lands, tenements, rents and other possessions whatsoever. And that they by the name of Masters or Governors and Commonalty of the Mistery of Cooks of London may have power to plead and be impleaded before any Judges whomsoever in any Courts or Actions whatsoever. And that the aforesaid Masters or Governors and Commonalty and their successors may make lawful and honest meetings of themselves and Statutes and Ordinances for the wholesome government, supervision and correction of the Mistery aforesaid, according to necessity and when and as often as need shall require, lawfully and freely without let or hindrance of us or our Heirs or Successors, Justices, Escheators, Sheriffs, Coroners or other Bailiffs or Ministers of ours, or of our Heirs or Successors whatsoever, so as that the said Statutes and Ordinances may be in no way contrary to the Laws and Customs of our Realm of England. Further we will grant for us, our Heirs and Successors as much as in us lies, that the Masters or Governors of the aforesaid Commonalty for the time being and their Successors for ever may have the supervision, scrutiny, correction and government of all and singular men of the said Commonalty of Cooks using the Mistery of Cooks in the same City and suburbs thereof. And the punishment of them for their defaults in not perfectly executing doing and using the Mistery aforesaid, so as the punishment of this sort be executed by reasonable and fit means. And we will grant for us our Heirs and Successors as much as in us lies, that neither the said Masters and Governors and Commonalty of the said Mistery of Cooks, nor their Successors, nor any one of them shall by any means hereafter, within the aforesaid City and suburbs thereof, be summoned or put upon any assizes, inquests, inquisitions, attainder or other recognizances within the said City and the suburbs thereof, to be laid before the Mayor and Sheriffs or Coroner of the said City for the time being or to be summoned by any his officer or minister or officers or ministers, although the same juries at inquisitions or recognizances may have been summoned by virtue of a writ or writs of us or our Heirs. But that the said Masters or Governors and Commonalty of the Mistery aforesaid and their successors and every of them may against us and our Heirs and Successors and against the Mayor and Sheriffs of our City aforesaid for the time being and their officers and ministers whatsoever be thenceforward for ever acquitted and absolutely exonerated by these presents. And lastly we for the consideration aforesaid of our especial grace do for us our Heirs and Successors grant to the said Masters or Governors and Commonalty of the said Mistery of Cooks and their successors, this liberty, namely that they may for ever thereafter admit and receive persons able and sufficiently instructed and informed in the said Mistery of Cooks approved of by the Masters or Governors of the same Mistery for the time being and presented to the Mayor of the aforesaid City for the time being unto the same Mistery of Cooks, according to the liberties of the said City, to have and enjoy according to the custom of the said City and no other persons whomsoever, not by any other means any command or request of us or of our Heirs and Successors, by letters in writing or otherwise, howsoever made or done to the contrary notwithstanding. And albeit the same Masters or Governors and Commonalty and their successors shall use this privilege for ever thereafter against any command or request of us, our Heirs or Successors, or any others in form aforesaid to be made. Yet they shall on that account in no way incur nor any of them incur fine, contempt or loss against us, our Heirs or Successors or loss or evil whatever in their goods or persons against others whomsoever any Statute or Ordinance or Act to the contrary hitherto declared, made, ordained or provided notwithstanding. In testimony whereof etc..

Witness the King at Westminster the 11th day of July.
By writ of Privy Seal etc..

The Charter of King Henry VIII

National Archives, National Archives, C 66/631, membrane 1. Translated from the Latin original.

The King to all to whom etc.. We have seen the Letters Patent of the Lord Edward the Fourth, late King of England, made in these words:
[Here follows the Charter of Edward IV verbatim]
Now we, the letters aforesaid and all and singular in them contained, having ratified and granted for us and our heirs as much as in us is, do accept and approve and to our well beloved and now Masters or Governors of the Mistery aforesaid and their successors, do ratify grant and confirm by these presents as in the Letters aforesaid is reasonably witnessed.

Witness the King at Westminster the 11th day of July.
Five marks paid into the Hanaper.*

* The Hanaper was an office of the Court of Chancery, the name derived from the fact that public documents were originally kept in a hanaper or hamper.

The Charter of Queen Elizabeth I

This Charter does not appear in the C66 series of Patent Rolls in the National Archives but in Guildhall Library Ms 9989, *Abstract of Company charters etc 1461–1735 (compiled between 1735–64 by liveryman Wood)* it is recorded that Queen Elizabeth I, in the first year of her reign, on 2nd November, 1559, granted a Charter, which recites the Patent of 10 Henry VIII and confirms the same, and appoints a Master and three Wardens.

The First charter of James I

The *Abstract of Company charters*, referred to above, also states that King James I, in the second year of his reign (1604) granted a Charter which recites the Patents of Queen Elizabeth I, Henry VIII, and Edward IV and confirms them. It appoints John Harte as Master and Richard Scarlet and Arthur Harte as Wardens.

Second Charter of King James I (suppressed)

This is recorded in the *Remembrancia* of the City and is discussed in Chapter 4 of this book. The Charter does not appear to have been enrolled, but was placed in the Council Chest.

The Third charter of King James I

National Archives, C 66/2079, membrane 1

Granted 19th May, 1616. This recites the previous charters and continues:

The many services heretofore done and performed and as yet continued to our noble progenitors, Kings and Queens of England, as also to ourselves since our first coming unto the Imperial Crown of this Realm by our well beloved subjects, the honest freemen of the said Mistery of Cooks of our said City of London, in their own persons as well as at the Royal Feast of our Coronation, at the entertaining of our dear brother the King of Denmark, the marriage of my well beloved daughter the Lady Elizabeth, our annual Feasts of St George, as at the entertaining of foreign Princes and upon all other occasions when they are thereunto required.

The charter gives power to sell beer and ale, with victuals, at home without license and grants several other privileges, and appoints and confirms two Masters, two Wardens and twenty-two Assistants and a Clerk. This is the first mention of the Assistants. The Masters appointed are Thomas Norman and John Stokes and the Wardens, Nicholas Pinfold and Robert Wood. The Clerk appointed is Robert Glover. Among the Assistants is John Shield, a Benefactor of the Company.

The Charter of King Charles II

National Archives, C 66/3011
16th February, 16 Charles II (1663)

This Charter recites in full the Charter of Edward IV and its ratification by succeeding monarchs and ratifies and confirms the same. It also ratifies the Act of Common Council that ordains that all freemen using the trade of Cooks within the City and not being free of the said Company of Cooks, should be translated from such Company they were free of to the Company of Cooks.

Among other privileges granted by the Charter are the following:

Whereas we are given to understand that the Masters or Governors and Commonalty of the Mistery of Cooks of our said City of London have of late times been called in question, and some them have been required to take licences to victual as Common Alehouse keepers used to do, which we much mislike, because it doth infringe their ancient privilege. We therefore of our special grace and of our Princely favour to our said subjects, the Masters or Governors and Commonalty of the Mistery of Cooks, for Us and our Heirs and Successors, do you will, command and grant that the said Masters or Governors or Commonalty of the said mistery of Cooks and their successors, and all men free of the said Mistery and who exercise the said trade, shall not at anytime hereafter be taken, called or reputed to be Common Victuallers, Tipplers, or Alehouse Keepers, but that they shall for ever hereafter be persons able to sell, as within their houses, shops, cellars, and other places, as also out of them, meat, bread, beer, ale, salt, sauce and all other victuals, fit and wholesome for the bodies of men, freely, according to the aforesaid custom of the said Mistery of Cooks, without any other license from Us, our Heirs and Successors, from any of our Justices or other officers and without any let, trouble, disturbance, interruption, or denial of Us, our Heirs or Successors or of any Mayors, Sheriffs, Bailiffs, Justices of the Peace, Constables, Headboroughs [Petty Constables] or any other our officers or ministers whatsoever, any Law, Statute, Act, Ordinance, Provision, Proclamation or other restraint, matter, cause or thing whatsoever to the contrary thereof in anywise notwithstanding.

Power is given for the said Master or Governors to search and survey Shops, Cellars, Houses, Rooms and other places of Cooks and to seize works and stuff which they shall find falsely made.

Power is also given that they the said Master or Governors of the Mistery aforesaid, with the assent and consent of twelve or eight at the least of the best most ancient and sufficient men of the same Mistery being Assistants of the same once in every year at the accustomed time of election heretofore observed amongst them, shall and may chose and elect of the most ablest and expert men of the said Mistery of the Assistants who have not borne the office or charge of one of the Masters or Governors of the said Mistery, two discrete persons, freemen of the same Mistery of Cooks, to be the two Assistant Wardens of the said Company for that year, the one whereof who is the last elected to be called the Renter Warden.

Edward Corbett and John Knowles are appointed the two Masters of the Company, from the date of these presents unto the 14th day of September commonly called Holy Cross alias Holyrood now next issuing. Thomas Paine and John Symonds are appointed the two Assistant Wardens. The names of the twenty-five assistants appointed for and during their natural lives follow.

Grant that on the said feast day, commonly called Holy Cross alias Holyrood day, if it be not Sunday and if it be, then on the next day following, yearly for ever hereafter the Masters or Governors, Wardens and Assistants of the said Mistery for the time being or the greater part of them for that intent and purpose to be assembled at or in their Common Hall for the time being shall and may nominate two persons who have formerly been in office as Wardens, according to the former custom of the same Mistery, to be the two Masters or Governors of the said Mistery for the year then next following. And shall at the same time elect, choose and nominate out of the said Assistants, two persons to be Assistant Wardens of the said Mistery; which said Masters or Governors and Wardens so as aforesaid nominated elected and chosen shall be and continue Masters or Governors and Assistant Wardens of the said Mistery unto the end and term of one whole year then next ensuing.

Provision that if the Master die during his year of office a new Master be appointed and if an Assistant die, a new one be appointed in his place.

Power to appoint one honest and discrete person Clerk of the Company to be elected and chosen yearly at the accustomed time of Election heretofore observed.

Power to make meetings in Common Hall.

Power to make Ordinances etc..

Power to fine for transgressions of Ordinances etc, the same fines to be used and employed to the use, benefit and behoof of the poor and decayed members of the said Mistery.

Power to make and use one Common Seal to serve for the ensealing of Grants, Leases etc.. and power to break, deface or alter and make new the same Seal as to them shall seem most meet.

Power to receive and take of all and all manner of person or persons using the trade of a Cook in London the like quarterage and quarterly payments as they are accustomed to take and receive of such persons as are or shall be hereafter freemen of the Mistery of Cooks and not any other or greater sums and if any such person shall make default of payment of the same that then shall he forfeit twelve pence in the name of a pain.

Power to have, purchase and enjoy any messuage, lands, tenements and hereditaments not exceeding in yearly rent two hundred pounds.

All Masters, Wardens, Assistants and Officers to take oaths of allegiance and supremacy of the the Holy Evangelists before the Lord Mayor and Chamberlain of the City of London before acting as Officers.

The payable fine on the Charter is 20 nobles. The cost of the Charter defrayed by a subscription among the members.

The Charter of King James II

National Archives, C 66/3263, membrane 1
This Charter is dated 7th May, 1685 and is enrolled in Chancery, I James II.
It recites that the Governors and Commonalty of the Mistery of Cooks of London had surrendered all their powers and authorities concerning the election of Masters, Wardens, Assistants, and Clerk and that the Surrender had been accepted.

The Charter confirms the previous Charters and gives the Company fresh powers.

It nominates Thomas Humphreys and Anthony Spencer as Masters, John Smith and John Pether, Wardens, and names twelve Assistants, with power to make up the number of Assistants to twenty-six. It stipulates that the Clerk to be elected must be approved by the King under the Privy Seal or Sign Manual.

Act of Parliament of 2 William and Mary, 1690

The Charter of James II was annulled and made void and the Company reverted to the Charter of 16 Charles II.

Inspeximus of 58 George III, 1817

On 10th December, 1817, the Company obtained an Inspeximus of the Charter of King Charles II, which stated that the Letters Patent granted by King Charles II had been inspected and remained duly on record in the Chapel of Rolls and, after quoting the whole of the Charter verbatim, it exemplified the said Letters Patent.

Supplemental Charter of 2 George VI, 1938

The company obtained a supplemental Charter on 31st May, 1938, giving power to hold lands etc of the clear yearly value of £20,000.

APPENDIX SIX

The Bye-Laws

In 1686 the Lord Chancellor, George, Lord Jeffreys and the two Lords Chief Justice, Edward Herbert and Thomas Jones, examined and approved the Bye Laws proposed by the Cooks' Company. The forty six clauses are summarised below:

If any controversy shall at any time arise between any Brethren of this Society relating to the trade of a Cook, complaint must first be made to the Masters or Governors, before any action at law is undertaken. The Masters or Governors will endeavour to settle the matter. The penalty for ignoring this procedure is *6s 8d.*

The said Masters or Governors may at any time enter into the shops, cellars,houses, rooms and other places of all and every Member of the Company, to search, view and see the workmanship of the Member. Should any refuse the penalty is £3 *6s 8d* for each occasion.

The Masters, Governors or other office holders may not intermeddle with receipts or payments of any money upon the account of the Company, or with any goods or estate belonging to the Company; within eight days of the Feast of All Saints they must make full account in writing of all that has been within their stewardship and deliver the same to incoming officers, so that the Company's estate and goods may not in anywise be conveyed away, misspent or embezzled. For every month's delay in doing this penalty will be £5 and failure to pay any outstanding debts will attract a penalty of £10 per month.

Anyone who disposes of or sells the services and terms of their apprentices, before their apprenticeships have expires, is liable to a penalty of £10 for each offence.

If any Member of the Company is willing to work as a Journeyman at any Feast or Business of Cookery, then no other Member may set to work any apprentice as a workman unless the Master of that apprentice is also working there. The penalty for this is 20*s*.

No Member of the Company shall be Master Cook at any more than two Corporations at any one time, the penalty being £10 for the first month of an offence and 40*s* for every subsequent month.

Every Member of the Company must appear when summoned by the Clerk or the Beadle and if they do not do so, having no reasonable excuse, they shall pay 2*s* for the first offence, 3*s* for the second, and double fee every subsequent offence.

Some Members of the Company have been constantly employed in the Cities of London and Westminster and four miles compass and have given very good satisfaction, but other Members, envying their conditions, have by sinister practices and indirect means made it their business to circumvent and undermine such persons. In future no Member shall get or procure by any means of craft or subtlety from any other Member the service as a Cook without the special licence, consent and agreement of him who shall be in possession thereof, upon pain of forfeit of £10 for the first month and £5 for every subsequent month.

Every Member shall pay 6*d* for their Quarterage, with a penalty for late payment of 5*s*.

No Member shall strike, slander, revile, abuse or defame in words or otherwise the Masters or Governors or any other Member of the Company but at all times shall be of good behaviour and civil conversation. If any Assistant infringe this he shall be expelled and put out of his place as Assistant and may not be chosen again until he has paid a fine not exceeding £5; any other Member infringing this rule shall pay a fine not exceeding 20*s*.

Any Member who employs the Beadle to warn or summon another Member, with whom he is in dispute, to appear before the Master or Governors, Wardens and Assistants shall pay the Beadle 4*d*, and the Masters or Governors shall pay the Beadle 12*d* for every foreigner he shall find who is employed by any Freeman of the Company, contrary to the Charter and Ordinances.

No Member of the Company may bind an apprentice before he has been presented to the Masters or Governors, so that the said Masters or Governors may see that he has fit limbs and features for the said art of Cookery; the binding must take place at the Common Hall of the Company, where the Indentures shall be made by the Clerk. The name will be entered in the Register and the Masters or Governors shall receive the usual fee of *2s 6d*, and the Clerk for drawing and engrossing *2s*. No more than two apprentices may be taken at any one time without the consent of the Masters and Wardens, on penalty of £5 for the first month and 40*s* for every month thereafter. Those who have served as Masters or Governors or Assistants make take three apprentices at any one time

If any member of the Company shall dress or cause to be dressed any Breakfast, Dinner, Supper or Feast within the Cities of London and Westminster or four miles compass, then the Master Cook or Cooks concerned shall give notice thereof to the Masters or Governors, who may then come and see that the business is well and honestly done, as well for the content of such as bear the charge thereof as also for avoiding of evil report and scandal to the Company. Whenever the Master Cook requires two further workmen from the Company, one shall be an Assistant, and if six workmen are needed two shall be Assistants and so on proportionately, so that every third workman shall be an Assistant. If no warning of a Feast is given the penalty shall be 20*s*, and for every Assistant who is not employed when he should be the fine is 20*s*.

The Company Charters and other documents shall be put into several chests and boxes and the keys of these will be passed to the new Masters and Wardens on their election. All the plate shall be in the custody of the Renter Warden, who must also keep the accounts, which must be truly kept and accounted for, against a penalty of £500. Any Member of the Company refusing to serve in the office of Renter Warden shall pay £20.

Every Member who is entrusted with the keys of the chests shall bring them to the Hall every Quarter Day, and those who are to leave the City shall give such keys to one of the Masters and anyone who fails to do this will be fined 10*s*.

Every year three Stewards shall be chosen by the Court. They shall at their own expense provide a dinner for the Court and Livery, each expending at least £10 of their own money; should anyone refuse to serve as Steward they will be fined £13 *6s 8d*.

Any Member who is appointed to work at the Guildhall Feast but refuses to do so shall be fined 10*s* for each offence.

The Masters and Wardens for the time being shall provide two competent dinners for the Assistants and their wives during their year in office, and if any one shall refuse tom do so the fine will be £10.

Any Member who refuses to accept office as Master or Warden shall pay £10.

Any Member who refuses to accept office as an Assistant shall pay £10.

When the Election Feast is held in the Common Hall the new Masters and Wardens shall, at the Company's charge, allow to the three Workmen who attend the Feast three aprons, the price of which should not exceed 10*s*.

Any Member of the Company who aids or assists any of the Lord Mayor's or Sheriffs' Cooks in any business of Cookery not qualified according to these Ordinances shall be fined 40*s* for every offence.

The Masters and Wardens and other persons concerned shall, within three months of the Guildhall Feast, give a true account in writing of all the money due to Members of the Company for dressing the said Feast, and report to the Court every Member who is in default, through absence or otherwise. Such Members shall be fined a sum not exceeding 20*s*. The Masters or Wardens shall be fined £5 if in default.

Any Assistant who is absent on Election Day shall be fined 2*s*

If any of the Masters or Governors are absent from any public business of the Company, such as waiting upon the Lord Mayor, attending burials and other such services with no reasonable excuse they shall be fined 6*s* 8*d* for each offence.

No Member of the Company may remove from the Hall books, evidences, deeds, papers or writings concerning the Company without the permission of the Court, the fine being £6 13*s* 4*d* for each offence.

It is for the good of the Company that expert Cooks dress the Dinners, Suppers and Feasts of the Lord Mayor and Sheriffs, so no Member of the Company whose Master serves as Lord Mayor or the Sheriff shall, during their year of office, undertake any work outside his Master's dwelling houses, unless such work is at the proper cost and charge of their Master, and the penalty for doing so is £5 for each offence.

Every member of the Company who shall happen to be Cook to the Lord Mayor or Sheriffs shall, for that year of his office, appoint an Under Cook to assist him, who must not be a foreigner or an apprentice but a freeman of the Company. Penalty for breaking this rule is £6 13*s* 4*d*.

No member of the Company may set on work any Cook or Under Cook working for the Lord Mayor or Sheriffs. Penalty 20*s* for each offence.

Regarding dinners dressed in Livery Halls, any Member of the Company who is Cook to a particular Livery, shall, if a dinner there is dressed by another Member of the Company, bear half the charges and be entitled to receive half of the profits derived from such events, upon pain of forfeiting 40*s*.

To avoid and as far as possible suppress the profane sin of swearing, if any Member swears an oath or curses another Member he shall pay the sum of 12*d*.

Whereas the Company has of late been scandalised and abused by some drunken persons free of this Society, who in their drunkenness and debauchery have railed against the Masters, Wardens and Assistants, it is ordered that hereafter any Brother of the Company who is found drunk in Hall shall pay 5*s* for every offence.

Inconvenience has arisen by Members of the Company bringing a multitude of guests to the Hall when not authorised to do so, it is ordered that on Election Day the Masters and Governors may have two couples as guests and the Wardens one couple. Any Member introducing other guests without authority shall forfeit 6*s* 8*d* for every offence.

In recent years the Masters or Governors had allowed property and land leases of a longer term of years than is usually granted by other corporations; it is therefore ordered that no new leases may be granted until those leases now in being are less than three years from expiry. Such new leases must be for no longer than twenty one years and be at a reasonable yearly rent.

The Court shall elect new Members of the Livery and submit the names of those chosen to the Lord Mayor and Court of Aldermen for their approval. The Masters shall then instruct the Beadle to clothe the new Member in a Livery gown and the Master shall put on his shoulder a party coloured hood made after the usual manner, after which the Masters and Wardens shall shake hands with the new Member saying *Brother, you are admitted into the Clothing of this Company*. The new Member shall pay £10 as an admission fee, and 5*s* to the Clerk and 2*s* 6*d* to the Beadle. Any Member refusing to come onto the Livery and with no valid excuse shall pay £20.

Because many seek to be admitted to the Company by redemption although they are not Workmen, in future no one who has not been brought up as a Cook shall be admitted by redemption. As the Court of Alderman has settled the fine for every Freeman coming in by redemption at £5 (for the City's use) the Company shall charge £5 for admission by redemption, payable to the Renter Warden.

Because some ill-disposed Brethren have, for private gain, taught several persons that are not bound Apprentices to raise and make all kinds of Bakemeats and Pies, it is ordained that anyone who does this in the future shall pay £10 for every offence.

To make members of the Court more decent and comely it is ordained that they shall wear those gowns that are commonly called Court Gowns, and any Assistant found without his gown shall pay 12*d* for each offence.

The Clerk and Beadle should be diligent in carrying out their duties, for which they shall receive the following fees: the Clerk, 2*s* for engrossing indentures for apprentices, 2*s* 6*d* for every person admitted to the Freedom, 5*s* for every person coming on the Clothing, 10*s* for every person becoming or declining the role of Steward, 5*s* for every person becoming an Assistant, together with all other fees and perquisites which have been due to his predecessors. The Beadle shall receive: 1*s* for every apprentice, 1*s* 6*d* for every Freeman, 2s 6*d* for every Liveryman, 2*s* 6*d* for every Steward, 2*s* 6*d* for every Assistant together with all other fees and perquisites which have been due to his predecessors. Any Member refusing to pay these fees shall be fined 13*s* 4*d*.

Any person admitted to the Company by Servitude shall pay the usual fees and take the usual oath to be obedient to all the lawful ordinances of the Company.

As recently several Members, out of selfish and sinister ends, have made servants or apprentices brought up in the Trade of Cookery free of other Companies, henceforth this will attract a fine of £10 for every offence.

If any Member of the Court shall reveal any of the lawful secrets, conferences or consultations of the said Society he shall be fined a sum not exceeding £5 or 40*s* for ordinary Members of the Company.

Every Member of the Company shall contribute his portion of common expenses, such as taxes charged upon the Company or monies spent on the welfare and good estate of the Company, as assessed by the Court; every person refusing to pay shall be charged a reasonable fine, not exceeding £5.

No leases, demises, annuities, grants, gifts, bargains or sales of any kind shall at any time be granted of pass under the Common Seal of the Society unless authorised by the Court and anyone acting contrary to this shall be disenfranchised and shall pay for each offence the full sum of £100.

For the better avoiding of disorders, noises and confusions in the Court or Assemblies every Member shall keep silence at the command of the Masters or Wardens and only one person shall speak at a time. Every Member shall speak bareheaded and address himself to the Masters or Wardens. Penalty 1*s* for each offence.

All penalties and forfeitures shall be to the Masters and Governors and may be sued for and recovered in any of His Majesty's Courts of Record or by distraining the goods and chattels of the offender.

The Oaths to be administered to the Members of and Servants to this Company, appended to the Bye Laws

The Master's Oath

You do swear that you will, to the best of your skill and power, execute and justly and indifferently cause to be executed all the good and lawful Ordinances and Orders made or to be made for the conservation, order and government of the Trade, Art or Mistery of Cooks, without sparing any person for affection, reward, fear or promise of reward during the time of your continuance in your office of Master or Governor and that you will make or cause to be made a just and true account of all such goods, plate, sum and sums of money as shall come into your hands according to the Orders and Ordinances of this Company and lastly that you shall well and truly execute the office or place of Master or Governor of the said Mistery of Cooks of London in all things appertaining to the said office according to the best of your skill and knowledge, so help you God.

The Wardens' Oath is the same, substituting only the word Warden for Master or Governor.

The Assistants' Oath

You do swear that you will be aiding, counselling and assisting from time to time and at all times hereafter to the Masters or Governors and Wardens of this Company (for the time being) in all things concerning the well ordering and government of this Company, according to your best knowledge, direction and understanding and that you will come to and attend all their lawful summons, unless you have a sufficient excuse for such failure or omission. The lawful Ordinances and Orders of this Company and every of them you shall to your power preserve and keep and all the lawful secrets of this Company to the prejudice and hurt of this Company, and all other matters and things belonging to the place of an

Assistant, you shall truly and faithfully execute and perform according to the best of your skill and knowledge, so help you God.

The Freemen's Oath

You do swear that you shall be true to our Sovereign Lord the King and to his Heirs or lawful successors, Kings or Queens of this realm. You shall be obedient to the Masters or Governors and Wardens of this Company (for the time being) in all lawful things that you will be willing and ready to come to all their lawful summon, unless you have a sufficient excuse for such failure or omission. The lawful Ordinances and Orders of this Company and every of them you shall to your power observe and keep and not disclose to any person not free of this Company or to any person or persons free thereof that may tend to the prejudice and hurt of this Company. So help you God.

The Clerk's Oath

You do swear that you shall be obedient to the Masters or Governors, Wardens and Assistants of this Company in all lawful things. You shall come to all their lawful summons when you are thereunto required unless you have a sufficient cause to be absent. All the lawful secrets of this Company you shall keep and not disclose to any person or persons not free of this Company, and finally in all things you shall well and truly execute your office of Clerk to this Company according to your best knowledge and skill and understanding. So help you God.

The Beadle's Oath

You do swear that you shall be true to our Sovereign Lord the King that now is and to his Heirs and lawful successors, Kings or Queens of this realm and that you will be obedient to the Masters or Governors, Wardens and Assistants in all lawful things. You shall justly and truly execute or cause to be executed all such summonses as the Masters or Governors, Wardens and Assistants shall order you to execute and all the lawful secrets of this Company you shall keep and not disclose to any person whatsoever without the direction of the said Masters or Governors and Wardens or any one of them and finally in all things you shall well and orderly behave yourself in your office of Beadle of this Company. So help you God.

APPENDIX SEVEN

A Schedule of the plate, implements, goods and other things belonging to the Worshipful Company of Cooks, London, taken in the year 1746

In the Cellar

A sliding partition for a coalhole; two small wine cellars with locks and shelves, two locks on the doors and a door to each wine cellar.

In the Little Kitchen

An iron grate complete [with] iron back; a falling dresser with two iron legs, shelves round the same; a cupboard with shelves, a dresser with drawers and cupboards under it and iron lock and key to the door.

In the Yard

A small leaden cistern & cock

In the Great Kitchen

A pair of iron racks; 3 spits, 2 iron dripping pans, 2 stands, 3 iron trivets, one copper hung complete with a wooden cover; 5 stoves; two large fish pans; a leaden cistern with a leaden pipe and two brass cocks; an iron curb round the stoves and 3 iron grates to the stoves; two ovens with iron sides; one iron slice; a large fir dresser; a large brass skimmer; one cold rack supported with four supporters; a chopping block; a small dresser and two shelves over it; a double door with lock and key; & bench; 2 supporters for the spit at the range; a wooden form.

In the Pantry

A dresser with two shelves over it and cupboards under it; 3 other shelves; 2 doors one with a lock & key, the other with a latch; a hanging shelf; 2 wooden chests, two iron ditto.

In the Little Pantry under the Great Stairs

The same complete with shelves round it; a glass light and lock and key to the door.

In the Great Parlour

A marble chimney piece and hearth; a Compass Stove and iron tongs, poker and shovel and fender; a month clock; a six-leaved leather screen; twelve leather chairs; a looking glass with an ebony frame; a large oval wainscot table; a long cloth covering the table; cloth squabs to all the seats; two folding doors with brass lock and key, 2 bolts and sliding spring brass pins; round the room 4 double sash windows, 4 locks under the windows; a bench at the head of the long table; the King's Arms; the room wainscoted and the Company's Arms over the Chimney; 2 stone cheeks to the chimney and stone hearth; a plan of the Company's estate in a frame.

Mr Henshaw's Office

The office wainscoted round 5 shelves, a broad shelf with cupboards and drawers under it; two sliding sash windows with an old man's head painted on one of them; a nest of holes for paper on each side of the chimney; 2 cupboards with folding doors and sliding shelves for books and a smaller ditto over an iron Wand Stove, iron blower, iron fender and brass brush; the chimney set round with tiles; 2 outward shutters with iron bolts; a door with lock and key; 4 cane chairs.

The Clerk's Office

Three sash windows wainscoted and painted all round; shelves round the office; lock and key to the door; a sash over the door and two Turkey worked chairs.

Under the Piaza

A warehouse with a wooden partition, the inside wainscoted almost to the top, and wooden bench under it; 2 long wooden tables; 2 wooden forms; 6 wooden horses; 3 wooden tables; pallasadoes with 4 iron supporters; a wooden bench; 2 leaden pipes; a large passage door with 2 bolts; a large brassbound lanthorn with 4 brass sockets therein and an iron chain; 2 dozen leather buckets with the Company's Arms.

The Servant's Room in the Staircase

The same wainscoted, a cupboard & shelves; two sash windows.

In the Dining Room up one pair of Stairs

A beaufet with shelves; cupboard and shelves and glass doors; 2 sash windows; a wooden chimneypiece; marble slab; Gally tiles; 2 sash doors; a brass lock and key to the door and iron lock to the sash door.

In the Room Adjoining

White Gally tiles to the chimney; glass sash lights round the room; an iron lock and key to door.

In the Landing Place

Two iron locks, one to the Necessary House, the other to the stairs

In the Old Hall

A chimney set with Gally tiles, a fire stone hearth; marble foot pace[?]; a steel compass stove with fender, tongs, shovel, and poker; 7 cane chairs; 4 wooden forms; a brass lock and key to the doors; a picture of King Edward the 4th presenting the Company with their Charter.

In the Pantry

Dresser and shelves round the same; double door lock, key & bolt; a cupboard with shelves with lock and key to the doors; a cupboard under the stair with lock and key.

In the Great Hall

Three large tables with seats at the back of them; 10 forms; 6 cloth squabs; two tables of Benefactors, the Company's Arms and ornaments over the door; a double door with brass lock & bolts & iron bar; a brass branch; brass pins round the room; a butler's office with shelves.

The Little Room at the end of the Great Hall

A press with the Company's writings in it.

In the Clerk's Bedchamber

A double door going into the leads with lock and key & 2 bolts; a closet with a door, lock and key; a chimney piece set with Gally tiles and marble stones for a foot pace; a pair of steps to go into the leads; an iron lock and key to the door; a door going from the stair head into the Clerk's dining room with lock and key.

Plate etc
One large cup & cover gilt
Four large cups, two gilt
Nine wine cups
Three tankards
One large salver
Twenty two silver spoons
One nut bowl
11 5*l* pie plates
24 4*l* ditto
19 six inch stands
2 dozen saucers
10 butters cups
11 dozen plates
3 flagons
3 chamber pots

Pewter
4 7*l* dishes
24 5*l* dishes
24 4*l* dishes
12 3*l* dishes
6 2*l* dishes
4 deep dishes
A plate warmer

Linnen
Eight table cloths
Fifteen napkins
Four kitchen cloths
3 dozen and 8 knives
2 dozen forks
Twenty five wine glasses

The Beadle's Apartment adjoining the Hall

A door lock and key and hatch at the foot of the stairs; the room 2 pair stairs forward, wainscoted all round; a stove, fire shovel, tongs, poker and fender; the Beadle's staff; the Bell and Hammer; the arms of the Militia; 2 buff coats, 2 guns, 2 swords, 2 bayonets, and 2 pouches; 2 doors lock and key and bolt; the Company's Balloting Box

In the Room Backwards

An iron grate, trivet, shovel, tongs, poker and fender and gridiron; a dresser and 3 shelves; a lead weight; folding doors; the Beadle's gown.

A similar inventory survives from 1752 in Guildhall Library Ms 9999

APPENDIX EIGHT

An Act for regulating the Company of Cooks of the City of London

The 26th George II, 1753, May 9th

Whereby it is enacted, that, from and after the 29th of September next, every person occupying, using or exercising the Trade of Cook, within the City of London, or Liberties thereof, shall be made Free, in the Company of Cooks, and that no person now using, or hereafter using the said Trade, shall be admitted by the Chamberlains into the Freedom or Liberties of this City, of or in any other Company than the said Company of Cooks.

And it further enacts that every person, after the said 29th September, 1753, using the Trade of a Cook not being Free of the said Company of Cooks shall forfeit and pay five pounds for every offence. The same to be recovered by action of debt in the name of the Chamberlain.

This Company having received many informations and complaints that several persons, Cooks by Trade, have been made Free of other Companies and do act contrary to the above Charters and Acts; and that several persons, as well as those who are intitled and ought to take up their Freedom, by Patrimony and Servitude, of the Company, do neglect to take up the same respectively and yet do exercise the said art, contrary to the said Laws and Acts. Notice is hereby given, that all persons concerned do conform to the said Charters and Acts, otherwise they will be sued for the penalties above-mentioned.

APPENDIX NINE

Orders for Confirmation Day

Guildhall Library, Loose papers, Ms 9997

31 Oct 1782
Method of drinking to new Masters and Wardens on confirmation days.

Silence being proclaimed by the Beadle
The clerk pronounces "Sir Alex Kennedy" (giving the title to any dignified person that may happen to be present) and Gentlemen
The late Master drinks to the new Master, wishing him health to go through his Office;
Then the late Second Master or Upper Warden drinks to the new Second Master or Upper Warden; the late Second Warden drinks to the new Second Warden wishing him etc.., and the late Renter Warden drinks to the new Renter Warden wishing him etc..

The King, the Queen, Prince of Wales and the rest of the royal family

Prosperity to the City of London and the trade thereof;

Gentlemen and Ladies, visitors. The Master and Wardens drink your health and are happy in the pleasure of your company;

Masters and Wardens; the Gentlemen and Ladies, visitors drink to your health and thank you for your polite attention to them.

Orders for Confirmation Day 20 Oct 1809

The new Master and Wardens to be Sworn in the last business before the rising of the Court; notice to be given to them to attend for that purpose; the Master, Wardens and Clerk to be habited in their gowns during dinner; about 7 o'clock the installation of the Master and Wardens shall take place; the ceremony shall be as follows:

After the eighth toast, the Master and Wardens elect and four Seniors who have passed the Chair to retire to an adjoining room to be habited in gowns, during which time the Music shall play some favourite national air. When ready, the Clerk shall give notice that the Master and Wardens elect are about to be admitted to their several offices agreeably to the laws of the company and request that silence be preserved during such time. The Clerk then crowning the Master and after making his obeisance to the Chair shall join in the procession in the adjoining room. When the procession enters the room, the trumpets shall flourish and the band to play.

Order of the procession:

The Beadle in his gown with his staff
The Clerk in his gown, wearing a hat and holding in his hand
open the register of the election and the written proclamation.
The Master elect [all in their gowns]
The Second Master or Upper Warden elect
The Second Warden elect
The Renter Warden elect
Four Seniors of the Court passed the chair singly

On the arrival of the procession opposite the Master's Chair, the band will cease playing and the trumpets to flourish.

The Clerk will then proclaim that the Master, having been elected Master or Governor of this company for the year ensuing, the late Master drinks to him, wishing him health to go through his Office (the new Master making his obeisance to the Chair).

The Clerk will then remove the crown from the head of the late Master and place it on the head of the new Master.

The like ceremony as to the Upper Warden, Second Master and Renter changing caps.

After each proclamation the trumpets shall flourish.

When done the late Master will give the health of the new Master and Wardens and retire from the chair and the new Master will take the same as also the Wardens their chairs.

The Clerk's toast,
The new Master taking the chair will give the health of the late Master;
Then the Ladies;
Then the Visitors.

About half past seven the Ladies will retire.

About half past eight admittance to the Ballroom begins.

No dance to be called after two o'clock.

Music engaged as long as the Master of the Ceremonies shall direct.

Mr Yates to provide the refreshments.

The Orders for the Confirmation dinner in October 1815 include a display of the colours and a stipulation that the Company's bowls and plate should be used.

APPENDIX TEN

Letter to the Master from an Injured Freeman, 1773

Printed in William Kahl, 'The Cooks' Company in the Eighteenth Century' in *The Guildhall Miscellany*, Vol II, 1961, 71–81

Sir

Your being at this time Master of the Worshipful Company of Cooks makes me so bold as to address you on the behalf of myself and my brother Freemen of the said Company. Several of us being at this time out of employ, whereas it need not be, for there is room enough in the City for us, but the places are occupied by foreigners, some of whom never served any time at all. For at this time six of the most capital shops employ foreigners and give them better wages than Freemen; so we Freemen not finding any work waited on the Masters in the City, who had foreigners at work, and asked of they pleased to give us the preference, we being Freemen and every way capable of work, more than the foreigners they employed. But they refused us work and when we urged our rights, they bid us defiance, which us puts under disagreeable circumstances of attending my Lord Mayor to prevent the foreigners from having their licences renewed. . Notwithstanding which a Master of our business, one of the most capital, got a licence for his man, for three months, under the false pretence of being a pastry cook, a kitchen cook, and a confectioner, whereas I prove, he is never a one of the three, having served no time at all to any business. Thus, Sir, is our Freedom made useless to us if we can receive no benefits, by being Free, I have always understood that when a Master of any business licensed a man, it was upon oath he could not get a Freeman to do his business, whatever may be urged to the contrary. Shall I make so bold, Sir, as to desire you, for a few minutes to reflect, was you in our situation, whether you would not think it hard to be out of work, whilst foreigners are employed. Some of us have wives and families to provide for, which how can we do whilst we are out of employ, and all the necessaries of life are so extreme dear, I have thus endeavoured to make a short sketch of the difficulties we at present labour under, not at all doubting but you will have a feeling for us, your brother Freemen, as it is in your power to redress our grievances. By ordering the Beadle of the company to see the foreigners turned out and the Freemen employed, or by any other means as your better judgment shall think proper. May I presume under submission to your judgment when the Company shall meet, to have this letter read and then you will be able to judge whether the facts advanced are not strictly true, and as such I make not doubt, but that you, Sir, as a Freeman, Friend and Protector of Company rights, will exercise that power you are invested with, in redressing our just complaints. I beg pardon for this trespassing upon your time, but one more thing to add I have and it is this, that I am credibly informed, there is a law in our Company restricting any Master from having any more than two apprentices at a time. But there are some Masters, at this time, who have three and four apprentices at one time. By which means our trade if overrun with hands, will in time come to decay. Therefore I humbly hope you will see this law put in force, as it will be of equal benefits to the Masters as well as the Men. I am sorry to be so troublesome to you, Sir, but trust your goodness will pardon me, for thus making you acquainted with facts which otherways you might not have known. Therefore, with submission, I beg leave to subscribe myself,

Your Obedient humble Servant
An Injured Freeman

Index